Work Organisation Labour & Globalisation

Volume 1, Issue 1, Winter, 2006-7

First published in 2007
by Analytica Publications Ltd.
46 Ferntower Road
London N5 2JH
United Kingdom
www.analyticapublications.co.uk
phone: +44 (0)20 7226 8411
fax: +44 (0) 7226 0813
email: orders@analyticapublications.co.uk
(for subscriptions and editorial queries)

in association with Merlin Press Ltd.
96 Monnow Street
Monmouth NP25 3EQ
United Kingdom
www.merlinpress.co.uk
phone: +44 (0)1600 775663
fax: +44 (0)1600 775663
email: orders@merlinpress.co.uk
(for single copy or trade sales)

Published in Canada by Fernwood Publishing
32 Oceanvista Lane
Site 2A, Box 5
Black Point, NS B0J 1B0
Canada
www.fernwooodpublishing.ca

Edited by Ursula Huws
Design by Andrew Haig Associates
Printed in the UK by Antony Rowe Ltd., Eastbourne

ISBN: 978-0-85036-582-5
ISSN: 1745-641X

Printed and bound by CPI Antony Rowe, Eastbourne

The spark in the engine:
creative workers in a global economy

edited by Ursula Huws

About this journal

The globalisation of world trade in combination with the use of information and communications technologies is bringing into being a new international division of labour, not just in manufacturing industry, as in the past, but also in work involving the processing of information.

Organisational restructuring shatters the unity of the traditional workplace, both contractually and spatially, dispersing work across the globe in ever-more attenuated value chains.

A new 'cybertariat' is in the making, sharing common labour processes, but working in remote offices and call centres which may be continents apart and occupying very different cultural and economic places in local economies.

The implications of this are far-reaching, both for policy and for scholarship. The dynamics of this new global division of labour cannot be captured adequately within the framework of any single academic discipline. On the contrary they can only be understood in the light of a combination of insights from fields including political economy, the sociology of work, organisational theory, economic geography, development studies, industrial relations, comparative social policy, communications studies, technology policy and gender studies.

Work Organisation, Labour and Globalisation aims to:

- bring together insights from all these fields to create a single authoritative source of information on the new global division of labour, combining theoretical analysis with the results of empirical research in a way that is accessible both to the research community and to policy makers.
- Provide a single home for articles which specifically address issues relating to the changing international division of labour and the restructuring of work in a global knowledge-based economy.
- Bring together the results of empirical research, both qualitative and quantitative, with theoretical analyses in order to inform the development of new interdisciplinary approaches to the study of the restructuring of work, organisation and labour in a global context.
- Be global in scope, with a particular emphasis on attracting contributions from developing countries as well as from Europe, North America and other developed regions.
- Encourage a dialogue between university-based researchers and their counterparts in international and national government agencies, independent research institutes, trade unions and civil society as well as policy makers. Subject to the requirements of scholarly peer review, it is open to submissions from contributors working outside the academic sphere and encourages an accessible style of writing in order to facilitate this goal.
- Complement, rather than compete with existing discipline-based journals.
- Bring to the attention of English-speaking readers relevant articles originally published in other languages.

Each issue addresses a specific theme and is also published independently as a book. The editor welcomes comments, criticisms, contributions and suggestions for future themes. For further information, visit the webssite: http://www.analyticapublications.co.uk

Editorial board

Contents

The spark in the engine:
creative workers in a global economy

Ursula Huws

Ursula Huws is professor of international labour studies at the
Working Lives Research Institute at London Metropolitan University, UK, the director of Analytica and the editor of this volume.

ABSTRACT

Introducing this volume, this paper summarises the contents and offers an analysis of the place of creative work in a global economy, focusing in particular on the restructuring of global value chains and the commodification of knowledge in a process which simultaneously opens up the possibility for new creative tasks for some workers whilst deskilling others. It concludes with a discussion of the contradictions that this presents for creative workers who may be offered a choice between disappointing their own creative aspirations or collaborating in their own exploitation.

Introduction

There are few greater pleasures in life than the satisfaction that comes from making something original and beautiful, whether this is a musical performance, a crafted object or the solution to an intellectual puzzle.

One of the most famous celebrations of the joy of creative work is by William Morris whose utopian 1890 *News from Nowhere* was set in a future time in which:

> 'all *work is now pleasureable; either because of the hope of gain in honour and wealth with which the work is done, which causes pleasurable habit, as in the case with what you may call mechanical work; and lastly (and most of our work is of this kind) because there is conscious sensuous pleasure in the work itself; it is done, that is, by artists.'(Morris, 1890)*

This 'conscious sensuous pleasure in the work itself' isn't limited to artists. Studs Terkel, in his remarkable 1974 collection of interviews with people about their work, elicited descriptions of it across an astonishingly broad spectrum of tasks and occupations.

Here for instance is a book restorer:

> '*I'm just a swabber...I'm not an artist...It isn't very skilled work...It's just knowing what books need, if you want to preserve them. It's just something you do... A mechanic takes care of a tire and he knows... But if you bind good books, you make something really good, really and truly good.' (Turkel, 1974:268)*

And a hairdresser:

> '*Once in a while a hairdo will disturb me because I feel I didn't do it quite right. I'll brood over it for a little while. I like to feel I've done the best on each one each day.' (ibid:217)*

And a housewife:

'I'll sit here and I'll bake a pie and I'll get to see everybody eat it. This is my offering. I think it's the greatest satisfaction in the world to know you've pleased somebody.' (ibid:258)

Some poetry can be generated from even the most apparently boring and pressurised labour processes. Here, is a supermarket checkout operator:

'I use my three fingers – my thumb, my index finger and my middle finger. The right hand. And my left hand is on the groceries … I got my hips pushin' on the button and it rolls around on the counter. When I feel I have enough groceries in front of me, I let go of my hip. I'm just movin' – the hips, the hand, and the register, the hips, the hand and the register…If you've got that rhythm you're a fast checker…If somebody interrupts to ask me the price, I'll answer while I'm movin'. Like playin' a piano.' (ibid:241-2)

Perhaps because of some dogged refusal to believe that the long hours spent labouring could be entirely futile, and the amazing human ability to extract meaning and pleasure from any daily experience, there is a sense in which nearly all work can be experienced as creative, at least some of the time.

When most people these days speak of creative work, however, they have a somewhat narrower range of tasks in mind – typically those that involve 'having ideas' for new products or processes, adapting existing ones for new purposes or creating content for the mass media. Richard Barbrook (2006) has comprehensively catalogued the many collective nouns that have been coined to describe these workers. The 70-odd terms he lists include Helen Wilkinson's (1999) 'elancers', David Brooks' (2000) 'bobos' ('bourgeois bohemians'), Franco Bifo Berardi's (2001) 'cognitariat', and John Brockman's (1996) 'digerati' as well as Richard Florida's (2002) rather better known 'creative class'[1]. William Morris, incidentally, preferred the term 'intellectual proletariat' to refer to creative workers (Morris, 1886).

Why the urge to classify these workers? And why, particularly, now? With the simultaneous spread of digital technologies and globalisation of trade in the last years of the 20th century they have assumed a new importance as sources of 'added value' or 'intellectual property' (IP). In the 'knowledge-based economy' that public policies increasingly aspire to[2], creativity is regarded as the essential raw ingredient of economic growth.

If, as the European Council put it in its famous 2000 Lisbon Declaration,

'The shift to a digital, knowledge-based economy, prompted by new goods and services, will be a powerful engine for growth, competitiveness and jobs.' (Lisbon European Council, 2000:1)

then creative workers are the spark in this engine.

Whilst regions and cities compete to attract creative industries (Ross, this volume), corporations carry out 'knowledge audits' (Bontis, 2001, Sveiby, 1997), measure their 'intellectual capital' (Edvinsson & Malone, 1997), rate how their employees perform on

---

1   All dates and citations here are from Barbrook (2006)

2   See, for instance, the European Union's official adoption, at the 2000 Lisbon Summit, of the 'strategic goal for the next decade: to become the most competitive and dynamic knowledge-based economy in the world' (Lisbon European Council, 2000:1)

the MBTI-Creativity Index (Weiner, 1990), pour resources into 'knowledge management' (Tiwana, 2002) and ensure that their employees' ideas are copyrighted and patented, whilst the World Trade Organisation acts as a global police force to protect this newly appropriated 'knowledge'.

Creative workers would appear to be in demand as never before, but their creativity is also subject to control and contestation as never before.

Contents of this volume

This volume takes these creative workers for it subject. First, Andrew Ross sets the scene with an account of the 'mercurial career of creative industries policies' illustrated by the examples of the UK, the USA and China. One of the most influential shapers of these policies has been Richard Florida, whose consultancy services have contributed to the development of many of them. His central thesis – that creating 'cool cities' will attract creative talent which will in turn generate economic growth – is challenged in the next paper by Richard Shearmur, who draws on a detailed analysis of urban growth and graduate migration in Canada to demonstrate that the reality seems to be exactly the opposite: graduates move to where the economic growth is taking place, not vice versa.

Next, we have a series of empirical accounts of the working lives of the creative workers these policies seek to attract. Sybille Reidl, Helene Schiffbänker and Hubert Eichmann present a study of creative workers in Vienna which paints a picture of people who clearly enjoy their work, but unless they are lucky enough to work for the well unionised national broadcasting authority or in a highly regulated profession like architecture, pay a high price for this in long hours, precariousness and stress that reaches out into their personal lives. This theme is picked up by Bettina-Johanna Krings in a qualitative study that looks into what being a creative worker means for women in Germany who have, within a generation, moved from a typically home- and family-centred model of life to a work-centred 'breadwinner' model. The different strategies adopted to cope with this change range from giving up the idea of motherhood altogether to living in a permanent state of stress from the effort of juggling the demands of work and daily life. Ashika Thanki and Steve Jefferys describe the informalised labour market of the media industries in London and show how the need for personal contacts to find work and the precariousness of the workforce have reinforced the dominance of the industry by a white middle-class elite, serving not only to marginalise Black and minority ethnic workers in the workforce but also to perpetuate racism in programme content.

Bob Hughes places the concept of the 'creative' in a historical context, describing its evolution into an instrument of management control, drawing on his own experience in the advertising industry in the 1970s and 1980s to show how the division of the workforce into 'suits' and 'creatives' served to infantilise the 'creatives' and alienate them from craft-based trade unionism as well as from progression to positions of authority.

In a study of the values of new media workers in Madrid, Armando Fernández Steinko also takes up the issue of infantilisation, placing it in the context of traditional forms of organic solidarity that exist in Southern Europe. Because of the precariousness of the new economy labour market, the young workers in his study are still likely to be living with their parents well into their thirties and transfer their unquestioning attitudes to authority from the extended family to the small firms for which they typically work, and he explores the implications of this for their ability to develop a critical perspective on their work and on the world in general.

A paper by Simone Dahlmann and Ursula Huws illustrates the impact of offshore outsourcing of editorial work from the UK to India, describing the shock experienced by the British workers when they discovered that the skills in which they took pride were so easily replaceable, and the stress and insecurity experienced by the new Indian workforce as a result of having to meet the company's demands for 'flexibility'.

Finally, two papers explore workers' organised resistance to the precarisation of their jobs and the restructuring of the industries that employ them. Catherine McKercher and Vincent Mosco examine how the culture and sense of craft identity of their members led to a failure of two Hollywood trade unions to unite, despite overlapping membership, technological convergence between different media and mergers between the employers with whom they negotiate. Leif Schumacher looks at the video games industry, where workers in California have taken class action suits against their employers to win the right to overtime pay. Ironically in order to do so they had to argue that their work was *not* 'creative' because it involved working to tight supervision under conditions that bore more resemblances to a Fordist assembly-line than to the unstructured autonomous working conditions described in many accounts of the new economy. These Taylorised working conditions, he argues, cast doubt on the hypotheses that new autonomous forms of work are emerging and that what Marxist autonomists (Hardt and Negri, 2000) call the 'multitude' of 'immaterial workers' will adopt quite different forms of resistance from their 20th century forerunners.

Taken together, these accounts paint a highly contradictory picture. Across the world, motivated no doubt in part by the 'cool' of the new economy and media industries, and the enticing promise of autonomy, self-expression and social prestige, young people in large numbers seek out creative work even when they know that, compared with other kinds of work, it is precarious, competitive and may well involve long hours and poor rewards, and that the odds against achieving individual stardom are overwhelming. They are often prepared to pay a high price for this - prolonged economic dependence on parents or partners, a constrained social life, and no guarantee of long-term security, pension rights, paid holidays or the kind of slack that makes it possible to deal with unforeseen developments in their private lives.

Why are they so willing to strike this unequal bargain? and what happens when their desire for creative fulfilment, or Morris's 'conscious sensuous pleasure in the work itself' collides head-on with the employer's need to cut costs and standardise processes?

I will return briefly to these questions at the end of this paper. But first, I will present a more structural account of the role played by creative work in thecommodification process in the hope that this will shed some light on these contradictions.

The place of creative work in the commodification process

Two things lie at the source of every commodity: natural resources (whether mineral, vegetable or animal); and human creativity and ingenuity. Capitalism's trick is to appropriate these in order to create a profit which can be reinvested to create more commodities, and further profit, in an ongoing (albeit turbulent) process of development. Continuous expansion is thus one of its essential features. The expansion is both an expansion into new areas of human life (exemplified by new commodities that meet demands that were previously met outside the money economy or not at all, for instance new drugs, or new entertainment media), and a spatial expansion – into new parts of the world. Furthermore, it has several different dimensions. The expansion may be driven by the need to seek out new sources of raw materials, ranging from DNA to fossil fuels (Altvater, 2006); to find new markets (Luxemburg, 2003); or to find new places to invest the surplus, or 'sites of accumulation' (Harvey, 2003). It may also be looking for somewhere to dump the detritus resulting from all these other activities. Or, finally, the quest may be for new supplies of labour (Froebel, Heinrichs and Krey, 1977; Huws, 2003). These different drivers are dynamically interconnected with each other. For instance new groups of workers drawn into the production process will also constitute a new market for the commodities produced; investments in new infrastructures will create access to new sources of raw material and open up new sites for production, and so on.

One of the puzzles confronting those who seek to understand the dynamics of capitalist expansion has, for many years, been this: what happens when it runs out of room to expand? In theory, this could happen in relation to any of these dimensions: the world could, for instance, run out of some raw materials; markets could become saturated; we could drown in our own waste; there could be an epidemic of such proportions that the supply of labour dries up; or some other unforeseen catastrophe could take place. Some have speculated that terminal crises of capacity have only been avoided by the destruction of war and the rechannelling of surplus into investments in arms manufacture (Kidron, 1967). This is not the place for a detailed discussion of such extreme eventualities. It is, however, useful to remind ourselves that the scope for expansion is not unlimited and, as fewer and fewer areas of the world's population remain outside the market economy, the pressures increase: pressures to invent new commodities, competitive pressures to make them better or cheaper than anyone else, pressures to reach new consumers and persuade them to buy more, and pressures to do all these things more quickly, because, with the instantaneous access to information created by the internet, the moment in which any given supplier has a market advantage is becoming shorter every day.

In order to understand the place of creative work in all this, it is important to remember that everything we now have, at least everything that is produced within the money economy, whether this is products, processes, infrastructure or 'knowledge', is the result of past creativity. The technical division of labour across an economy is the result of processes of commodification which took place in the past and which continue to evolve. Before the first industrial revolution, for instance, all the functions involved in the production of a piece of cloth might have been carried out, if not by the same person, probably within the same household, including spinning, dyeing, designing, weaving, quality control, marketing, sales and so on. In industrialised fabric production these tasks may be divided not just between different workers but even between different industries, with a complex geographical division of labour. In the process splits have taken place between mental and manual tasks: between 'head' and 'hands'. Most of the manual tasks have been automated and routinised; the mental ones have been further divided up into 'executive', 'clerical', 'professional' and 'technical' functions. And some of these would fall into most people's definitions of 'creative': for instance some of the activities involved in the research and development of new fibres and dyes, the design of new fabrics, the invention of creative ways to market them and various ancilliary activities like designing the companies' websites or producing their annual reports. But what is important to remember is that they *all* have a distant ancestry in the 'craft' of those artisanal textile workers. The same could be said of a myriad other activities.

The sequence of events can be schematically summarised as follows. In the beginning, we have a worker or group of workers carrying out some task that involves the exercise of skill. Following Michael Polanyi (1967) we can describe this skill as 'tacit', a word that describes an ability or facility or knowledge that we have without being able to define precisely what it consists of. Sometimes it may even not be perceived as a skill but as a 'gift' or a 'talent' or inherited aptitude. The possession of this tacit knowledge gives these workers some bargaining power in the labour market; nobody else can do what they do, or at least not as well or as quickly. And, of course, the more they have managed to restrict access to this knowledge (for instance through long apprenticeships, or difficult-to-get qualifications, or membership of hard-to-enter guilds, or the requirement to swear oaths of secrecy), the greater will be their ability to insist on high pay or favourable conditions. For their employers, therefore, they constitute something of an obstacle to rapid expansion.

In order to cheapen production processes, or rapidly expand production (usually, but not necessarily involving the mechanisation or automation of all or parts of the process) this tacit knowledge must be *codified*, that is, it has to be analysed and broken down into its component parts so that these can be turned into a set of instructions that can be replicated by less-skilled people or a machine (Braverman, 1974). This stage can also be referred to as standardisation. Codification does not necessarily mean simplification. It can result in highly complicated algorithms, models, databases or programmes requiring abstruse knowledge that is only available to a small highly trained group of workers. Nevertheless, codified knowledge is systematised, rational and calculable.

Once tasks have been standardised, they can be counted easily, because each unit in each stage of the process is essentially the same. This makes it possible to specify tasks numerically and to manage workers, not by standing over them and making sure that they are really working, but by measuring their outputs, or standardised 'performance indicators'. And, once these outputs have become measurable, a price can be determined for them. No longer an indefinable part of a bundled-together collection of skills and knowledge, they have become separate, quantifiable entities in a division of labour.[3] They have become *tradeable*. And once work can be managed by results, if those results

---

3   Work that can be managed by results can in principle also be paid by results although this need not necessarily be the case. It is perfectly possible - and indeed most often the case - for a group of workers to be paid by the hour even though the products of their labour are sold individually and their services individually priced by the employer.

can be readily transported (whether in the form of physical components or of digitised information that can be sent electronically), then there is no longer any need for it to be carried out in the same place, or by the same organisation. This can lead to changes in the division of labour within an organisation (e.g. merging or breaking up traditional structures into separate cost or profit centres, automation of processes, and/or relocating them to other sites) or it can lead to subcontracting them to other organisations. Spatial and contractual restructuring may be combined in many different configurations – for instance a function may be outsourced with a transfer of personnel to an external company, on an adjacent site; it may be relocated in its entirety to another company in another country; it may continue to be carried out on the same site but by employees of a temporary agency or a subcontractor; or it may be carried out by freelancers. A global company may decide to centralise a particular function on a single site in one country or, conversely, to decentralise it to a dispersed network of agents (Flecker & Kirschenhofer, 2002). The point is that once any task has been reduced to standard components, or modules, these modules can be reconfigured in a huge variety of ways, to suit the particular needs of any given organisation at any particular point in time. The greater the degree of standardisation, the greater the scope for reconfiguration, and the more potentially complex the global division of labour.

This is, of course, a highly schematic overview, but it is one that seems to be applicable to the development of all commodities, whether these are goods or services (Huws, 2003). It is a process which is self-replicating: every time a process becomes standardised, the division of labour becomes more complex; and each time this happens, new processes are required, inorder to develop and manage this new division of labour. Each time, a new split between 'head' and 'hands' takes place, some manual jobs are automated out of existence while others become less skilled and more routine, whilst simultaneously new non-manual jobs are created to manage the machines and the manual workers. Meanwhile, the 'head' jobs are themselves subject to rationalisation and standardisation processes, leading to further sub-divisions. The overall effect is a continuous elaboration of the technical division of labour. In this fracturing, more and more separate steps are involved in the development of any given commodity. If we think of a complex modern commodity like a mobile phone, it becomes apparent that determining what parts of its value have been contributed by what worker would be a task of forensic magnitude – so many fractions of so many standardised processes, so much codified knowledge, extracted from so many workers, living and dead, so many ancillary activities involved in getting it from the germ of an idea to the consumer, are involved.

It is not just new consumer products that are constantly entering the market as a result of these processes. Their production also involves intermediary inputs in the form of other commodities, including the machinery used to produce them, the infrastructure and services required to make them run, and a range of other business services, each of which, to the extent that it is standardised and capable of being traded at a profit, can also be regarded as a commodity, whether this is the provision of accountancy or an outsourced customer service call centre; an insurance policy or website management; logistics services or market research.

So, where do creative workers fit into this picture? First and most obviously we have to point out that, using a broad definition, some measure of creativity can be said to be involved in just about any tacit process, whether it is recognised as such or not. Often, indeed, an activity is only appreciated as creative when it has already been replaced by more stand-ardised, automated processes. When skills become obsolete, they usually morph very quickly from the taken-for-granted abilities of the lowly tradesperson into 'creative' crafts carried out as educational stimulation for school children, leisure activities for the idle, therapy for the mentally ill or the manufacture of luxury one-off products for sale to the rich. Suddenly, making pottery, embroidery or ornamental ironwork is no longer just the result of training, or patience or a 'knack' but requires 'talent', 'flair' and 'artistry'.

The results of workers' past creativity is thus the raw material for what we already have. But new creativity is constantly needed at every stage in the process described schematically above. It is needed to analyse what is being done tacitly and imagine how this knowledge can be codified and standardised. It is needed to invent the machines that can replicate it and formulate the instructions to run these machines. It is needed to find ways to persuade the old workers to change their ways (or depart peacefully) and to train the new ones. It is needed to devise ways to change the spatial and organisational structures within which work is organised and to manage these, and to make sure that all the separate units are communicating with each other. It is needed to persuade people to buy the products and understand how to use them. It is needed to carry out research and invent new products and processes. It is needed to adapt existing products and processes for new purposes. It is needed to provide content for the exponentially growing (and technologically diversifying) mass media: to educate, entertain and inform the public and cater to their aesthetic and spiritual needs. Finally, it is needed for a number of functions traditionally carried out by government ranging from providing health services to waging war.

The emergence of new forms of creative work does, not, of course mean the death of all the old forms. There remain many spaces in the system for lucky individuals to exercise autonomy and gain huge satisfaction from their work, whether this is making music, designing buildings, making films or writing novels. These spaces are, however, becoming more constrained, because of the increasing dominance of a few giant media conglomerates, the bureacratisation of funding processes, and the sheer pressure of competition.

What does this mean for creative workers?

Creative workers are in an extraordinarily ambiguous position in all this. They are, on the one hand, agents of change. Without new ideas, the whole system would grind to a halt. The expansionary logic underlying capitalism means that it cannot stand still. Failure to innovate means being overtaken by the competition which means eventual displacement from the market, however good the product. A constant supply of new ideas is therefore absolutely necessary. On the other hand, in the process of innovation, what preceded it is rendered obsolete. Whether it is visible or not to the creative worker (and often it is), the process of creation is therefore also a process of destruction, sometimes the destruction of another worker's livelihood. Mike Hales (1980) described some of the contradictions that arise here from the perspective of a systems analyst whose job is to redesign other people's labour processes. Having to deal with the knowledge that they may have harmed another person's life chances may also do damage to traditional allegiances and solidarities but it is only one of many challenges creative workers face.

More acute, for many, is the problem of the ownership of their own ideas. Ideas, unlike words, images or music (which can be copyrighted) and designs (which can be patented) do not form part of any regulated market. Whilst being an 'ideas person' may be your greatest asset, the moment you have communicated that idea to someone else it ceases, legally speaking, to be yours. In parting with it, whether to an employer, a potential employer or a client, you are therefore taking the risk that you may not get the credit for it or, indeed, even be rewarded for it at all. Once others have this idea, your usefulness to them may well be at an end. Even if you are an employee and your employer continues to employ you whilst using your idea, this idea might only have a short shelf-life. If it is a good one, the chances are that it will be quickly and widely copied. If it is bad then it is likely to be dropped. Every idea is therefore like a little grenade, with the capability of damaging the person who throws it as well as making an impact where it is thrown. It is a cliché of the creative industries that you are only as good as your last idea, but, especially in precarious labour markets with a rapid turnover in ideas, this is increasingly the reality for many workers.

Ideas are not the only assets of creative workers, of course; they also produce intellectual property in forms that can be legally protected by patents and copyright, as well as possessing abundant knowledge, experience and what has come to be known as 'social capital' (Bourdieu, 1983) – reputations and networks of contacts. But, just like the tacit knowledge of artisanal weavers, these too are subject to appropriation, standardisation and incorporation into new commodities. Creative workers are not only the architects of commodification; they are also its victims.

'Knowledge management' practices explicitly target these workers. They are asked to pool their contacts in common address books; to participate in brainstorming sessions where their ideas are recorded;[4] to write manuals explaining the programmes they have developed; to run training courses for their junior colleagues or 'mentor' them; to share their 'frequently asked questions'; to participate in the development of standard procedures whose descriptions will be incorporated into quality standards, or even outsourcing contracts for others to abide by; to suggest the 'performance indicators' that will be used to determine their future pay and promotion; to place their work in progress or powerpoint presentations onto corporate or university intranets; and to contribute to the development of 'knowledge databases'.

Two consequences of this development deserve comment here. First, by participating in these practices creative workers are contributing to their own dispensibility. By sharing their knowledge they are cheapening it, and rendering themselves more easily replaceable. However, because they rarely work alone, but are typically working in teams with an internal division of labour, they cannot afford *not* to share this knowledge. Not only will the quality of the overall product (and hence, perhaps, their personal reputations) be adversely affected if there is poor communication within the team; and not only will they have to do more work if their colleagues don't have the skills to help them out; they also want to learn as well as teach. The exchanges of knowledge that go on within a collaborating group do not just have a synergistic effect in creating a whole that may be greater than

---

4   Under the guise of 'total quality management' (Feigenbaum, 1951) policies, such brainstorming techniques are also often used to extract productivity-enhancing ideas from manual workers.

the sum of its parts; they can also generate considerable intrinsic job satisfaction for those involved, as well as adding to the resources they can bring to future work. If the workers are insecure about their future employment (as is often the case when people are working on projects with a fixed term), then considerable tension can be generated between the urge to co-operate and the urge to compete (Meil, 2004).

Second, even if the workers in question have secure jobs and have not participated in a process of explaining themselves out of work, the very process of codifying their knowledge contributes to a change in the quality of their work. As soon as it is embedded in standardised protocols, specified quality standards and performance indicators, the work starts to lose its spontaneity and the workers their autonomy. The very qualities that attracted them to creative work in the first place start to disappear under the weight of daily routines that involve filling in endless time sheets and job sheets, checking boxes to ensure that standard routines have been followed and documenting every step of the work. This presents a challenge for managers. How can they control this volatile workforce without stopping the flow of new ideas? How can they manage the risk that many of these ideas may be duds? How can they generate an impression that they have provided a funky, fun place to work whilst making sure that productivity stays high? At what point does the coop become so confining that the geese stop laying the golden eggs?

But this development also creates enormous dilemmas for creative workers themselves. Starting from an urge to express themselves or create something meaningful or beautiful they want to give their all to the task in hand. But every extra contribution they make may involve a further degree of self-exploitation – in terms of putting in extra time, accepting lower pay or poorer conditions, or handing over their knowledge in ways that may contribute, either directly or indirectly, to constructing new bars for their own cages, or those of others.

At its harshest, the deal they are offered on the labour market can come perilously close to that of the mother brought before Solomon to decide the fate of her baby[5]: give up the thing you love, the product of your own creation, to someone else, or see it maimed or killed. It is a vivid example of the sort of alienation attributed to proletarian workers by Karl Marx[6]. Whether we should argue that this alienation has now spread to parts of the bourgeoise or that creative workers now form part of the proletariat is a debate that I have taken up elsewhere (Huws, 2003).

The eager young people flocking to enter creative jobs doubtless have a range of different reactions to this situation. Compared with their parents, or their less adventurous schoolmates, many will undoubtedly feel that they have won a better and freer lifestyle. And they may well attribute to personal inadequacy or bad luck some of the negative experiences they have on the labour market. Yet they are intelligent, educated, critical people with a wide knowledge of the world and an overview of the processes they are involved in. They have to

---

5   Bible,1 Kings 3:16-28,

6   In Chapter 4 of *The Holy Family*, Karl Marx and Friedrich Engels, say that, 'The propertied class and the class of the proletariat present the same human self-estrangement. But the former class feels at ease and strengthened in this self-estrangement, it recognises estrangement as its own power and has in it the semblance of a human existence. The class of the proletariat feels annihilated in estrangement; it sees in it its own powerlessness and the reality of an inhuman existence. It is, to use an expression of Hegel, in its abasement the indignation at that abasement, an indignation to which it is necessarily driven by the contradiction between its human nature and its condition of life, which is the outright, resolute and comprehensive negation of that nature.' (Marx & Engels, 1844)

be, because it is precisely for these qualities that they are recruited. Innovation can only come from 'thinking outside the box'. And employers are aware of this. But the imperatives of expansion in a context of competitiveness and rapid change impel them, willy nilly, to embark on precisely those processes that involve putting people *into* boxes.

What happens in the minds and imaginations of creative people in the process of being inserted into those boxes is terribly important, not just for their own futures but for those of the organisations for which they work and, more generally, for the future of society as a whole. Will they resist and start to bite the hands that feed them? And if they do, will this resistance have any effect? Or will they simply be discarded and replaced by the next wave of starry-eyed youngsters? If they don't actively resist, will they actively co-operate and hasten the commodification process with all the waste and environmental destruction that entails? Will they subside into a cynical semi-acceptance that guarantees them some personal security but does at least offer some passive resistance to the worst excesses of the market? Or will they transfer their energy and originality and idealism to other arenas – outside the boxes – and contribute to the project of imagining and designing alternative social and economic models? The papers in this volume open up a discussion of such questions, as well as giving us a rich descriptive picture of the working lives, attitudes, fears and employment prospects of creative workers.

I will end as I began, giving the last word to William Morris, who was quoted at the beginning of this paper. His utopian future in which all labour is creative and unalienated is contrasted in *News from Nowhere* with a an old man's recollections of the 19th century, in words which still seem apposite in the 21st.

'In the last age of civilisation men had got into a vicious circle in the matter of production of wares. They had reached a wonderful facility of production, and in order to make the most of that facility they had gradually created (or allowed to grow, rather) a most elaborate system of buying and selling, which has been called the World Market; and that World Market, once set a-going, forced them to go on making more and more of these wares, whether they needed them or not. So that while (of course) they could not free themselves from the toil of making real necessities, they created a never-ending series of sham or artificial necessaries [sic], which became, under the iron rule of the aforesaid World Market, of equal importance to them with the real necessaries [sic] which supported life. ...Once they had forced themselves to stagger along under this horrible burden of unnecessary production, it became impossible for them to look upon labour and its results from any other point of view than one - to wit, the ceaseless endeavour to expend the least possible amount of labour on any article made and yet at the same time to make as many articles as possible. To this "cheapening of production", as it was called, everything was sacrificed: the happiness of the workman at his work, nay, his most elementary comfort and bare health, his food, his clothes, his dwelling, his leisure, his amusement, his education - his life, in short - did not weigh a grain of sand in the balance against this dire necessity of "cheap production" of things, a great part of which were not worth producing at all.' (Morris, 1890)*

REFERENCES

Altvater, E. (2006) 'The social and natural environment of fossil capitalism', Panitch, L. & C. Leys (eds.) *Coming to Terms with Nature,* Socialist Register, 2007, London: Merlin:37-59

Barbrook, R. (2006) *The Class of the New,* London: Openmute

Bontis, N. Assessing knowledge assets: a review of the models used to measure intellectual capital. *International Journal of Management Reviews,* 2001, Volume 3 No 1, pp 41-60

Bourdieu, P. (1983) 'Forms of capital' in J. C. Richards (ed.) *Handbook of Theory and Research for the Sociology of Education,* New York: Greenwood Press.

Braverman, H. (1974) *Labor and Monopoly Capital: the degradation of work in the twentieth century,* New York: Monthly Review Press

Edvinsson, L. & Malone, M. (1997) *Intellectual Capital: Realising Your Company's True Value by Finding its Hidden Brainpower,* New York: HarperBusiness

Feigenbaum, A. V. (1951) *Quality Control: Principles, Practice, and Administration,* New York; London: McGraw-Hill

Flecker, J. & Kirschenhofer, S. (2002) *Jobs on the Move: European case studies in relocating eWork,*IES Report 386, Brighton: Institute for Employment Studies

Froebel, F., J. Heinrichs & O. Krey (1977) *The New International Division of Labour,* Cambridge: Cambridge University Press

Hales, M. (1980) *Living Thinkwork: Where Do Labour Processes Come From?,* London: Free Association Books

Hardt, M. & A. Negri (2000) *Empire,* Cambridge, MA: Harvard University Press

Harvey, D. (2003) 'The "new" imperialism: accumulation by dispossession', Panitch, L. & C. Leys (eds.) *The New Imperial Challenge,* Socialist Register, 2003, London: Merlin:43-63

Huws, U. (2003) *The Making of a Cybertariat: Virtual Work in a Real World,* New York: Monthly Review Press

Kidron, M. (1967) 'A Permanent Arms Economy', *International Socialism* No.28, Spring

Lisbon European Council (2000) *Presidency Conclusions,* 23-24 March, retrieved, November 1, 2006 from http://www.consilium.europa.eu/ueDocs/cms_Data/docs/pressData/en/ec/00100-r1.en0.htm

Luxemburg, R. (1913; reprinted 2003)*The Accumulation of Capital,* London: Routledge (reprint)

Marx, K. & F. Engels (1844) *The Holy Family or Critique of Critical Criticism: Against Bruno Bauer and Company.* Retrieved on October 30, 2006 from http://www.marxists.org/archive/marx/works/1845/holy-family/ch04.htm

Meil, P. (2004) 'Spanning the distance: challenges for competency, control and quality of work life', *ICT, the Knowledge Society and Changes in Work Workshop,* The Hague, 9-10 June

Morris, W. & E. Belfort Bax (1886) *Socialism from the Root Up,* Chapter 22: 'Socialism Militant' [Part 1]. Retrieved November 2, 2006 from the William Morris Internet Archive, http://www.marxists.org/archive/morris/works/1888/sru/ch22-1.htm

Morris, W. (1990) *News from Nowhere,* Chapter 15: 'On the Lack of Incentive to Labour in a Communist Society'. Retrieved, November 2, 2006 from the William Morris Internet Archive, http://www.marxists.org/archive/morris/works/1890/nowhere/chapters/chapter15.htm

Polanyi, M. (1967),*The Tacit Dimension,* Garden City, NY.: Doubleday

Sveiby, K. E. (1997), *The New Organizational Wealth: Managing and Measuring Knowledge-Based Assets,* San Francisco, Ca.: Berret-Koehler

Terkel, S. (1974) *Working,* Harmondsworth, UK; New York, USA: Penguin

Tiwana, A. (2002), *The Knowledge Management Toolkit: Orchestrating IT, Strategy, and Knowledge Platforms* (2nd Edition), Upper Saddle River, NJ: Prentice Hall, 2002

Wiener, I.B. (ed) (1990) *Journal of Personality Assessment:* Vol. 54. Nos. 3 & 4

Nice work if you can get it:

the mercurial career of creative industries policy

Andrew Ross

Andrew Ross *is Professor of Social and Cultural Analysis at New York University in the USA.*

ABSTRACT

Driven by the belief that culture-based enterprise can be promoted as a driver of economic development, governments all over the world have developed policies aimed at boosting their creative industries. These policies ought to present some new, long-term opportunities for cultural workers, but in practice they seem more likely to universalise the traditionally precarious work profile of artists. Focusing on the career of creative industry policy in the UK, the USA and China, this paper calls for an assessment of its model of job creation from the standpoint of quality of work life.

The newfound affection of governments all over the world for boosting their 'creative industries' presents a conundrum. This emerging policy consensus assumes that culture-based enterprise can be promoted as a driver of economic development for cities, regions and nations that want to keep up, catch up, or not be left out of the knowledge society. At the very least, then, the policy spotlight ought to present some new, long-term opportunities for cultural workers accustomed to eke a fragile, makeshift living out of art, expression, design, and performance. So far, however, the terms and framework of the kind of development envisaged by policy-makers seem guaranteed merely to elevate this traditionally unstable work profile into an inspirational model to be emulated by employees in related industrial sectors. If the creative industries become the ones to follow, jobs, in short, may well look more and more like gigs; nice work if you can find it.

The shift in nomenclature – from the rusty coinage of 'cultural industries' to the newly minted 'creative industries' – is usually credited to the UK's incoming New Labour administration of 1997, whose zealous modernisers renamed the Department of National Heritage as the Department of Culture, Media and Sport (DCMS), and promoted, as its bailiwick, a paradigm of self-directed innovation in the arts and knowledge sectors of the economy. In the pages that follow, I will summarise how this policy paradigm has fared in the years since the establishment of the DCMS. Focusing on its career in the UK, the USA, and China, I will describe some of the reasons for its enthusiastic reception and will try to assess its model of job creation from a qualitative standpoint. For while statistics about the growth and productivity of the creative sector have been legion, there has been precious little attention to the quality of work life with which it is associated.

The concept of the creative industries was initially introduced in Australia by Paul Keating's government in the early 1990s, but its definitive expression, in the founding documents of Blair's DCMS, bore all the breathless hallmarks of New Economy thinking: technological enthusiasm, the cult of youth, branding and monetisation fever, and ceaseless organisational change (DCMS, 1998). Regardless, the paradigm survived the New Economy burnout, and was further endowed with statistical and fiscal backing from the Treasury and the Department of Trade and Industry. While this renewed interest stemmed, in large part, from militantly optimistic estimates of the export trade potential of 'British creativity', few could have predicted that the creative industries model would itself become such a successful export. In the space of a few years, it had been adopted as a viable development strategy by the governments of countries as politically and demographically disparate as Russia, Brazil, Canada, and China, to name just a few of the largest. As the global competition for talent heats up, it has been relatively easy to persuade bureaucrats that high-end human capital and intellectual property are the keys to winning a permanent seat in the knowledge-based economy. But those same officials are ever tormented by the task of finding the right kind of industrial strategy to deliver the goods. On the face of it, the carefully packaged policy of the 'creative industries' appears to fit the bill.

It may be too early to predict the ultimate fate of the paradigm. But sceptics have already prepared the way for its demise: it will not generate jobs; it is a recipe for magnifying patterns of class polarisation; its function as a cover for the corporate intellectual property (IP) grab will become all too apparent; its urban development focus will price out the very creatives on whose labour it depends; its reliance on self-promoting rhetoric runs far in advance of its proven impact; its cookie-cutter approach to economic development does violence to regional specificity; its adoption of an instrumental value of creativity will cheapen the true worth of artistic creation (Hesmondhalgh and Pratt, 2005). Still others are inclined simply to see the new policy rubric as 'old wine in new bottles' – a glib production of spin-happy New Labourites, hot for naked marketisation but mindful of the need for socially acceptable dress. For those who take a longer, more orthodox Marxist view, the turn toward creative industries is surely a further symptom of an accumulation regime at the end of its effective rule, spent as a productive force, awash in financial speculation, and obsessed with imagery, rhetoric, and display (Arrighi, 1994, 2005).

Scholars and activists with ties to the labour movement can ill afford to be quite so cynical or high-minded in their response to these developments. Industrial restructuring over the last three decades has not been kind to the cause of secure, sustainable livelihoods, and indeed many of the changes have been aimed directly at destroying the power of trade unions. In OECD countries, the traditional cultural industries have been a relatively significant union stronghold with a long and fruitful history of mutual support between craft-based locals. While capital owners have succeeded in offshoring production wherever possible, the power of organised labour has held on in core sectors, especially those dependent on a heavily localised urban supply of skills and resources that cannot be readily duplicated offshore. In some cases, the migration of an industry to new regions has even helped to generate a pioneer union presence. For example, when Walt Disney created Disney World in Central Florida in the 1960s, he had little option but to bring along the unions, instantly making his company the largest union employer in the state.

Certainly, new patterns of investment, rapid technological change, and global production have all taken their toll on employees' capacity to engage in collective bargaining. But fair labour at union rates and conditions remains an institutional feature of cultural industries (film, radio, TV, theatre, journalism, musical and other performing arts) as they were classically constituted from the 1930s. By contrast, the non-commercial arts have long been a domain of insecurity, underpayment, and disposability, interrupted only by those few who can break through into an often lucrative circuit of fame. Maps of the 'creative industries,' as pioneered by the DCMS, include the traditionally unionised commercial sectors, but the entrepreneurial paradigm touted by the policy-makers defiantly points away from the fair standards commonly associated with a union job. The preferred labour profile is more typical of the eponymous struggling artist, whose long-abiding vulnerability to occupational neglect is now magically transformed, under the new order of creativity, into a model of enterprising, risk-tolerant pluck. So, too, the quirky, nonconformist qualities once cultivated by artists as a guarantee of quasi-autonomy from market dictates are now celebrated as the key for creative souls with portfolio careers to integrate into the global value chains that are central to the new topography of creative markets.

Even more challenging, from a strict labour perspective, is the rapid flourishing of activities tied to self-publication or amateur content promotion. The most admired artefacts on the new information landscape are websites like YouTube, Flickr, YourGallery, and MySpace, which, along with the exponentially expanding blogosphere, attest to the rise of amateurism as a serious source of public expression. Hailed as a refreshing break from the filtering of editorial gatekeepers, they are also sources of free, or cut-price content – a clear threat to the livelihoods of professional creatives whose prices are driven down by, or who simply cannot compete with, the commercial mining of these burgeoning, discount alternatives. The physical construction of the World Wide Web has itself been a mammoth enterprise of free, or undercompensated labour (Terranova 2000); its adoption as a commercial delivery model (based on the principle of 'disintermediation') has taken its toll on jobs and small businesses in the brick-and-mortar world of sales, distribution and retail; and its use for unauthorised file-sharing has been legally opposed by all the entertainment unions as a threat to their industries' workforce. The rapid flowering of these networked media channels has hastened on the process – initiated with the onset of a consumer society in the early twentieth century – by which the burden of productive labour is increasingly transferred on to the user or consumer.

Nor is the web-enabled 'liberation' of individual creators an easy escape from corporate capture. Self-generated Internet buzz has been hailed as a viable avenue for artists looking to market their work independently of the entertainment majors. Recent examples include: the musical careers of Sandi Thom, the Arctic Monkeys, Lily Allen, and Gorillaz; films like *The Blair Witch Project,* and *Snakes on a Plane;* and

Chinese Internet celebrities like the brazen blogger known as Sister Hibiscus and the Sichuanese mountain girl known as Tianxian MM. Arguably, the largest beneficiaries of these innovations are the corporate majors, for whom the profitable cooption of amateur strategies has long been a studied preoccupation: as in 'cool hunting,' the adoption of 'indie' aesthetics and attitudes, the manufacture of microbeers, and the tactic of viral marketing among college students. In traditional media enclaves, the allied discount practice of reality-based programming is by now an indispensable principle of profit. Nothing has more radically undermined union efforts to preserve the integrity of pay scales for talent in the media industries than the use, in TV and radio, of amateurs on reality (and talk) shows of every genre and description.

Where unions side with corporate employers – in the IP clampdown against file-sharing, for example – there is every justification for lamenting the conservative character and outcome of 'business unionism'. But in non-unionised industries like IT and software design, the labour implications of non-proprietary activities waged against the big corporate powers are equally fraught. For example, the cooperative labour ethos of the FLOSS (Free/Libre Open Source Software) networks of engineers and programmers has been lauded as a noble model of mutual aid in the public service (Stallman, 2002: Weber, 2004). But FLOSS has been much less useful as a model for sustainable employment. Seduced by the prospect of utilising unpaid, expert labour, tech multinationals have increasingly adopted open source software like Linux, reinforcing concerns that the ethical principle of free software for the people equals free labour for corporations.

Like corporations in pursuit of non-proprietary public goods, national economic managers are keen to discover fresh and inexpensive sources of value – hidden in off-the-chart places or unexploited cross-industry connections – that can be readily quantified as GNP. The biggest returns are in high-tech industries, of course, and so it is not surprising that the creativity bandwagon is being driven by the much lionised experience of lucrative fields like software design. The original inclusion of this sector in the DCMS map of the creative industries helps to explain why governments have been so willing to promote the new policies[1].

But what if the newfound interest of states and corporations were a genuine opportunity for creative labour? After all, creatives, in any field, yearn for attention and recognition, and habitually bemoan neglect on the part of institutional authorities. So, too, wasn't the demand for creative, meaningful work in factories and offices a rallying cry of the 1970s 'refusal of work'? Calls to humanise the workplace by introducing mentally challenging tasks and employee innovation have long been pushed as an alternative to the humdrum routines of standard industrial employment. Could some of those hopes be realised through the elevation of creativity to a keystone of industrial policy? Critics of the new policy paradigm have an obligation to look for emerging profiles of a 'good job' that might stand the test of time in

---

1   The DCMS boosted employment by 500,000 and income by £36.4bn by adding in the UK's software sector. Even so, influential DCMS consultant John Howkins, author of *The Creative Economy* (2001) regrets that the majority of science-based industries were left out of the DCMS definition, seeing no justification for excluding them from the rubric of creativity other than the administrative claim of another government department, Trade and Industry. (Howkins, 2004)

an economic environment where the ground now shifts underneath workers with disturbing frequency.

A Very UnBritish Coup

At the dawn of the post-war Labour government, its policy architect, Aneurin Bevan, depicted Britain as 'an island of coal surrounded by a sea of fish'. It was a memorable image of the nation's natural assets, and it captured his own party's mid-century appetite for nationalising them. Fifty years later, in the wake of de-nationalisation, film honcho David Putnam offered an update: Britain had become 'an island of creativity surrounded by a sea of understanding' (Ryan, 2000: 16). Not a winning phrase, for sure, but Putnam's characterisation was an equally faithful reflection of the temper of the New Labour government he would shortly join as an advisor on science and culture. From the outset, Tony Blair's Cool Britannia would be a massive PR campaign to persuade the world that the country Napoleon once mocked as a nation of shop-keepers was now a nation of artists and designers, with the future in their enterprising bones. 'Creative Britain' was rolled out under the kleig-light scrutiny of the tabloid media, and, for several years, resembled one never-ending launch party, with artists and arts grandees playing front-page Eurostar roles ordinarily reserved for sports and movie celebrities.

The real story behind Creative Britain was much more prosaic, of course. By the 1990s, the nation's economy was no longer driven by high-volume manufacturing, fuelled by the extractive resources that Bevan had extolled. Like their competitors, Britain's managers were on the lookout for service industries that would 'add value' in a distinctive way. In the bowels of Whitehall, an ambitious civil servant came up with a useful statistic. If you lumped all the economic activities of arts and culture professionals together with those in software to create a sector known as the 'creative industries', you would have, on paper at least, a revenue powerhouse that generated £60 billion a year. (In 2000, revised and improved estimates put the figure at £112 billion). Even more illustrative, the sector was growing at twice the rate of growth of the economy as a whole. For an incoming government, looking to make its mark on the sclerotic post-Thatcher scene, the recent performance and future potential of the creative industries were godsends. Britain could have its hot new self-image, and Blair's ministers would have the GNP numbers to back it up. Unlike Bevan's coal and fish, or Thatcher's North Sea oil, creativity was a renewable energy resource, mostly untapped; every citizen had some of it, the cost of extraction was minimal, and it would never run out.

As far as cultural policy went, almost every feature of the old dispensation was now subject to a makeover. When the Arts Council was established in 1945, its first chair, the serenely mischievous John Maynard Keynes, described the evolution of its famous 'arms-length' funding principle as having 'happened in a very English, informal, un-ostentatious way – half-baked, if you like' (Keynes, 1945: 142). Keynes would have us believe that Britain acquired its arts policy, like its empire, in a fit of absent-minded-ness. In truth, it was simply falling in line with every other Western social democracy by acknowledging that the market failure of the arts should be counteracted through state subsidies. Keynes's batty boosterism – 'Let every part of Merry England be merry in its own way. Death to Hollywood' – was a far cry from the regimen of requirements demanded fifty years later by Chris Smith, the first DCMS minister, who declared *ex officio* that he did not believe in 'grants for grants' sake' (Smith, 1999: 14).

To qualify for public funding under Smith's department, artists had to show a demonstrable return on investment; they had to prove that their work furthered public goods like diversity, access, relevance, civic pride, community innovation, and social inclusion. DCMS policies asked artists to play directly functional roles in society: assisting in the improvement of public health, race relations, urban blight, special education, welfare to work programs, and of course, economic development (Smith, 1998). Politicians began to recount visits to homeless shelters or hospitals where the introduction of some worthy arts program had transformed the lives of residents. Soon, they were speculating on how a savvy application of arts skills could help reduce crime, truancy, teenage pregnancy, poverty, and neighbourhood degradation. Naturally, most working artists, suspicious of their newly designated role as instruments of social policy, saw these functions as more appropriate to glorified social workers than to traditional creative practitioners. For those who had never hewed to the principle of arts autonomy, and who subscribed instead to the more progressive ethos of service to political ideals, New Labour was demanding that artists be socially conscious in passive and complicit ways, and to eschew any real opposition to the state. Harold Rosenberg spearheaded a similar complaint in the 1930s, when he declared that the New Deal's WPA programs, offering a government wage in return for socially useful art, heralded the death of the bohemian avant garde, as a radical force, at least (Rosenberg, 1975).

But to see the policy changes simply as a way of reining in, and exploiting, artists' often wayward citizenly energies is to miss much of the rationale for the shift in government focus. Nicholas Garnham has argued that the new policy paradigm was driven, in large part, by innovation fever around IT development, and therefore should be seen primarily as an extension of information society policy (Garnham, 2005). The key creatives and the highest economic performers in this scenario were the engineers and technologists whose entrepreneurial efforts as change-agents in New Economy start-ups rode the trend of business management away from the stifling, cumbersome domains of the large hierarchical corporation. The IT industry buzz around creativity caught the imagination of British politicians who saw a convenient bridge to other sectors that were potentially rich in IP exploitation. Indeed, by 2003 the figures for software, computer games, and electronic publishing clearly dominated (at 36.5 per cent) the revenue statistics for the creative industries as a whole (Prowse, 2006).

With the Creative Industries Task Force lighting the way, every region of Britain soon had its own Cultural Consortium, along with designated 'creative hubs' and 'cultural quarters.' Development of the sector has been recently acknowledged by Gordon Brown, Blair's heir apparent, as the vital spark of the future national economy. Pushed as an all-purpose panacea, the development formula was even embraced as common sense by left-leaning academics weaned on critical cultural policy studies (Hartley, 2004). Most conspicuously, the triumph of the paradigm was achieved in the absence of any substantive data or evidence to support the case for culturally-led regeneration (Oakley, 2004). After all, what quantitative measures are useful in assessing the impact of cultural activity, in any given community, on reducing crime, binge-drinking, adult illiteracy or sexual intolerance? Common sense observation tells us that these results are much more likely to be offshoots of the gentrified demographic changes typically associated with cultural quartering.

Despite the lip service paid to supporting independent artistic initiatives, which are liable to evolve in unforeseen shapes and sizes, the preferred framework for business development in this sector remains some version of the New Economy start-up, a micro-business or SME structured to achieve a public listing, or geared, in the short-term, to generating a significant chunk of IP by 'bringing ideas to the market.' Thus, in the Creative Economy programme, the latest DCMS productivity initiative 'to make Britain the world's creative hub,' the government offers its services as a broker between creative entrepreneurs and potential investors in the understanding that creators are not always the best placed to exploit their ideas. Though they might win awards, they will remain commercially weak, incapable of breaking through to the market, unless they are incubated and groomed for growth or for hitting the jackpot.

While creative work can surely be organised and channelled in this enterprising way, and to patently profitable ends, it has yet to be shown that the nature of the enterprise produces good work, never mind good jobs. The productivity statistics that orbit, halo-like, around creative industry policy, do not measure such things, nor has there been any DCMS effort to date that assesses the quality of work life associated with its policies. This omission is all the more remarkable if we consider the high status that governments, historically, have accorded cultural creativity when it comes to maintaining a nation's quality of life in general. A fuller, multi-faceted appraisal of creative worker profiles would go a long way to answering the questions that labour advocates have about this sector.

The Great American Bootstrap

In the British case, as I have shown, the state has taken a more active role in cultural policy, elbowing aside the 'arm's length' tradition, but only to ensure that reliance on state assistance will diminish as rapidly as possible. Government action, in the creative industries model, is aimed at stimulating and liberating the latent, or untutored, entrepreneurial energies that lie in reserve in every pocket of cultural activity; a hand up, in other words, rather than a hand-out.

The American case-history is complicated, from the outset, by the selective lip service paid to the First Amendment. As Toby Miller and George Yudice have argued, the widely accepted claim that the USA does not dabble in cultural policy because it strives to maintain a strict constitutional separation between the state and cultural expression, is somewhat disingenuous. The state, for example, has long nurtured the entertainment industries – especially Hollywood – through tax credits, a range of other subsidies, and lavish trade promotion (Miller and Yudice, 2003). These myriad forms of market protection have been extended, more recently, to the US-based media Goliaths – General

Electric, Disney, Time Warner, Viacom, Liberty Media, NBC, News Corporation – whose conglomerate operations and properties dominate almost every sector of cultural expression in the USA. Their ability to secure government-granted monopoly franchises brings untold wealth and power (McChesney, 2004). Who could maintain that this long-established reliance on government largesse does not amount to cultural policy in all but name? Nor is the practice limited to domestic operations. Though the USA took the best part of two centuries to become a net IP exporter, its strong-arm overseas efforts to enforce the IP rights of Hollywood and other content exporters through international agreements such as TRIPS (Trade Related Intellectual Property Rights) along with those brokered by the WTO (World Trade Organisation) has been a driving preoccupation of US trade policy since the 1960s. Indeed, from the perspective of many developing countries, IP protection vies, currently, with the projection of pre-emptive military force as the dominant face of US power abroad. In the case of the conflict in Iraq, for example, State Department plans to privatise that country's economy gave extraordinary prominence to the sanctity of IP rights.

While the state's market protections for these industries are not necessarily content-specific, cultural content has long been an active component of US foreign policy. This was especially the case during the era of the Good Neighbor policy in Latin America, when Nelson Rockefeller headed up the Office of the Coordinator of Inter-American Affairs (Yudice, 2004). It would be impossible, moreover, to ignore the explicit use of targeted cultural policy in the Cold War in the staggering range of activities sponsored by CIA fronts like the Congress for Cultural Freedom (Saunders, 2000). While more formally abstract, the profile of free artistic expression promoted by government agencies like the USIA (United States Information Agency) to highlight the virtues of living in the 'free world' was no less ideological. With the end of the Cold War, the propaganda value of the autonomous artist evaporated overnight; the spectacle of American artists strenuously exercising their freedoms was no longer serviceable. In 1997, the same year as the New Labour turnaround, the National Endowment for the Art's policy document, *American Canvas,* laid out a remarkably similar template for applicants to follow, in order to apply their work to socially useful ends, 'from youth programs and crime prevention to job training and race relations' (Larson, 1997). Just as in the British case, the artist was reconceived as the model citizen-worker – a self-motivated entrepreneur who is able to work in a highly flexible manner with a wide range of clients, partners and sponsors.

While American fine arts policy, strictly speaking, has been mired in the moralism of the Culture Wars, the commercial cultural industries have been consumed with the gold rush to secure ownership of IP rights in every domain of expression. For the most part, they have enjoyed a 'first mover' advantage in global markets, and so there has been little need for the change in nomenclature that New Labour initiated, or for institutional authorities to view creativity as a development strategy for 'catching up.' Instead, in the USA, the creative industries are more routinely, and bluntly, referred to as copyright or IP industries.

By contrast, it is in urban policy that the USA has witnessed the most visible expression of the turn to creativity. The 'creative cluster' was pioneered in the 1990s as a development strategy for cities that had lost their industrial job base (Landry, 2000). These often involved costly investments in museums or heritage centres, in the hope of attracting a steady tourist stream, if not the kind of destination paydirt eventually achieved by the Bilbao Guggenheim. In the USA, this strategy dovetailed with the fiscally disastrous policy of building downtown stadia, mostly at taxpayer expense, for major league sports teams (Rosentraub, 1997). In the world of inter-urban competition, managers of second and third tier cities were persuaded that they had no alternative but to enter into this beggar-thy-neighbour game of attract-ing prestige (Cagan and DeMause, 1998). Unlike the sports teams, the museums and heritage centres were not nomadic franchises of a monopoly cartel, but they were often a harder sell in provincial cities.

Richard Florida's 2002 book, *The Rise of the Creative Class*, gave city managers a new rationale for upgrading their competitive status. Urban fortunes, he argued, depend on the ability to attract and retain the creative workers whose capacity to in-novate is increasingly vital to economic development. Since these cherished souls are highly mobile, they are choosy about their live/work locations, and the cities they tend to patronise are rich in the kind of amenities that make them feel comfortable. Tolerance of ethnic and sexual diversity, for example, rates high on Florida's indices of liveability. Though Florida estimated the Creative Class in the USA to be 38 mil-lion strong (lawyers and financiers are lumped along with artists, entertainers and architects) its demographic was unevenly distributed, and heavily skewed toward liberal enclaves in the blue states (Florida, 2002). Aspiring cities in pursuit of better regional leverage in the 'creative economy' would need to become eligible suitors by submitting to a makeover, somewhat along the lines of the television programme *Queer Eye for the Straight Guy*.

Civic leaders rushed to embrace Florida's vision, express-ordering a 'creative strategy' from Catalytix, his private consultancy group. Announcing that Detroit, Dearborn, and Grand Rapids would soon be 'so cool you'll have to wear shades,' Michigan governor Jennifer Granholm commanded her state's mayors to adopt hipsterisation strategies that were part of a new 'Cool Cities' commission (Michi-gan, 2004). A hundred signatories from almost 50 cities gathered in Tennessee to agree on the Memphis Manifesto, a blueprint for turnaround communities willing to compete for creative talent (Creative 100: 2003). In 2004, the US Mayors' annual conference passed a resolution on the role that creative industries could play in revitalisation. Jobs in these sectors, it was agreed, were unlikely to be outsourced to other countries, and could prove more sustainable than the high-tech employment that cities had spent so much money trying to attract in the previous decade. Aside from the domestic impact, the mayors also acknowledged the potential for global export: overseas sales of creative products were estimated at $30billion (US Mayors, 2004).

The zeal for jumping onto the creativity bandwagon was also inspired by some supporting data. A 2004 mapping of the country's creative industries by the non-profit body Americans for the Arts showed almost three million people working for 548,000 arts-centric businesses (2.2 per cent and 4.3 per cent, respectively, of US employment and businesses). One in 24 US businesses was estimated to be arts-centric, and these belonged to the fastest growing sector of the economy (Americans for the Arts, 2004). The World Bank reported that more than half of consumer spending was on outputs from creative industries in G7 countries, and that, globally, creative industries accounted for 7 per cent of world GDP (Nabeshima and Yusuf, 2003). The export data encouraged the view that the competition for creative talent was being waged on a global scale. In 2005, Florida published his alarmist sequel, *The Flight of the Creative Class*, warning that the Bush administration's domestic and foreign policies were driving the best and the brightest overseas (Florida, 2005). City officials in Europe and East Asia responded by rolling out the red carpet for Florida's consultancy. In tune with the hapless efforts of Midwestern mayors to attract gay college graduates, the Governor of Singapore relaxed his city-state's prescriptions against homosexuality (Economist, 2000).

The solutions being prescribed for strivers hoping to move up in the creativity rankings are easy to satirise: Jamie Peck has described them as 'another variant of the Papua New Guinean cargo cults, in which airstrips were laid out in the jungle in the forlorn hope of luring a passing aircraft to earth' (Peck, 2005). Nonetheless, the cures are advertised as low-cost, and almost pain-free, often consisting of little more than image regeneration around public amenities, such as the creation of bike paths, the makeover of some centre-city ex-industrial warehouses or the stimulation of hip entertainment and consumption zones. Compared to the lavish tax exemptions and infrastructural outlays used to attract large corporations, creativity initiatives are soft budget items, requiring minimal government intervention with little risk of long-term commitments from the public purse. Moreover, traditional Chamber of Commerce businesses can rest easy that no significant public resources will be diverted away from serving their interests. As Peck observes, 'for the average mayor, there are few downsides to making the city safe for the creative class – a creativity strategy can quite easily be bolted on to business-as-usual urban-development policies. The reality is that city leaders from San Diego to Baltimore, from Toronto to Albuquerque, are embracing creativity strategies not as alternatives to extant market-, consumption- and property-led development strategies, but as low-cost, feel-good complements to them' (Peck, 2005, 763).

Left wing critics of these development strategies have pointed out that cities high in the creativity rankings also top out on indexes of class polarisation and social inequality; that the gentrification of creative neighbourhoods drives out those most likely to innovate; and that Potemkin cultural zones which are too obviously staged for consumption scare away the precious recruits (Marcuse, 2003: Maliszewski, 2004: Peck 2005). Moreover, those unlucky enough to be designated as uncreative have little to look forward to but trickle-down leavings since they will almost certainly be performing the low-wage service jobs that support their lifestyling superiors. Right-wingers has been even harder on the Florida cult, seeing nothing but a policy to elevate liberal havens as models of growth (Malanga, 2004: Kotkin, 2004, 2005). In fact, they argue, Republican cities that don't rate as particularly creative. Low-tax, business-friendly suburban cities, like Phoenix, Houston or Orlando are the ones with the best performance on job and population growth.

If the creative city is a liberal plot, it is a far cry from the liberal city of the post-war economy, which relied on federal block grants to oversee the basic welfare of its citizens. With budgets cut to the bone, and the citizenry increasingly cut off from institutional protections, American urban policy-makers have all but embraced the accepted neoliberal wisdom that self-sufficient entrepreneurial activity is the best, if not the most just, stimulant to growth. The individual career portfolio of the young, freelancing creative is a perfect candidate for this profile of self-reliant productivity. Whether the policies will generate employment remains to be seen. They cannot do worse than their stadium-based predecessor. Surveys over the last three decades have shown that the presence of professional sports teams or their facilities failed to register any significant impact on employment or city revenue (Noll, 1997). Indeed, one Chicago economist estimated that if the public money expended on a typical stadium project were dropped out of a helicopter over the city in question, it would probably create eight to ten times as many jobs.

But, unlike the helicopter drop, the creative jobs in question will not be scattered over a wide area. They have a tendency to cluster, and in zones that become socially exclusive in a short space of time. If the creative cities campaigns do result in more jobs, and if they prove to be economic accelerators, they will almost certainly intensify the polarisation of city life between affluent cores and low-income margins; any significant spoils will be captured in the zones of growth, and by a minority of creative workers at that. In this context, Florida's nostrum, that creativity is everyone's natural asset to exploit, is difficult to distinguish from any other warmed-over version of American bootstrap ideology.

China's Leap Forward

The creative industries policy model is a very recent import in mainland China, but the PRC is arguably the most important of the many developing countries that have seized on it to help drive its national economy towards the most prized IP fruit at the top of the value chain (Keane, 2004). The British Council (an unabashed leader in the policy export field) defines a state in 'transition' to full exploitation of its creative economy as 'one which has moved beyond the development stage but is still unable to protect intellectual property rights in creative goods and services'. To say the least, leading IP exporters like the UK have a vested interest in seeing Chinese authorities enforce IP rights protection in their 'transition' to fully-fledged capitalism. They are more ambivalent about the prospect of aiding the transition from a labour-intensive 'Made in China' economy to an innovation-based 'Designed in China' economy with domestic control over patents and IP rights. Nonetheless, this is the direction of the PRC's breakneck growth, and it is fully backed by a powerful, state-driven economy in the lock of a long-term policy of technonationalism. Whether the drive applies only to high-tech sectors, with large-scale capitalisation, or whether it extends to 'softer' creative domains, where smaller enterprises tend to flourish, remains to be seen. Because of the market's jumbo size and the broad spread of the industrial operations involved, the result will surely affect livelihoods everywhere. We have seen this in the case of manufacturing and white collar services, and there is no reason to think that creative occupations will be any different.

For China's policy cadres, there are good reasons to welcome the shift in nomenclature from 'culture' to 'creativity'. The watchful officials who oversee all media content have been accustomed to subordinate cultural policy to the goals of developing a market economy. The Cultural Revolution, by contrast, is officially remembered as a period when too much primacy was given to culture, and the economy was in the passenger seat. Most of China's leadership cadre since the philosophically colourful rule of Mao have been sober engineers, sworn to uphold the technonationalist project. Policy about culture has been restricted, and thereby relegated, to the traditional domain of heritage arts and crafts, while the ongoing partial commercialisation of state-owned media, especially new media, is a politically fraught endeavour. On the face of it, creativity is a much safer term to promote. Not only is it is unlikely to be inducted into a top-down political program of the kind that flourished in late Maoism. It is also understood to originate with individuals, whose appetite for self-expression is widely tolerated as long as it avoids politically sensitive topics. Indeed, if this appetite can be steered into appropriate industrial channels, then government elites can well imagine that they will have contained an otherwise volatile source of public dissidence.

But political expediency is not the primary reason for jumping onto the creativity bandwagon. The push for creative industry *(chuangyi gongye)* policy could not have arrived at a more relevant time for the Asian giant's economic development. China's march forward cannot be sustained unless it proves it can generate its own intellectual property by jumpstarting home-grown innovation rather than imitating or adapting foreign inventions. Speaking at a national conference on innovation in January 2006, Premier Wen Jiabao declared that 'independent innovation' *(zizhu chuangxin)* would be at the core of the country's development strategy over the next 15 years. Nothing less than the honour of the nation was at stake. Accordingly, leading brokers in the creative industries field are lobbying hard to have the concept fully incorporated into the nation's Eleventh Five-Year Plan (Rossiter, 2005).

The government can point to fledgling industrial design achievements in hard technology such as automobiles, white goods, and semiconductors, while global firms in a whole range of advanced industries have rushed to set up offshore R&D centres, employing local talent, in Shanghai and Beijing's free trade zones. But the creative sectors where the country's designers are expected to enjoy a running start are in video games, animation, advanced computer graphics and multimedia communications – fields directly relevant to consumer electronics and digital media. Online gaming (officially recognised as a 'competitive sport' by the state's sports agency) and mobile-media (in a country with several hundred million cell phone users) are already proven as dynamic sectors, and government backing in these areas is readily available. Moreover, the potential for promoting cultural nationalism, and limiting foreign content through the use of Chinese theming is bottomless. Producers of multimedia genres can draw on a reservoir of several centuries of myth and legend as well as courtly and folk narratives that are well-known elements of the national patrimony.

China's foreboding bureaucracy stands in the way of creative producers, who depend on permits from a range of different industry regulators (the Ministry of Culture, State Administration of Industry and Commerce, State Administration of Radio, Film, and Television, Ministry of Information Industry, and the General Administration of Press and Publication), each with its own prescriptions for a cultural field or genre (Cunningham, Keane, Ryan, 2005). This licensing system, which also functions as an instrument of content surveillance, is particularly fraught for new (or cross-) media production which customarily straddles several of these traditional industries. The more high-tech the activity, the more chance producers have of falling under the rubric of the Ministry of Science and Technology whose top-level mandate to back innovation generates the most fast-track results (Claydon Gescher Associates, 2004). Even so, the focus there is on getting big companies publicly listed. This policy of 'securing the big and letting go the small,' as Jing Wang observes, is a 'vision contrary to that of the creative industries,' and so the preferred PRC policy is to push the creativity initiatives in Hong Kong with the mainland export market in mind (Wang, 2004).

It took two decades of liberalisation to wean China's state-owned enterprises off the state subsidy system of non-performing bank loans. Many of the new creative industries post-date state ownership and are being developed with a minimal number of public purse-strings attached in the expectation that start-ups will become self-sufficient in the short term. If they fail to reach the threshold for market entry, or if they cannot secure the necessary licenses, creative producers will take their chances in the unauthorised grey economy where precariousness and uncertainty are a way of life. For new entrants who successfully navigate the ministerial agencies, government support is short-term, and highly conditional not only on the commercialisation of products but also on finding private investors or sponsors as soon as possible. The resulting imposition of entrepreneurial enterprise often results in unorthodox forms of investment that flout legality and transparency, exposing producers to chronic risk.

Though it is the world's most unionised economy (the national labour federation claims as many as 150 million members), China's trade unions are ineffective (mostly providing social services), and have only a weak foothold in the commercialised sectors where the new creativity initiatives are being launched. Mainland enforcement of labour laws and standards is notoriously feeble, and the labour markets that have formed in the most dynamic sectors of the economy are the most volatile and unstable, prone to high turnover and a chronic workplace culture of disloyalty, both on the part of employers and employees. In a country where, only yesterday, livelihoods were guaranteed by an 'iron rice bowl,' and fewer and fewer workers, whether skilled or unskilled, expect their current employer to be around for very long, job-hopping has become a national pastime. Moreover, it is in the high skill sectors, where contracts include no stipulations on maximum working hours, that seventy-hour workweeks are increasingly an expectation on the job (Ross, 2006). The new focus on creative industries is being developed in the heart of this superflex work environment, where pressures from market exposure and project deadline crunches combine to inject extra anxiety into the perennially immature labour markets that plague cultural production.

Unlike 'British creativity,' for example, which is a recognisable global commodity with a proven historical track record, the Chinese counterpart must be laboured into being in a media environment where content is still largely a state monopoly, and it must do so in the teeth of longstanding Orientalist stereotypes about the static and derivative nature of Chinese society. For sure, there are Chinese equivalents of the working-class characters in the film, *The Full Monty* (a feelgood allegory of New Labour's policy), laid off and down on their luck, but tapping into their latent creativity to stage their own entrepreneurial comeback. Yet they are unlikely to be lionised as 'model workers,' unless they produce some credible IP; nor is a one-party government obliged to sell the creativity paradigm to socially marginal and underemployed populations, as is the case in a democratic polity like the UK.

To ensure the market capture of IP, most of this activity is being placed in locations that are under surveillance. The Chinese government has endorsed the construction of creative industry zones in selected cities with proven talent pools: a constellation of creative districts in Beijing; multiple centres in Shanghai developed under the auspices of the Creative Industries Association; the 'Window of the World' zone in Nanjing, 'Creation 100' in Qingdao; and further-flung outposts in technology-driven urban economies like Xian and Chengdu (Sun, 2006). Investors who set up in these locations will enjoy the same kind of trade, tax, and operational incentives as in the export-processing and high-tech zones familiar from earlier phases of the reform era. Overseas investors with unrealistic expectations of fast profit will doubtless enter into the same kind of informal agreements as before, conceding technology transfers in return for the promise of government, or market, access. In the case of the new sectors, however, the proximity to fresh IP will render the transfers ever more sensitive to the foreign owners, and ever more attractive to home-grown entrepreneurs and the officials who back them.

As is the case in the high-tech manufacturing sector, the labour market for industry creatives is a tight one. In New York, an estimated 12 per cent of workers are from the creative sector, with the figure reaching 14 per cent and 15 per cent in London and Tokyo respectively, but in Shanghai, it stands at only one per cent[2]. To ease the bottleneck, in 2004 Beijing announced a massive training and recruitment scheme to produce more than a million additional 'gray-collar' employees; the category includes software engineers, architects, graphic artists, and industrial designers (Xinhua, 2004). If the government succeeds, then the current labour shortage, and the accompanying wage spiral, may be short-lived. But the cause of the instability does not lie simply in the lack of supply. Workers are now as footloose as global corporations, and less likely to commit to employers beyond the short term. In stunning contrast to their parents, Chinese youth who are entering the urban labour markets have been weaned in a socio-economic environment where loyalty to anything other than the family is either an anachronism or a liability. Having witnessed the shredding of securities in all aspects of their lives, Chinese people of a certain age have truly seen all

---

2   These figures were cited by Li Wuwei, chairperson of Shanghai's Creative Industry Association, at a January 2006 session of the Shanghai People's Congress (SPC). [http://www.designtaxi.com/news.jsp?id=1807&monthview=1&month=1&year=2006]

that was solid melt into air, and their children have been raised to believe they must be authors of their own lives.

The advent of the creative industries sector as a tentative object of state attention comes at a moment well before the maturing of the requisite labour market. Will this sector produce its own version of the exploitation endemic to the low-wage, labour intensive sweatshops of South China's export-processing and assembly zones? Will we see the same ominous combination of demographic pressure, sky-high turnover, lax regulation, and cut-price bidding emerge in the microbusinesses and SMEs of the creative economy? If so, then China's pivotal position in the global economy means that its creative sector, like its other industries, could set norms that will affect wages and working conditions in other parts of the world. The 'China price,' so feared by domestic producers in OECD countries, may well come to be associated with 'Designed in China' just as it has been the overseas hallmark of 'Made in China.' This is already beginning to happen in architectural and software firms, where the quality of the work being out-sourced to mainland China is leaping up the value chain. The downward pressure felt on employees will not just be felt onshore. For most young Chinese, the pristine oppor-tunity to work at a creative craft under their own initiative is likely to come at the cost of a high-stress worklife dictated by chronic uncertainty, where self-direction morphs into self-exploitation, and voluntary mobility is a fast path to disposability.

Conclusion

The conditions for the emergence of creative industries policy differ from state to state, as do the resources available in any country to fit the policy requirements. At the very least, the quicksilver adoption of the concept can be taken as evidence of the ready globalisation of ideas about governance. But there are other, more tangible reasons for its mercurial career: its core relationship with the exploitation of intellectual property; its connection, in urban development, with property revaluation; its potential for drawing marginal cultural labour into the formal, high-value economy; and the opportunity to link dynamic IT sectors with the prestige of the arts. Most mundane of all, the creative policy requisites are generally cheap to implement, involving relatively small investments on infrastructure and programmes, and even smaller outlays on human capital, since the latter rely mostly on stimulating the already proven self-entrepreneurial instincts of creative workers, or on mining the latent reserves of ordinary people's creativity. The returns on these slight investments, if they are realised, promise to be substantial. In sum, it is fair to observe that all of the above-mentioned at-tributes are familiar features of global capital formation, with managers and investors who are ever on the lookout for fresh sources of value, labour, and markets.

While the rage for creative industries policy has sparked scepticism, and even contempt, from radically-minded artists and artist groups, mainstream organisations have gone along with it in general, seeing the potential for greater economic leverage, more direct access to patronage, and an expanded range of partners and clients. To the degree to which the policy returns are envisaged as a high-stakes lottery – with hot tickets in the hands of those quickest to go to market – there are indeed likely to be some handsome winners, reinforcing the residual Rom-antic concept that creativity resides in select geniuses (albeit a genius for business). Yet, for most of the players, the lottery climate of sharpened risk will only accentuate the precarious nature of creative work, with its endemic cycles of feast and famine, and generally reinforce the income polarisation that is by now a familiar hallmark of neoliberal policymaking.

So, too, the rhetoric about taking creativity seriously has won admirers in unlikely places. For one thing, it feeds into longstanding demands for humanising the workplace. Who would pass up the promise of inventive, mentally stimulating alternatives to the repetitive routines of assembly lines or data entry pools of the recent past, not to mention the dark Satanic mills of yore? A self-managed working life free from rigid supervision and conformity, where independent initiative was prized above all? But business owners can also take heart from the proposition that such workplace permissiveness is not so much a concession to pushy emp-loyees as a proven source of profit in and of itself. Indeed, the record of work restructuring shows how easily the original worker demands for liberation from boredom – dating to the 1970s 'refusal of work' — have been interpreted as opportunities to increase productivity and shed 'surplus' employees. Managerial innovations in the last three decades have been devoted to freeing up the workplace in ways somewhat different from the employees' Utopia – by stripping away layers of security, protection, and accountability. So, too, technological innova-tions have also made it possible to prise work away from its fixed anchoring in a single job with a single job-holder; work tasks can now be broken down, reassigned all over the world, and the results recombined into a new whole through the use of work-flow platforms.

Consequently, wherever work has become more feelgood and free, it has also become less just, and this formula has perilous consequences for an industry that takes creativity as its watchword (Ross, 2002). Job gratification, for creatives, has always come at a sacrificial cost – longer hours in pursuit of the satisfying finish, price discounts in return for prestige, and disposability in exchange for mobility and autonomy. Yet there is nary a shred of attention to these downsides in the statements and reports of the creative industries policymakers; only a passing concern that the 'instrumentalising' of culture might bring undue harm to the cause of aesthetics, as evinced by Tessa Jowell, Blair's successor to Chris Smith as DCMS Minister in the UK (Jowell, 2004).

If sustainable job creation is to be a true goal of the new policymaking, then it would be best to acknowledge from the outset the well-known perils of precariousness that afflict creative work, and then build in some guarantees of income and opportunity to protect those who won't ever win the IP jackpot prizes. There is no shortage of documentation on these perils, dating back to the rise of culture markets in the late 18th century. Policy-makers would do us all a favour if they put aside the productivity statistics and solicited some hard analysis about what it takes to make a 'good' creative job as opposed to generating opportunities for occasionally finding 'nice work.'

REFERENCES

American for the Arts (2004) *Creative Industries: Business & Employment in the Arts. Retrieved on June 6, 2006 from* http://www.artsusa.org/information_resources/research_information/services/creative_indus-tries/default.asp

Arrighi, G. (1994) *The Long Twentieth Century: Money, Power, and the Origins of Our Times,* London: Verso

Arrighi, G. (2005) 'Hegemony Unravelling,' *New Left Review* 32, 33: 24-80, 83-116

Cagan, J. & N. deMause (1998) *Field of Schemes: How the Great Stadium Swindle Turns Public Money into*

Private Profit, Monroe, Me.: Common Courage Press

Claydon Gescher Associates (2004) *Changing China – The Creative Industry Perspective: A Market Perspective,* A market research report for UK Trade and Investment. Retrieved on June 6, 2006 from www.uktradeinvest.gov.uk

Creative 100 (2003) *The Memphis Manifesto,* Memphis: Memphis Tomorrow and Mpact

Cunningham, S., M. Keane, Michael & M. D. Ryan, Mark (2005) 'Worlds apart? Finance and investment in creative industries in the People's Republic of China and Latin America'. *Telematics and Informatics* 22(3) : 309-331,

DCMS (UK Department of Media, Culture, and Sport) (1998) *Creative Industries Mapping Document*
Economist, The (2000) 'The Geography of Cool': April 13

Florida, R. (2002) *The Rise of the Creative Class: And How It's Transforming Work, Leisure, Community, and Everyday Life* New York: Basic Books

Florida, R. (2005) *The Flight of the Creative Class,* New York: Harper Business

Garnham, N. (2005) 'From Cultural to Creative Industries: An Analysis of the Implications of the 'Creative Industries' Approach to Arts and Media Policy-Making in the UK', *International Journal of Cultural Policy* 10, 1: 15-30

Hartley, J. eds. (2004) *Creative Industries,* Oxford: Blackwell

Hesmondhalgh, D. & A. Pratt eds. (2005) 'The Cultural Industries and Cultural Policy', special issue of *International Journal of Cultural Policy,* 11, 1

Howkins, J. (2002), 'The Mayor's Commission on the Creative Industries', in Hartley, ed. *Creative Industries,* 117-125

Jowell, T. (2004) 'Government and the Value of Culture', Department of Media, Culture, Sports, and Media, UK

Keane, M.(2004) 'Brave New World: Understanding China's Creative Vision,' *International Journal of Cultural Policy,* 10, 3: 265-279

Keynes, M.(1945) 'The Arts Council; Its Policy and Hopes,' in Wallinger, M. & M. Warnock eds. *Art for All?: Their Policies and Our Culture,* London: Peer

Kotkin, J. & F. Siegel (2004) 'Too Much Froth,' *Blueprint* 6: 16-8

Kotkin, J. (2005) 'On Uncool Cities', *Prospect,* October,. Retrieved on May 28, 2006 from http://www.prospect-magazine.co.uk/article_details.php?id=7072

Landry, C. (2000) *The Creative City: A Toolkit for Urban Innovators,* London: Earthscan

Larson, G. (1997) *American Canvas: An Arts Legacy for Our Communities,* Washington D.C.: National Endowment for the Arts

Malanga, S. (2004) 'The Curse of the Creative Class', *City Journal* (Winter): 36-45

Maliszewski, P. (2004) 'Flexibility and its Discontents', *The Baffler* 16: 69-79

Marcuse, P. (2003) 'Review of "The Rise of the Creative Class"', *Urban Land* 62: 40-1

McChesney, R. (2004) *The Problem of the Media: US Communications Politics in the 21st Century,* New York: Monthly Review Press

Michigan, Department of Labor and Economic Growth (2004) *Cool Cities,* Lansing: State of Michigan
Miller, T. & G. Yudice (2003) *Cultural Policy,* London: Sage

Nabeshima, K. & S. Yusuf (2003) 'Urban Development Needs Creativity: How Creative Industries Can Affect Urban Areas,' *Development Outreach,* special issue on Unknown Cities, World Bank. Retrieved on June 10, 2006 from http://www1.worldbank.org/devoutreach/nov03/article.asp?id=221

Noll, R. (1997) *Sports, Jobs, and Taxes: The Economic Impact of Sports Teams and Stadiums,* Washington D.C.: Brookings Institution Press

Oakley, K. (2004) 'Not So Cool Britannia: The Role of the Creative Industries in Economic Development', *International Journal of Cultural Studies* 7: 67-77

Peck, J. (2005) 'Struggling with the Creative Class', *International Journal of Urban and Rural Research* 29,4: 740-770

Prowse, M. (2006) 'Creation Myths?', *The Quarter,* 2, Spring

Rosenberg, H. (1975) 'The Profession of Art: The WPA Art Project', *Art on the Edge: Creators and Situations,* New York: MacMillan: 195-205

Rosentraub, M. (1997) *Major League Losers: The Real Cost of Sports and Who's Paying for It,* New York:

Basic Books

Ross, A. (2002) *No-Collar: The Humane Workplace and its Hidden Costs,* New York: Basic Books

Ross, A. (2006) *Fast Boat to China: Corporate Flight and the Consequences of Free Trade – Lessons from Shanghai,* New York: Pantheon

Rossiter, N. (2005) 'Interview with Su Tong: 'Created in China', translated by Du Ping, *My Creativity* (Nettime) mailing list, May 26

Ryan, Mark (2000), Wallinger, M. & M. Warnock, eds., *Art for All?: Their Policies and Our Culture,* London: Peer

Saunders, Frances Stonor (2000) *The Cultural Cold War: The CIA and the World of Arts and Letters,* New York: New Press

Smith, C. (1998) *Creative Britain,* London: Faber & Faber

Smith, C. (1999) 'Government and the Arts', Wallinger, M. & M. Warnock, eds., *Art for All?: Their Policies and Our Culture,* London: Peer

Stallman, R., L. Lessig & J. Gay, Joshua, eds. (2002) *Free Software, Free Society: Selected Essays of Richard M. Stallman,* Boston, Ma.: Free Software Foundation

Sun, M. (2006) 'Creative Industry, New Force in Beijing's Economy', *Beijing This Month,* June 14

Terranova, T. (2000) 'Free Labor: Producing Culture for the Digital Economy', *Social Text,* 18: 33

US Mayors, (2004) Adopted Resolution on the Creative Industries Index, Boston, 72nd Annual Meeting

Wang, Jing (2004) 'The Global Reach of a New Discourse: How Far Can "Creative Industries" Travel?' *International Journal of Cultural Studies,* 7, 1: 9-19

Weber, S. (2004) *The Success of Open Source,* Cambridge, MA: Harvard University Press.

Xinhua (2004) 'China Badly Needs "Gray-Collars" for Manufacturing', *China Daily,* March 21

Yudice, George (2004) *The Expediency of Culture (Uses of Culture in the Global Era),* Durham: Duke University Press

The new knowledge aristocracy:
the creative class, mobility and urban growth

Richard Shearmur

Richard Shearmur *is Canada Research Chair in Spatial Statistics
and Public Policy in the Spatial Analysis and Regional Economics Laboratory, Institut National de la Recherche Scientifique,
Urbanisation, Culture et Société at the University of Québec at
Montréal in Québec, Canada.*

ABSTRACT

Many policy-makers, particularly in North America, have been seduced and influenced
by the ideas of Richard Florida, who suggests that cities and regions can be economically
revitalised if they make themselves attractive to the mobile and talented 'creative class'.
This suggests that economic growth is caused by an influx of such people. This paper
argues that it is more plausible to suggest the reverse – that the 'creative class' is attracted to economic growth and that Florida's theories have the unintended consequence
of justifying the investment of considerable public resources in support of the lifestyle
choices of this already privileged class, in effect sustaining a new knowledge aristocracy
at the expense of the immobile majority.

On 27th January 2005 Richard Florida unveiled his analysis of Montreal's economy
(Stolarick *et al.*, 2005) during a fine luncheon in one of Montreal's upmarket ho-
tels. Backed by, amongst others, the Chamber of Commerce, *Culture Montréal*[1] and
Montréal International[2], this $85 a head ceremony gathered the municipal, economic
and cultural glitterati of Montreal: for thirty minutes we listened to Dr.Florida explain
how winning cities need to attract and retain 'talent'. The best way for them to become
attractive to these very mobile and well educated people is to, amongst other things,
encourage cultural activities, the lifestyle that these people enjoy, and – particularly
– 'tolerance'.

Obviously, this flattering message went down very well with the audience. No one in
the room – except maybe the waiters – could doubt that he (or she) was included in the
rather wide definition that Florida (2002) gives of 'talent' and of the 'creative class' (i.e.
educated and innovative people – vague terms, but which, in practice, gather together
most people in design, development and managerial occupations). How pleasant to nod
off to a post-prandial address that reminds one of one's own importance. Such an address
is all the more pleasant when it emphasises the urgency to (re)model the city to meet
our needs. It is therefore to the honour of 'creative' Montrealers that the message was
received with a certain amount of scepticism.

---

1   An organisation that gathers Montreal's cultural elite and that lobbies for more funding.
2   A provincially funded organisation the purpose of which is to market the Montreal agglomeration
to outside companies and potential – usually wealthy or educated – immigrants.

This scepticism has parallels in some more fundamental questions of development economics, theorisation, and the bridge between theory and public policy raised by Florida's ideas. In this paper I will try to present a number of elements, both theoretical and empirical, that explore the reservations that can be formulated with regard to his thesis. It is not my intention to deny that there exists a link between economic growth and people with talent, education, know-how or creative abilities. However, it is important to look closely at this link and to see whether it applies to *urban* and *regional*[3] growth, and, if so, to question the direction of causality. Florida suggests that a city merely needs to attract the creative class in order to benefit from subsequent economic growth. I will argue that it is highly probable that the opposite is true, and that educated or talented people are mobile, well informed, and attracted to opportunities in faster growing regions.

In the first part of the paper I briefly review the literature on the link between human capital and economic growth (usually of *countries*) as well as income growth (of *individuals*). Research on the growth of *regions*, however, tends to emphasise that migration is attributable to opportunities available in the destination region. Regional growth, which is a question of location rather than of growth generation, is linked to industrial structure, geographic location relative to major markets, local culture and diffuse agglomeration economies that cannot be attributed to any isolated factor.

In the paper's second section I examine the distinction that Florida makes between human capital and 'talent', a distinction that is a little difficult to follow and which carries with it some particularly problematic connotations. In the final section of the paper I present some empirical results from Canada that call into question any simple link between human capital and regional growth. These results tend to demonstrate that educated people move towards regions that grow fast: hence growth would tend to be a cause, rather than a consequence, of the in-migration of 'talent' (although it is undeniable that some feedback is involved).

Human capital and growth

Human capital theory, growth and regional development

For over fifty years economists have been investigating the link between education and economic growth. Lewis (1955) and Schultz (1959) – who received the economics Nobel Prize in 1979 – were amongst the first to theorise this link and to place it in a far wider context. Indeed, Lewis (1955), in his book *The Theory of Economic Growth*, strongly insists upon the role of human and institutional capital in the process of national development. According to him, it is property rights, the organisation of markets, religion, attitudes towards risk and change – and education and training – that are the basis for development. No simple causality exists between any unique factor and development: rather, it is the complementarities and synergies that arise from different combinations of these factors that lead to growth.

Becker (1964) subsequently formalised the link between human capital and growth

---

3   In this text 'city' and 'region' are used interchangeably to denote small open economies within a country.

by integrating the concept to Solow's (1956) growth model. Indeed, despite the important theoretical advances of Lewis and Schultz – which remind one of certain principles of institutional economics behind recent work in the field of regional development (Nelson & Winter, 1982; Cooke et al., 2004) – human capital was only fully accepted by the community of economists once it had been formally integrated into mathematical models. Solow (1956) had identified an unexplained per capita growth 'residue' (over and above growth what could be explained by classic factors such as quantities of labour and capital) which he attributed to technological change. Becker (1964), in order to explain technological change itself (in order to make it endogenous to the model), integrated the qualitative change of labour, the increase in its stock of 'human capital', to the model.

It is important to emphasise that labour's know-how was assimilated to capital, because capital has an important property: like physical capital (tools, machines, infrastructure, etc.), human capital can be increased by investment (most notably in education and training). For an individual, human capital therefore corresponds to a stock of knowledge and know-how that enables him or her to obtain an income. By increasing this stock, an individual can increase his or her income.

Becker's (1964) idea, which was initially intended to explain technological progress in economic growth models, has been used to explain differences in standards of living and growth between countries. Romer (1989), for instance, has examined the stock of human capital at the scale of a country, and has shown that countries with a greater stock of this type of capital tend to have higher standards of living. Furthermore, increases in this stock lead to increasing standards of living. The desire to endogenise technological progress has thus given rise to a wider school of thought, that of endogenous growth theory (Lucas, 1988; Martin & Sunley, 1998). This theory (in fact a number of different theories that share similar basic principles) suggests that a country's level of growth is determined endogenously by its accumulation of (and by its capacity to generate) physical capital, human capital and technological know-how. In short, it is undeniable that theoreticians have, during the course of the last fifty years, integrated into their models the idea that an individual's income and a country's standard of living are partly attributable to human capital. Empirical studies tend to show that this is the case for countries (Barro & Lee, 2000; Romer, 1989) and for people (Constantinos & West, 1991; Card, 1999): positive correlation is found between education levels (individual attainment for people, average levels for countries) and income. Human capital theory explains the causal relationships for individuals, and endogenous growth theory (together with the work of Schultz (1955) and Lewis (1959), to name but them) explains the causal processes at the level of countries.

There exists, however, another approach to examining growth that seems to contradict those just described. Indeed, theories of *regional* growth, which analyse the location of economic activity, emphasise labour mobility. Labour is deemed to move from region to region in order to maximise income: workers therefore move towards locations with high salaries (Courchene, 1986; Dicken & Lloyd, 1990). In a regional context, therefore, human capital does not necessarily benefit the region where it is located, even if it quite clearly benefits the individual who possesses it. People are mobile, and regional development theory assumes that they will migrate towards regions that offer the best opportunities. From an empirical perspective it has been verified that not only are people mobile, but that the most educated people – those best able to identify and benefit from new opportunities wherever they may be – are the most mobile (Cousineau & Vaillancourt, 1987; Antolin & Bover, 1997).

There are, however, two different points of view as to the consequence of this migration. On the one hand, it is argued that the influx of people will lower wages (by increasing the supply of labour) and that high wages will make employers seek out cheaper locations. In this context migration is merely a short term phenomenon leading to regional equilibrium as employers and labour move in opposite directions (Courchene, 1986). On the other hand, it is argued that cumulative processes are at play: the concentration of labour (and especially of qualified labour) will, indeed, lead to wage increases, but also to positive externalities (information spill over, innovation, division of labour, shared infrastructure…), the combined effects of which are often termed agglomeration economies. Such agglomeration economies attract further migrants to the same places, and lead to a cumulative growth process (Myrdal, 1959; Kaldor, 1970; Krugman, 1995).

These migration processes are not immediately compatible with Romer's (1989) or Lucas's (1988) empirical results or with endogenous growth theory. Indeed, as soon as one takes migration into account, a given (local) stock of human capital will not always have the expected (local) growth effect. Human capital is not an attribute of the region where it is located, and can easily move elsewhere. One of the theoretical problems yet to be fully resolved in this area is how to integrate cumulative regional growth models, which deal with the *location* of economic activity), with endogenous growth theories, which deal with the endogenous generation of growth within a particular area (Baldwin & Forsild, 2000).

These theories and observations can to some extent be reconciled if one remembers that Romer (1989) and Lucas (1988), together with most theoreticians of economic growth, have taken countries as their unit of analysis, and seek to understand what generates economic growth within a country. At the scale of a country – and notwithstanding the growing international migration flows that may yet invalidate this assumption – it is still reasonable to suppose that the stock of human capital is constant in the short to medium term, and that it will tend to increase as investment in education and training increases. In other words, we can assume that human capital is an attribute of countries. An economic reasoning premised upon concepts such as 'stocks' and 'investments' makes sense, since there is a given stock of human capital in a country, and investments in human capital can be appropriated at the (national) scale where they are made. Similarly, if one reasons at the scale of the individual, notions of a stock of human capital and investments therein make sense: my knowledge is my own stock of human capital (not someone else's) and if I study further I will add to it (and not to someone else's). But for a region or a city such reasoning does not work: regions are open systems with no migration controls, and migration, particularly that of qualified people, can be great. Investments made by one region in human capital can easily benefit another, and one region's stock can diminish if another region is more attractive (Cousineau & Vaillancourt, 1987).

A number of researchers have studied the correlation between education and urban growth (for example Simon, 1998; Shearmur, 1998), and correlations indeed exist between these two phenomena. However, in the light of the migration question it is difficult to impute a causal direction to these relationships. Simon (1998), whilst acknowledging this difficulty, concludes that human capital is a factor of employment growth in US metropolitan areas: his reasoning, though, is somewhat circular since his preference for this interpretation rests on the fact that it is compatible with human capital theory, the very theory he is attempting to corroborate. Shearmur (1998), who analyses the link between education levels and employment growth in disaggregated economic sectors, notes that correlations seem to be as expected by human capital theory during the 1980s (it is basic industries that grow faster in cities with high levels of degree holders), but that correlations are compatible with consumer driven growth in the early 1990s (it is retail and leisure sectors that are connected with employment growth during this period, suggesting that high education levels may – during some periods – be connected with growth merely through the local spending power of more educated people). In any case the evidence that education levels are connected to regional growth is not conclusive; indeed, the correlation between initial education levels and employment growth becomes weak to non existent if other growth factors, such as city size (as a proxy for agglomeration effects), proximity to major markets and industrial structure are introduced (Shearmur & Polèse, 2006).

A question that is in fact central to discussions of human capital and growth concerns the measurement of human capital. Above, I loosely defined human capital as 'a stock of knowledge and know-how that enables [a person] to obtain an income'. Human capital can thus be defined in an abstract but fairly clear fashion. However, as Krahn & Lowe (1998) and Field (2003) point out, when it comes to *measurement* this stock is in fact difficult to disentangle from social status and family background, i.e. from social capital. Thus, even if human capital can be *defined*, a question remains as to what is being *measured* by indicators of human capital: is it ability and knowledge, or is it social connections and status? Although this may make little difference in terms of outcome – both may lead to positive economic outcomes for an individual – from a theoretical and policy perspective the distinction is crucial. How can know-how and knowledge be measured? Many studies rely on simple indicators such as years of education or percentage of degree holders: these indicators certainly measure something, but is it intrinsic ability, is it social status, or is it acquired human capital? Furthermore, an increase in education levels over time does not necessarily signify an increase in human capital: given the strong competition for status and jobs, obtaining education credentials may merely be a product of 'credentialism' (Wolf, 2002) – an entrance requirement for a job irrespective of the skills involved. Given the problems associated with the use of formal education (or training) statistics, some researchers have investigated knowledge and know-how through interviews and tests (Boothby, 1993). But here too, given that the ability to perform in literacy or numeracy tests (for instance) is in part culturally determined, is it in fact possible to investigate human capital (as distinct from social capital) in this way? In short, although the concept of human capital is clear, it is very difficult to operationalise in a satisfactory way. Thus, even though these measurement problems are not the focus of this paper, it is important to remember that it is tenuous, at best, to assume that human capital can be measured unambiguously, and in particular to assume that it can be disentangled from social capital and status. Yet much of the empirical work purporting to demonstrate a link between human capital and growth – including, but by no means exclusively, Richard Florida's – fails to make this assumption explicit.

In sum, and even putting aside questions surrounding the measurement of human capital, there exist solid theoretical and empirical reasons for questioning any straightforward extension of human capital and endogenous growth theories to cities and regions, partly because urban and regional growth (a question of where economic activity will take place) is different from economic growth (a question of how economic activity is generated). Without claiming that these approaches have no application to the study of growth in small open economies (see Baldwin & Forsild, 2000), the high mobility of human capital (mobility is much lower internationally) and the effects of agglomeration economies (because of their spatial dimension these do not, by definition, act at a national scale) make it dangerous to suppose that these theories are applicable without modification at the urban or regional level. With these reservations in mind, we now turn to Richard Florida's theories.

The knowledge aristocracy and its mobility

Richard Florida places himself in the tradition of human capital theory, but makes two fundamental modifications to it, which have important consequences. First, he uses the notions of 'talent' and 'creative class', abandoning the term 'human capital'. Second, he transposes ideas developed in the context of economic growth analysis (and which are valid at a national and individual scale), to the question of urban and regional growth (which is basically a question of location).

It could be argued that the first modification is merely semantic, and of little fundamental relevance. Florida (2001; 2002; Gertler *et al.*, 2002) no longer speaks of human capital, but of 'talent' and 'creativity'. The declared purpose of this new vocabulary is to create a distance between his theory and some restrictive notions of what constitutes human capital. But although formal knowledge has often been used (for measurement purposes) as a proxy for human capital, the multiple facets of human capital – in particular the importance of informal types of knowledge – are well recognised and have been integrated into the literature surrounding the concept (though informal knowledge is often difficult to measure empirically, Livingstone, 1997; 1999). The continued use of the term 'human capital' carries through an important aspect of human capital theory: that human capital can be increased through investment (Ray, 1998). In other words, individuals (by way of experience or formal training) and countries (by way of investment in education or training) can, in theory, increase their human capital. The concept – for all its limits – remains fundamentally democratic in the sense that no one is, *a priori*, excluded from it[4].

In contrast, Florida (2002) writes of a 'creative class' made up of 'talented' people. This vocabulary carries very exclusive connotations. The 'creative class' must necessarily

---

4   Of course, if human capital in fact reflects social capital and status, then this argument does not hold in practice. But in theory at least, it is possible for everyone to increase their human capital even if maximum attainments are partly socially constrained.

be constituted in opposition to a 'non-creative class'. This other class – which, according to Florida, comprises about 70 per cent of the population – is not addressed by his theory. The notion of 'creative class' immediately raises the issue of this class's interests – interests that Florida actively encourages cities and regions to promote. The message that he sends to municipal and regional politicians and policy-makers is that cities should modify their local policies, their planning and their budget, in order to respond to the preferences of this creative class. Given that by definition this class comprises those people best suited to succeed in the 'new' or 'knowledge' economy – the knowledge aristocracy – this message boils down to saying that municipalities and regions should reinforce and subsidise their elites. Such 'talent welfare' is reminiscent of 'corporate welfare' policies relied upon by certain jurisdictions to attract companies (Shearmur, 2000).

The term 'talent' is no more neutral than 'creative class'. In general a 'talent' is considered as a gift, or as luck. Of course a 'talented' pianist (for instance) will no doubt have worked hard to perfect this talent, but at the origin this talent is a gift of nature. Florida insists on the great importance of 'talent' which, unlike human capital, cannot really be acquired. So, over and above the elitism inherent in the notion of 'creative class', it could be argued (with a little exaggeration) that Florida's message is, despite itself, one of social Darwinism: certain people are born lucky (with talent), and municipal and regional policies should promote their interests and desires. It is thus – from a Spencerian perspective – a means of reinforcing natural social selection (Spencer, 1857)[5].

Needless to say, these criticisms are not in line with Florida's own perception of his work, which he sees as representative of the US liberal tradition. He responds to a number of critiques (Florida, 2004), which he considers to be of two types. First, there are critiques of a cultural order, that often turn upon his gay index (which he uses as a proxy for tolerance), his bohemian index (a proxy for originality and innovation), and the idea that his 'creative class' excludes hard working small business men and women. This first set of criticisms principally reflects the divide that exists in the USA between a traditional and populist culture on the one hand and an urban and multicultural one on the other (Frank, 2005). Florida (2004) defends his positions well against these criticisms, and I will not enter these debates.

Second, there are critiques which dwell upon the elitism (avowed or latent) of Florida's creative class (Florida, 2004), which are along the lines of those presented above. Florida proposes two lines of defence. First, according to him, the attraction of 'talent' will end up benefiting everyone, since the whole population will benefit from urban growth. Second, he claims to be well aware that creativity exists in all walks of life and in all occupations.

Neither of these justifications is sufficient to refute the points raised. The idea that everybody will benefit from the success of an elite creative class is reminiscent of Ronald Reagan's economic policies premised on the trickle-down effect. According to this way of viewing the economy, it is necessary to reduce all administrative and policy hurdles to enrichment (such as progressive income tax, inheritance

---

5   It could be argued that Florida even goes further than Spencer. Spencer was against all government intervention, in particular intervention to help the poor. To my knowledge, he never advocated government intervention to help the rich.

tax, control of work conditions, welfare…) because, in the end, enrichment of the upper classes will pull all of society upwards: all boats rise on a rising tide. Given the widening gap between rich and poor in the USA since the early 1980's (Schluter, 1998), the trickle-down theory – which is not so much a theory as an ideological platform – has not been validated. Similarly, there is little empirical backing for Florida's contention that the prosperity of a city benefits all those who live there. Quite the contrary, in fact: economic growth – particularly when driven by elites (Hamnett, 2003; Donald, 2001) – often puts pressure on poorer people. The increased congestion and pollution that accompany fast growth often have, as first victims, the residents of poorer neighbourhoods. Poor neighbourhoods that are attractive are rapidly gentrified. Rising real estate prices put property ownership out of reach of many people. Studies of the distributional impact of urban and regional growth on the local (pre-growth) population are sorely needed, and Florida's statements in this regard are at the very least premature.

The second defence put forward by Florida is that creativity can be found in all walks of life and occupations. According to him (Florida, 2004), his theory of the creative class merely emphasises the fact that creativity is behind all economic growth. Were the theory limited to this, it would be banal and inoffensive. But the theory of the creative class goes much further, and Florida claims to be able to identify the creative class from a list of occupations. In his report on Montreal (Stolarick et al., 2005), he writes that the economy of the creative sector can be summarised by the TAPE formula: Technology and innovation, Arts and culture; Professionals and managers; and Education and training. These occupational categories leave little space for creative blue-collar municipal workers, seamstresses, or waiters; indeed, the TAPE occupations strangely resemble the professional profile of his audience on 27th January. It is not because Florida (2004) claims to recognise the existence of creativity in all occupations that his public policy prescriptions – or even his analyses – take much notice of it. In fact, the type of municipal and regional policy inspired by Florida's ideas is squarely aimed at attracting and retaining elites, often at the expense of other pressing, concrete but less visible municipal and regional responsibilities (Donald, 2001). In short, it could be argued that Florida firmly entrenches the connection between human capital and social status, not by recognising that educational or professional attainment is often an outcome of social status, but by confounding the two: human capital is social status. Human capital – by virtue of its command of economic power – must be respected and courted in a way similar to yesterday's aristocracy (Cannadine, 1999).

Florida's theory and growth prescriptions rest upon the idea that attracting individuals well endowed in talent and creative powers will lead to growth within the regions that succeed in doing so. But regional growth theories suggest that the reverse is true: that the economic motive for migration is the differential in opportunities and income that exist between the origin and the destination regions. This theory of migration accords with many facts: whether one considers international migrants from developing countries, Canadians migrating to the USA, or Quebecers from outlying rural regions migrating to Montreal, many share a common motive.

They are attracted by the better life that they expect at their destination. In other words, it is the fact that there is greater wealth (or better prospects of wealth) in other countries or regions that, from an economic perspective, motivates migration. In terms of causality, it is therefore wealth and/or growth that attract human capital. Florida claims, on the basis of static and qualitative analysis (not the analysis of migration flows), that the creative elite is no longer subject to such forces, and that it is now seeking out particular lifestyles. This is a fundamental departure from what we know about migration, and we will return to this in the empirical section of the paper.

The question of causality is at the heart of Florida's thesis, and this question is its greatest weakness. According to Florida it is the capacity to attract the knowledge aristocracy that determines growth. This conclusion rests upon qualitative analysis, theoretical reasoning (loosely based on human capital theory) and correlations. However, on the basis of the underlying motivations for migration, and if one rests one's analysis upon regional growth theory, then identical correlations can lead to very different conclusions. The well informed and highly mobile aristocracy has the information and the capacity to move to the most 'rewarding' areas – those where economic activity and growth are occurring (Angell, 1999). Furthermore, this interpretation is in accord with the ideas of sociologists such as Bauman (2002) and Urry (2000) who suggest that mobility – or the capacity to move – has become an important social determinant since it allows one to maximise the chance of success:

'Mobility becomes a most precious and sought after resource. If chances cannot
   be "fixed to a place" and made to last, one needs to go where the chances
   appear and when they appear'. (Bauman, 2002, p83)

A secondary aspect of Florida's theory – if one has accepted that the attraction of 'talent' will lead to growth – concerns the factors that will attract it. According to him, it is the availability of a certain lifestyle, and especially cultural and leisure amenities, that attracts the creative class. Thus, cultural industries are put forward as a key to economic growth, and it is easy to understand why the cultural milieu has quickly rallied round. However, even on Florida's own terms, the link between cultural industries and growth is somewhat circuitous: 'talent' creates growth, and, amongst the variety of things that attract 'talent', are cultural industries. This hypothesis is as questionable as the rest: although it is outside the scope of this paper to analyse the link between culture and the economy, it is probable that a historic investigation would demonstrate that cultural industries have tended to develop in cities and regions that were prosperous. For instance, I would suggest that the prosperity of Florence in the 13th and 14th centuries has a direct bearing on the subsequent explosion of renaissance art (and, conversely, that it is not Florence's artistic community – to the extent that it existed prior to its prosperity – that built the city's power and wealth). It is Lorenzo de Medici's wealth that permitted him to patronise Leonardo de Vinci and Michelangelo, not the patronage that led to his enrichment.

A few empirical results
So far I have raised some theoretical issues relating to Florida's ideas and have questioned the implication of the vocabulary that is used. In this section I present some

empirical results that allow one to better assess the direction of causality between migration, human capital and regional growth.

Factors of local growth in Canada

It is not possible, in this paper, to present a complete justification for the two regional growth models that will be presented below. These two models rest upon the work of Polèse and Shearmur (Polèse & Shearmur, 2002; Shearmur & Polèse, 2005, 2006) and their units of analysis are Canada's 152 urban agglomerations of over 10,000 people[6]. The theoretical reasoning that leads to the inclusion of each variable can be found in Shearmur & Polèse (2006), the basic idea being that local growth can be explained by a number of factors. First, geo-structural factors (the wider regional economy, distance to major markets, path dependent historical growth patterns) explain urban growth, hence the inclusion of two systems of geographic classification (metro/centre/periphery and regions). Second, a variety of theories such as those relating to agglomeration effects (hence the inclusion of city size) and human capital (hence the inclusion of initial education levels and their subsequent growth) are taken into account. Finally, income levels (as a proxy for local costs) and industrial structure (cities are classified into six different industrial profiles, and a diversity index is included) are also thought to influence local growth. These models draw upon a series of possible explanations of urban growth, and do not limit themselves to studying any single growth factor[7].

The dependent variable of the first model in table 1 is employment growth between 1996 and 2001, the dependent variable of the second model is mean salary growth over the same period. Geo-structural variables are important determinants of regional growth: indeed, the best predictor of employment growth is proximity to a metropolitan area (the cent variable), and a good predictor of both employment and salary growth is the region in which the city is located. City size has no effect on growth, but industrial structure and – in the case of salaries – diversity does. Cities with higher salaries tend to experience slower growth, all else being equal. Both models explain a high proportion of the variance in urban growth (62 per cent for employment, 53 per cent for salaries).

Turning now to the education variables, they behave the same way in each model. If the human capital model were applicable to urban areas, one would expect the initial stock of human capital (measured as the percentage of university graduates in 1996) to be positively related to growth: it is not. Given the other determinants of urban growth, cities with a high initial stock of educated people do not grow faster than cities with a lower initial stock. However, there is a strong association between increases in human capital and growth. This result seems to conform with Florida's theory, since according to him it is the attraction of 'talent' that leads to growth.

---

6   All data are drawn from the census. Data for the urban growth model are drawn from the 1996 and 2001 census; data for migration are from the 1981, 1986, 1991, 1996 and 2001 censuses. Note that for the 1996 to 2001 net migration model only 136 urban units are analysed, since only those south of the 55th parallel have been retained and a few urban areas are unavailable for reasons of boundary changes.

7   These models have been estimated using SAS GLM which permits classification and continuous variables to be analysed simultaneously. Only the coefficients of continuous variables are indicated in these tables.

Table 1: Employment and Income Growth in the Canadian Urban System, 1996-2001

Dependent variable: employment growth, 1996 to 2001					
	Variable	dl	F	Pr>F	Coeff
Classification of cities into 6 Canadian regions	reg	6	6.81	<.0001	-
Classification of cities into metro, centre, periphery	cent	2	10.69	<.0001	-
Log of population, 1996	lp 96	1	0.13	0.717	0.00
% of population with university degree, 1996	pg96	1	0.54	0.464	0.19
Increase of graduates, 1996-2001	pg9601	1	8.60	0.004	2.13
Index of industrial specialisation, 1996	sp96	1	1.40	0.239	-0.02
Mean salary, 1996	sal96	1	1.24	0.267	-0.09
Classification of industrial structure	ci96	7	3.93	0.001	-
	R2	0.62 n=152 urban areas			

Dependent variable: salary growth, 1996 to 2001					
	Variable	dl	F	Pr>F	Coeff
Classification of cities into 6 Canadian regions	reg	6	6.46	<.0001	-
Classification of cities into metro, centre, periphery	cent	2	1.57	<.211	-
Log of population, 1996	lp 96	1	0.37	0.546	0.00
% of population with university degree, 1996	pg96	1	2.65	0.106	0.21
Increase of graduates, 1996-2001	pg9601	1	6.94	0.009	0.95
Index of industrial specialisation, 1996	sp96	1	0.37	0.544	-0.02
Mean salary, 1996	sal96	1	7.22	0.008	-0.11
Classification of in dustrial structure	ci96	7	2.45	0.021	-
	R2	0.53 n=152 urban areas			

Source: Polèse, M. et R.Shearmur, 2005, *La production, l'attraction et la rétention des diplômés universitaires. Étude comparative de la région métropolitaine de Montréal et d'autres métropoles canadiennes et américaines*, Montréal : INRS-Urbanisation, Culture et Société, http://www.inrs-ucs.uquebec.ca/pdf/ProductionAttractionRetention.pdf

However, this result is also compatible with the alternative theory that growth attracts 'talent'. For this reason we will turn to migration data in order to attempt to understand the direction of causality.

Migration and the attraction of 'talent'

In figure 1 the evolution of net migration flows to (and from) major Canadian agglo-merations is presented. These flows are expressed as a percentage of the cities' initial number of graduates, and results are presented for four five-year periods between 1981 and 2001.

We can see that, over the entire period, net flows are high towards Toronto, Van-couver and Ottawa, are very modest towards Montreal, Winnipeg and Quebec, and are progressing over the period for Calgary and Edmonton. Florida, in his report on Montreal, insists quite strongly on the city's attractiveness to 'talent'; our results do not support his claim.

A closer look at Figure 1 suggests that it is more reasonable to conclude that the flow of graduates increases as economic performance improves. Calgary and Edmonton have benefited from very fast growth[8], especially in the late 1990s, because of their oil boom; migration flows seem to have reacted quite markedly to this boom. Vancouver, which relies heavily on Asian markets, saw its migration rates decline in the late 1990s (when the Asian crisis occurred); this decline in the flow of talents coincides with economic stagnation in Vancouver's (and in much of British Columbia's) economy. In the early 1990s a recession and 'jobless recovery' hit many white collar occupations, and principal-ly those in the financial sector. In the late 1990s, this sector strongly bounced back with the dot.com boom. Migration flows to Toronto, which has an economy strongly oriented towards white collar and financial occupations, declined in the early 1990s and bounced back in the late 1990s. Over the same period (early 1990s) the federal government began drastically cutting back on recruitment in order to control the budget deficit; over the same period, migration flows of graduates to Ottawa, seat of the federal government, declined. The high-tech boom that Ottawa subsequently experienced in the late 1990s coincides with renewed in-migration of graduates.

None of this evidence is conclusive: causality is always extremely difficult to pin down with statistics. However, there is considerable circumstantial evidence in Figure 1 to suggest that, overall, the migration flows of graduates react to economic conditions and structural changes, and not the reverse. It is simply not plausible to attribute Calgary and Edmonton's recent growth to the influx of graduates. Neither is it plausible to attribute Ottawa's and Toronto's early 1990s recessions to the decline in graduate in-migrants; nor can Vancouver's late 1990s economic troubles be assigned to its inability to attract graduates. In sum, Figure 1 allows us to state with confidence that, at least for Canada's major metropolitan areas, the flow of migrant graduates responds to local economic conditions and not the reverse.

---

8   In this section 'growth' is not merely that of employment or incomes, but a combination of fac-tors: in the cities mentioned growth consisted of rising incomes, house prices and employment, whilst decline consisted of stagnant housing markets, failing businesses and slower employment and income growth. The point being made is that 'growth' or 'decline' in these cities, however measured, can be explained by wider economic and structural factors. To the extent that migration appears to be correlated with this growth and decline, it cannot be argued that it is a cause of growth and decline. Rather, it appears to be a consequence of these wider factors.

Figure 1 : Net Flows of Graduates Towards the Principal Canadian Urban Agglomerations, 1981 to 2001

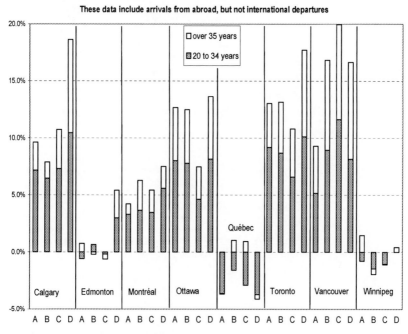

These data include arrivals from abroad, but not international departures

4 periods: A: 1981-86; B: 1986-91; C: 1991-96; D: 1996-01.

Source: Polèse, M. et R.Shearmur, 2005, *La production, l'attraction et la rétention des diplômés universitaires. Étude comparative de la région métropolitaine de Montréal et d'autres métropoles canadiennes et américaines,* Montréal : INRS-Urbanisation, Culture et Société, http://www.inrs-ucs.uquebec.ca/pdf/ProductionAttractionRetention.pdf

To conclude, we will test one final aspect of Florida's thesis: the idea that cultural amenities attract 'talent'. Is it possible that migration flows respond to the presence of cultural activities in urban areas? In order to address this issue a regression model has been estimated for net flows of graduates towards Canadian urban agglomerations. Between 1996 and 2001, 31 per cent of the variance in these flows could be explained by straightforward geo-structural variables associated with urban size. Graduates tend to flow towards larger cities, towards Alberta and British Columbia, and towards small cities located close to metropolitan areas.

The addition of a variable that measures cultural 'supply' (the local concentration of employment in the cultural sector) has no effect on the model: graduates are not particularly attracted to urban areas with a more developed local cultural sector. On the other hand, graduates tend to flow away from university towns; there is a strong negative relationship between the presence of university employment and graduate migration flows. This is not surprising since universities produce graduates, who then disperse across the territory.

Description of the variable	Variable	Coeff.	T	Pr>jtj
Intercept		-0.595	-4.04	<.0001
Metropolitan areas, population 500K+	AM	-0.042	0.59	<.211
Towns (50K-500K) <100km from metro area	ACA	0.007	0.20	0.546
Towns (10K-50K) <100km from metro area	**ACB**	**0.090**	**3.73**	**0.106**
Towns (50K-500K) >100km from metro area	APA	-0.058	-1.74	0.009
Towns (10K-50K) >100km from metro area	APB			0.544
Alberta	**AL**	**0.106**	**2.92**	**0.008**
Atlantic Provinces	AT	0.039	1.31	0.021
British Columbia	**BC**	**0.086**	**3.13**	
Ontario	ON	0.035	1.60	
Prairie Provinces	PR	0.033	1.07	
Quebec	QC	0.000		
Log of Population		**0.049**	**3.30**	
	r2	0.312		
	n	136		
Concentration of cultural jobs added* to model		0.000	0.53	
Concentration of university jobs added* to model		-2.261	-2.64	
*Each variable is added to the model separately				

Source: Polèse, M. et R.Shearmur, 2005, *La production, l'attraction et la rétention des diplômés universitaires. Étude comparative de la région métropolitaine de Montréal et d'autres métropoles canadiennes et américaines*, Montréal : INRS-Urbanisation, Culture et Société, http://www.inrs-ucs.uquebec.ca/pdf/ProductionAttractionRetention.pdf

In sum, Florida's ideas do not stand up to simple empirical tests. This does not mean that the processes he describes never occur: it is quite possible that some specific urban areas or regions have managed to develop by attracting graduates and by generating their own knowledge spillovers and agglomeration effects. What the results do quite clearly show is that Florida's theories cannot be generalised. It is therefore incorrect for Florida to claim that he has found the recipe for 21st century urban and regional growth. Had this message

9   It should be noted that only 136 urban areas can be analysed (rather than the 144 that are south of the 55th parallel) in these models. This is because flows could not be calculated for some urban areas owing to changes in geographic boundaries between 1996 and 2001.

remained hidden in academic journals, it would have had very limited consequences, and other more robust theories would eventually have proven their worth. However, the influence of these ideas over politicians and policy-makers is such that it is very important to demonstrate their limits, something I have attempted to do.

Conclusion

Florida's recent work has had the great merit – as Glaeser (2004) points out – of generating public debate about the factors and causes of urban and regional growth. This topic is rarely deemed newsworthy, and Florida has become its ambassador. His theory of the creative class is not devoid of merit; it rests to some extent on human capital theory, but also raises interesting questions about this theory's limits when it is applied to regional and urban growth, which is primarily a question of location. Indeed, the difference between endogenous growth theories on the one hand and regional growth theories on the other is an important source of the conceptual confusion surrounding Florida's ideas. Whereas endogenous growth theories attempt to explain how economic growth is generated, regional and urban growth theories attempt to explain where this growth will locate. By attempting to mix these theories without clearly conceptualising or distinguishing them, Florida has ended up generating a series of fascinating questions without really providing the answers.

At a different level, and despite his stated intentions, Florida has expressed his theories in a very elitist language. As any lobbyist well knows, choice of words is not without consequence, particularly when one is addressing politicians and policy-makers. Any theory of urban and regional growth that seems to actively promote the interests of a small and already privileged elite – in this case the knowledge aristocracy – is not a neutral theory. Although the author may not have wished to promote such an idea, there is little doubt that the success of his theory is partly attributable to the fact that it can serve to justify elitism. Furthermore, the popularity of his theory in the cultural milieu, which can be explained by the fact that it provides economic arguments justifying the financial support of cultural industries, cannot hurt its dissemination and media credibility. Without being fundamental criticisms of the theory itself, these points nevertheless raise important political and policy questions which are crucial when cities begin to apply recommendations derived from Florida's reports.

From an empirical perspective, Florida's theories are not verified in Canada. First, a city's initial endowment in 'talent' is not a predictor of future employment or income growth. Second, even if the increase in 'talent' is correlated with growth, an analysis of graduate migration flows shows that these flows increase towards fast growing regions and decrease towards slow growing ones, and that this growth can most plausibly be explained by reference to wider economic and structural factors. In other words, there is evidence that the attractive effect of growth on 'talent' is considerably stronger than the effect that 'talent' has upon growth. The presence of a cultural sector in a city has no effect on the attraction of 'talent'.

These results demonstrate that there are no general rules that associate 'talent' with urban growth, or that associate the attraction of 'talent' with local cultural endowment. This does not mean that there are no examples, in Canada, of cities in which the mechanisms described by Florida lead to growth. It simply means that these mechanisms do not operate everywhere and that the theory of the creative class – to the extent that it claims to be a general theory explaining urban growth – is false.

© Richard Shearmur, 2006

REFERENCES

Angell, I.(2000) *The New Barbarian Manifesto*, London: Kogan Page

Antolin, P. & O. Bover, (1997) 'Regional Migration in Spain: The Effect of Personal Characteristics and of Unemployment, Wage and House Price Differentials Using Pooled Cross Sections', *Oxford Bulletin of Economics and Statistics*, 59.2: 215-235

Baldwin, R. & R.Forsild, (2000) 'The Core-Periphery Model and Endogenous Growth: Stabilising and Destabilising Integration', *Economica*, 67:307-324

Barro, R. and J-W Lee (2000) 'International Data on Educational Attainment Updates and Implications', *NBER Working Papers* 7911, Cambridge (MA): National Bureau of Economic Research

Bauman, Z. (2002) *Society Under Siege*, Cambridge: Polity Press

Boothby, D. (1993) 'Is there a Literacy Problem?', *Canadian Public Policy*, 19: 18-28

Becker, G. (1964,) *Human Capital,* New York: National Bureau of Economic Research

Cannadine, D. (1999) *The Decline and Fall of the British Aristocracy,* New York: Vintage

Card, D. (1999) 'The Causal Effect of Education on Earnings', *Handbook of Labor Economics*, eds. O. Ashenfelter & D. Card, vol.3:1801-1863

Constantinos.C & E.G.West, (1991) 'Measuring Returns from Education', *Canadian Public Policy*, 17.2:127-138

Cooke, P., M.Heidenreich & H-J.Braczyk (eds) (2004) *Regional Innovation Systems: The role of governance in a globalized world*, 2nd edition. London; New York: Routledge

Courchene.T (1986) 'Le redressement régional, le système de transfert et le fédéralisme canadien', in *Essais sur le développement régional*, eds. Savoie, D. et A.Raynauld, Montréal: Presses Universitaires de Montréal

Cousineau, J-M. & F.Vaillancourt (1987) 'Investing in University Education' in *Still Living Together*, eds. Coffey.W and M.Polèse, Montreal: Institute for Research on Public Policy

Dicken, P. & P.Lloyd (1990) *Location in Space,* New York: Harper & Row

Donald, B. (2001) 'Economic Competitiveness and Quality of Life in City Regions: Compatible Concepts?', *Canadian Journal of Urban Research,* 10.2: 259-274

Field, J. (2003) *Social Capital,* London: Routledge

Florida, R. (2001) *Technology and Tolerance: The Importance of Diversity to High-Technology Growth*, Centre on Urban and Metropolitan Policy, Survey Series, Washington D.C.: Brookings Institution

Florida, R. (2002) *The Rise of the Creative Class*, New York: Basic Books

Florida, R. (2004,)'Revenge of the Squelchers', *The Next American City*, 5. Retrieved August 20, 2006 from http://www.americancity.org

Frank, T. (2005) *What's the matter with Kansas?*, New York: Metropolitan Books

Glaeser, E. (2004) 'Review of Richard Florida's "Rise of the Creative Class". Retrieved, August 20, 2006 from http://post.economics.harvard.edu/faculty/glaeser/papers/review_florida.pdf

Gertler, M., R.Florida, G.Gates & T.Vinodrai (2002) *Competing on Creativity: Placing Ontario's Cities in North American Context*, Ontario Ministry of Enterprise, Opportunity and Innovation and the Institute for Competitiveness and Prosperity. Retrieved, August 20, 2006 from http://www.competeprosper.ca/research/CompetingOnCreativity_061202.pdf

Hamnett, C. (2003) *Unequal City: London City in the Global Arena*, London: Routledge

Kaldor, N. (1970) 'The Case for Regional Policies' in *The Essential Kaldor* (1989), eds. Targetti. F & A.Thirlwall, New York: Holmes & Meier

Krahn, H. & G.Lowe (1998) *Work, Industry and Canadian Society*, 3rd edition, Scarborough, Ontario: International Thomson Publishing

Krugman, P. (1995) *Development, Geography and Economic Theory*, Cambridge: MIT Press

Livingstone, D. (1997) 'The Limits of Human Capital Theory: Expanding Knowledge, Informal Learning and Underemployment', *Options Politiques*, Juillet-Août 1997: 9-13

Livingstone, D. (1999) 'Beyond Human Capital: the Underemployment Problem', *International Journal of Contemporary Sociology*, 36.2: 163-192

Lucas, R. (1988) 'On the Mechanics of Economic Development', *Journal of Monetary Economics* 22: 3-42

Martin R. & P.Sunley (1998) 'Slow Convergence? The New Endogenous Growth Theory and Regional Development', *Economic Geography* 74: 201-227

Myrdal. G (1959) *Théorie Economique et Pays Sous-Développés,* Paris: Présence Africaine

Nelson, R. & S.Winter (1982) *An Evolutionary Theory of Economic Change,* Cambridge (MA) : Harvard University Press

Polèse, M & R.Shearmur (2002) *La périphérie et l'économie du savoir,* INRS-UCS et ICRDR : Montréal et Moncton. Retrieved, August 20, 2006 from http://www.inrs-ucs.uquebec.ca/default.asp?p=res

Ray, D. (1998) *Economic Development,* Princeton: Princeton University Press

Romer, P. (1989) *Human Capital and Growth: Theory and Evidence*, Brookings working paper no.W3173, Cambridge (MA): National Bureau of Economic Research

Schulter, C. (1998) 'Income dynamics from Germany, the UK and the USA: evidence from panel data', Working paper 8: Centre for Analysis of Social Exclusion, London School of Economics. Retrieved, August 20, 2006 from http://sticerd.lse.ac.uk/dps/case/cp/CASEpaper8.pdf

Shearmur, R. (1998) 'A Geographical Perspective on Education and Jobs: Employment Growth and Education in the Canadian Urban System, 1981-1994', *Canadian Journal of Regional Science,* 221.1:15-48

Shearmur, R. (2000) 'Quebec Signs on to the New Barbarian Manifesto', *Policy Options,* December 2000: 2-44. Retrieved, August 20, 2006 from http://www.irpp.org/po/archive/dec00/shearmur.pdf

Shearmur, R & M.Polèse (2005) *La géographie du niveau de vie au Canada,* 1971-2001, Montréal: INRS-UCS, 139p, http://www.inrs-ucs.uquebec.ca/pdf/GeographieNiveauVie.pdf

Shearmur, R & M.Polèse (2006) 'Do Local Factors Explain Local Employment Growth?: Evidence from Canada, 1971-2001', *Regional Studies,* forthcoming

Simon, C. (1998) 'Human Capital and Metropolitan Employment Growth', *Journal of Urban Economics,* 43: 223-243

Solow, R. (1956) 'A Contribution to the Theory of Economic Growth', *Quarterly Journal of Economics,* 70: 65-94

Spencer, H. (1857) 'Progess: Its Law and Causes', *The Westminster Review,* Vol 67:445-465

Stolarick, K., R.Florida & L.Musante (2005) *Montréal, Ville de Convergence Créatives : Perspectives et Possibilités,* Catalytix. Retrieved, August 20, 2006 from http://www.culturemontreal.ca/pdf/050127_catalytix_fr.pdf

Urry, J. (2000) *Sociology Beyond Societies: Mobilities for the Twenty First Century,* London: Routledge

Wolf, A. (2002) *Does Education Matter? Myths About Education and Economic Growth,* London: Penguin

Acknowledgements

An initial version of this paper was presented in French at a meeting of the Association d'Économie Politique du Québec, Montréal, November 2005, and will appear, in French, in the conference proceedings. This translation is a reworked version. I would like to thank my colleagues Mario Polèse and Christophe Ribichesi for discussions following the first paper; I of course carry full responsibility for the contents.

Creating a sustainable future?
the working life of creative workers in Vienna

Sybille Reidl
Helene Schiffbänker
Hubert Eichmann

Sybille Reidl *is a researcher at the Joanneum Research Centre at the Institute of Technology and Regional Policy in Vienna, Austria.*
Helene Schiffbänker *is a senior researcher at the Joannem Research Centre at the Institute of Technology and Regional Policy in Vienna, Austria.*
Hubert Eichmann, *is a senior researcher at Forschungs- und Beratungsstelle Arbeitswelt (FORBA), the Working Life Research Centre in Vienna, Austria.*

Abstract
This article looks at the sustainability of work arrangements in Vienna's creative industries. Based on a survey of over 900 people who work in five sub-sectors (advertising, architecture, graphics/design/fashion, film/video/broadcasting and multimedia), it finds that there is significant pressure on those working in these industries. This results mainly from the fact that most are self-employed and consequently their guarantee of future work is insecure and they lack strategies to develop their own micro-businesses. The respondents have, however, developed coping strategies to deal with these pressures. In general, therefore, those with a high risk strategy in combination with high levels of work autonomy are more satisfied than creative workers who are employed and have a steady income but little decision-making freedom. Despite this, issues such as social security raise doubts about the future sustainability of their work. Further information about the project can be found on www.forba.at/kreativbranchen-wien.

Introduction

The creative industries have generated increasing public interest in recent years, with the main focus on their economic and employment potential and on the systematisation of the creative industries sector. A significant impetus came from the European Commission (1998), which identified an employment potential of over four million jobs in the creative industries in Europe. The 'Creative Industries Mapping Document' (2001), funded by the British Departmentof Culture, Media and Sport (DCMS) provided a detailed (and continually updated) picture of the economic significance and employment relevance of many the subsectors of the creative industries. There have also been Austrian studies highlighting the economic and employment potential of the creative industries, e.g. two reports on the creative industries in Austria by KMU-Forschung Austria/IKM (2003 and 2006) and research into the economic potential of the creative industries in Vienna by WIFO/mediacult/ Kulturdokumentation (2003). Outside Vienna, several Austrian regions (e.g. Linz, Tyrol) have tried to assess the employment and economic potential of the creative industries (Lechner/Phillip 2006, Kalmar et al. 2005). This research has focused mainly on the development of economic clusters and on employment potential, but it also provides basic information on forms of employment and the availability of skills.

These sectors depend on knowledge and skills which are built up over time. Continuity of career patterns and sustainable working conditions are therefore of paramount importance. However, very little research has been done on the quality of work and life or on career patterns in the creative industries. The few Austrian studies available (overview by Schiffbänker/Mayerhofer 2003) relate more to classical groups of artists (e.g. in the fine or performing arts). Apart from this, most research has focused on the 'social situation', i.e. relatively easily measurable features of this type of work: its high educational requirements, its high ratio of self-employed or atypical workers with insecure incomes, at least in part, and the need for supplementary part-time or full-time employment in unrelated jobs. Therehave been almost no primary surveys of the socio-economic and socio-cultural aspects of work/life quality in broader sections of the creative industries in the private sector – e.g. in architecture, graphic design or fashion.

As with other knowledge-intensive industries, for broader creative industry sectors (as well as for artists in the narrow sense), a structural economisation is to be assumed inasmuch as these groups – regardless of their employment status – are becoming ever more directly subject to market constraints. In this process individual job descriptions are becoming broader and beginning to merge with others, e.g. the separation between creative work and customer work is losing its significance (for example among software developers, architects and designers), as are clear vocational demarcations. Consequently, research on the quality of work in knowledge-based and creative jobs has found a variety of different situations ranging from self-determina-tion and successful 'enterprising selves', to self-exploitation and insecure forms of work (Gottschall/Betzelt 2001, Pongratz/Voß 2003). But it is precisely among creative workers that insecure working conditions are compensated for by greater autonomy, intrinsic motivation potential and highly developed lifestyles and concepts of the self. This raises the question of sustainability and makes it necessary for studies of creative or knowledge-based workers, and for policy recommendations to take greater account of the connections between the objective features of this work and its subjec-tive meanings and needs[1].

---

[1]   It is difficult to classify 'creative' work in advertising, architecture, design etc. according to a clear-cut definition of creativity. Instead, as in most empirical research, we focus on people working in selected 'crea-tive' industries and/or occupations. Respondents from companies of a certain industry (e.g. advertising agencies) may produce some kind of artistic output (e.g. as graphic artists) or not (e.g. as customer adviser). Both the creative/artistic and non-creative/artistic work examined in our study refer to knowledge intensive work. Using this approach (sectors and occupations) we avoid the need to develop precise descriptions of creative or knowl-edge work (as well as the question whether Richard Florida's definition of a 'creative class' may be problematic). Despite this, it is possible to classify the industries we analyse as 'professional applied creative services', predomi-nantly falling outside classical definitions of 'artists' (cf. Hill & Johnson 2003).

Empirical base

Taking account of this context, the research project 'Sustainable Work and Employment in Vienna's Creative Industries', funded by WWTF (the Vienna Science and Technology Fund) was set up to address the following questions: How sustainable or insecure is work in the creative professions in Vienna? What conditions promote or hinder access to employment and job retention? To what extent are resources available to cope with or avoid excessive workloads? What differences are evident between men and women and between different subsectors and forms of work and activity? What are the key features of successful arrangements for sustainable work and employment?

The research project, conducted primarily by FORBA and Joanneum Research, focused on the sustainability of existing jobs in subsectors of Vienna's creative industries. This involved a detailed investigation of business processes, working conditions, careers and patterns of coping with work in the context of institutional and sector-specific conditions, with the essential point of reference being the sustainability of work and employment in creative industries. Sustainability in this context is understood as an enduring quality of life and work. This entails a difficult balance between resources, requirements and demands. The resources that were taken into account with respect to sustainability in this study were: *economic resources* (income, employment and social security); *social resources* (social capital, professional and private networks); *time resources* (working time, private time, reconciliation); *knowledge resources* (competences, vocational training); *health resources* (workload and coping strategies); and *biographical resources* (continuity of career perspectives, multiple jobs).

The target groups we chose to analyse were in the creative industries outside the classical branches of the arts, which are involved in the 'applied' sectors and can predominantly be classified as lying in the private sector of the creative industries: advertising; architecture; graphics/design/fashion; film/video/broadcasting; and multimedia.

At the beginning of the project, a separate analysis of the five different subsectors was carried out (see Eichmann et al., 2005). As expected, this showed a high level of heterogeneity in and between the sectors, demonstrating that 'creative industries' is just an umbrella term for funding policies. A common experience among those involved in the creative industries was a strong tendency towards 'self-economisation' (cp Pongratz and Voß 2003) by which we mean a need for workers to invest in their own work and career development. Sustainability in these occupational fields is not strongly institutionalised, which may result from the fact that labour supply is larger than demand. Four of the five sectors (architecture being the exception) are weakly regulated, dominated by project work and with unclear career prospects. These features, together with the highly demanding nature of the work, would suggest that working conditions in the creative industries are not very sustainable. For more detailed information about working and living conditions in the creative industries, we carried out fifty problem-centred qualitative interviews and a standardised quantitative survey. The results of this quantitative survey are the main topic of this article.

Background to the study

In 2005 an online survey was conducted in the five subsectors examined in this study. The questionnaire was distributed via multipliers (interest group representatives, educational institutions, databases). Despite the support of numerous multipliers, it was not possible to reach certain segments of the fields being studied, in particular creative workers in Vienna who are not included in the relevant databases. Because of this investigation method, which was chosen because of the uncertainty regarding the total numbers, it cannot be assumed that the survey is representative. In terms of basic research, however, the findings provide important information on the employment situation of those working in the selected five subsectors.

The study involved both people working in the creative industries and those working in creative occupations in other industries in Vienna as presented in Table 1. Those in the creative industries include both people whose jobs classify them as creative workers (field A) and people who have other types of job in these industries, for instance managers (field B). In total, 82 per cent of those who completed the questionnaire belonged in these two categories. It was also possible to contact creative workers outside the creative industries through professional associations and interest group representatives, for instance graphic designers working in the banking industry (field C) and these represented 18 per cent of our sample. This classification follows the methodology of Bernard Casey (1999).

Table 1: Classification of the creative sector by activity and industry

		Creative industries	
		yes	no
Creative activities	yes	Field A – examples: Camerawoman in a film production company; copywriter in an advertising agency	Field C – examples: Architect in the public services; Graphic artist in the banking industry
	no	Field B – examples: Marketing manager of a design studio; Secretary in an architect's office	Outside the creative sector

Source: FORBA and Joanneum Research, 2006

People employed in the creative industries and the basic terms on which they work

A total of 910 people from the fields of architecture, design/graphics/fashion, film/ broadcasting/video, software/multimedia/internet and advertising responded to the questionnaire. The data were weighted in accordance with the job count (Austria Statistics, 2004) and an expert estimate of the size of each sector. One third of the respondents were female and two thirds male. The picture that emerges from the data is of a small business structure, with almost half of the respondents working in companies with fewer than five employees. Figure 1 shows results from our survey that confirm a statement often made about employment relationships in the creative industries: namely that most of the respondents are neither employers in the conventional sense, nor employees, but something in between. It should be noted that the category 'self-employed' includes project and service contractors, new independents and freelance artists. 'Mobile workers' are people who have several different jobs at the same time.

Figure 1 Employment status by sector and overall (n=910)

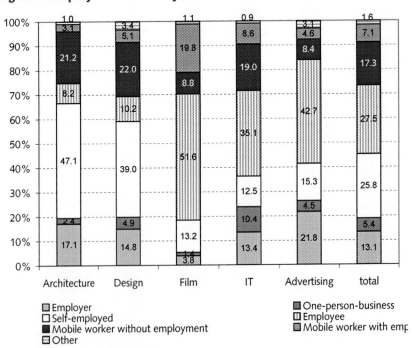

Source: FORBA and Joanneum Research, 2006

It is interesting to ask not only about the employment status of those working in the creative industries but also about what they would like it to be. These results (shown in Figure 2) show that, for the majority of respondents, their current situation coincides with their wishes Those most satisfied with their type of employment are those running their own businesses – 90 per cent of these would like to continue to do so in the future. In addition, however, 69 per cent of employees are also in their preferred employment relationship. Only 50 per cent of the self-employed, on the other hand, are happy with their situation. The other 50 per cent would prefer a change – 26 per cent would like to run their own business and 21 per cent would like to be employed. Half of

The spark in the engine: creative workers in a global economy

the mobile workers without employment would like to run their own businesses (most of this group have already set up a company but also have a variety of other forms of employment). In the case of mobile workers with employment, the percentage is somewhat lower, at 42 per cent. Two thirds of this group are already running their own businesses on a part-time basis, and a further third would like to do so. It should be noted that category 'call-off' in the graph refers to a small group of respondents who were interested in obtaining scholarships or Government assistance in their work. Overall, therefore, running one's own business is regarded as preferable to the increased security of long-term, full-time employment.

Figure 2: Current and Preferred Employment Status, in % (n=910)

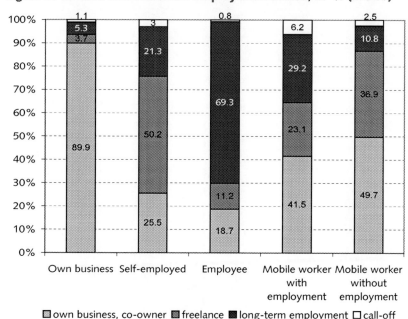

own business, co-owner ▨ freelance ■ long-term employment ☐ call-off

Source: FORBA and Joanneum Research, 2006

Our survey results found people in the creative industries working an average of 44 hours per week. In addition, a quarter of those questioned also worked in other sectors to give themselves some income security. Entrepreneurs, in particular, worked longer hours (52 hours per week inside and outside the creative industries, compared with 44 hours in total for employees). The creative industries also have a high degree of flexibility around when work is done, as Table 2 shows.

In addition to type of employment and working hours, income is a fundamental indicator of the basic (economic) terms on which a job is done. As shown in Figure 3, the average annual net income from work in the creative industries in 2004 was, in the case of these respondents, between €18,000 and €24,000. As was expected, there were marked differences between the sectors surveyed, which illustrate the heterogeneity of the five subsectors. Figure 2 shows the income distribution in each sector. Over 20 per cent of designers earn less than €6,001 a year (more than in any other sector), and only 10 per cent earn over €36,000. On the other hand, only two per cent of those in broadcasting earn under €6,001 a year, and 38 per cent earn between €24,001 and €36,000.

Table 2: Specific work practices in the subsectors, in % (n=910)

Subsector	Weekend work (at least once per month)	Night work (at least twice per month after 10 pm)
Architecture	72.4	58.7
Design/graphics/fashion	72.9	66.1
Film/broadcasting/video	90.1	81.3
IT	63.5	51.6
Advertising	59.2	44.3
Overall	72.1	60.9

Source: FORBA and Joanneum Research, 2006

Figure 3: Annual net income in 2004 by subsector, in % (n=817)

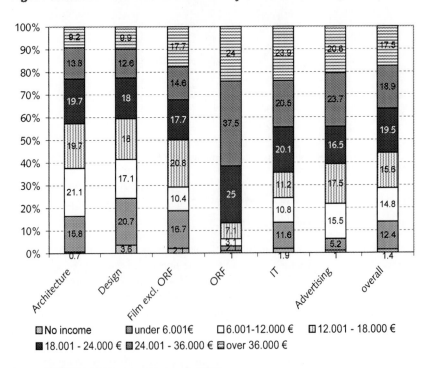

Source: FORBA and Joanneum Research, 2006

It should be noted that many people who earn relatively little in the creative industries work full-time in this sector. Only in the IT subsector do those earning less than €12,000 tend to be part-time, and the same applies to those in the film subsector earning less than €6,001.

Pressures

A central theme of the study was the pressures felt by those working in the creative industries and how they respond to these pressures. The most serious pressure identified by all those working in the creative industries was time pressure (58 per cent under pressure). Other overriding pressures were concerns about the future, such as the securing of future work (60 per cent under pressure), pension security (58 per cent under pressure) and general personal future financial position (57 per cent under pressure). Overall, with the exception of time pressure, future concerns created more pressure than present ones. Some people, however, also mentioned high personal demands (38 per cent under pressure) and the requirement to work on a number of projects simultaneously (35 per cent under pressure).

Pressure is increased by several factors: working in a situation characterised by lower fees for the work (primarily as a result of increased competition), uncertainty regarding future work and the resulting inability to plan. These work-related pressures can also affect a person's private life. Many respondents said that working in the creative industries left them too little time for their children and made it difficult to reconcile their work with their private life. This is also evident from the fact that substantially fewer women (less than 30 per cent) than men in the study had children to care for. The results showed that child care is still predominantly a woman's role in the creative industries, with only 30 per cent of the respondents saying that childcare was shared equally between partners.

However, many of the problems experienced by those working in the creative industries are offset by high levels of motivation and independence. People concentrate more strongly on the content of their work in order to forget what can sometimes be unfavourable working terms and conditions. This suggests that (from a subjective point of view) stress may sometimes be experienced as positive. If this ceases to be the case, then psychological and physical problems develop. This is, however, a relatively rare occurrence.

It is also noteworthy that the five subsectors analysed have a lot in common as regards pressures and resources. Two different groupings can be identified on the basis of marked differences between their working conditions and lifestyle: those working in architecture, design/graphics/fashion and film/broadcasting/video outside the ORF (Austrian Broadcasting Corporation) are highly atypical and have difficult working conditions and low income, resulting in greater levels of worry about the future. These people are also more motivated by the content of their work than by material rewards and more frequently place artistic demands uppermost in their career planning. Those working in the ORF, in advertising and in multimedia, on the other hand, have better employment and more conventional working conditions and a higher income.

Resources

In addition to financial and time resources, which as already noted are differently distributed among the respondents, the survey focused on the social resources and skills used to overcome the various pressures. A distinction can be drawn between professional and private coping strategies. Professionally, pressure can be significantly reduced by careful planning (72 per cent agree), self-confidence and composure (64 per cent agree) or seeking qualified support in the event of problems (55 per cent agree). Private coping strategies are also important: hobbies (59 per cent agree), long holidays (57 per cent agree) or the ability to switch off and not keep think about work during leisure time (47 per cent agree) help respondents to overcome the pressures on them.

In addition to these coping strategies, it is also possible to seek support from other people. Asked about the relevance of different 'sources of strength', most seek support from colleagues or through the professional networks on which 81 per cent say they rely. Many respondents also seek support from friends (69 per cent) or their partner or spouse (68 per cent). It is striking that 21 per cent of respondents turn to therapists, doctors or coaches for support.

Overall, despite the many pressures they experience, respondents see work in the creative industries as a positive challenge. The majority are motivated by the varied nature of their jobs and by being able to work in a self-determined way. Many have developed a range of professional and private strategies for coping with the pressures. They assess the growth in creative industries over the last five years as positive and expect this trend to continue in the future. The majority of respondents also believe they will always work in the creative industries.

Sustainability in the Creative Industries

It was necessary to analyse the data in more depth in order to find answers from the data obtained in the survey to questions such as: What does job satisfaction depend on in the creative industries? What creates pressures in the work and what relieves them? And what has the strongest influence on the state of mind of those working in the creative industries? For this purpose, variables were chosen and compiled into various indices which could be used in the next stage of the analysis to draw conclusions about the sustainability of the work.

The four key indicators of the subjective perception of the sustainability of a person's job situation in the creative industries were: job satisfaction; work pressures; respondents' stress levels (state of mind); and planned length of time in the sector.

The extent to which the presence or absence of these resources affects these indicators was investigated. Correlation and regression calculations were made to test which variables have a noticeable effect on these four key indicators. It should be noted here that all the variables integrated into the regression model were used, for reasons of logic and also because of the dependency relationships previously tested (using corresponding correlation measures) in explaining the key indicators.

Analysis of each of these indicators showed that job satisfaction was the one that could be described most clearly with the data available. By contrast, 'state of mind' and 'work pressure' are very difficult to represent numerically, because aspects of social desires and self-image always appear in the answers to the survey. Moreover, it is difficult to relate an unsatisfactory state of mind purely to the work context. Views here are undoubtedly coloured by what is happening in a person's private life. The picture of the factors affecting the state of mind and work pressure indices is, therefore, considerably less clear. Three main conclusions can, nevertheless, be drawn overall from this evaluation of employment sustainability.

First, at a micro level, a person's own coping strategies are critical in explaining job satisfaction, pressure and stress levels. Many respondents from the creative industries take it upon themselves to bring about improvements in situations where they are under pressure.

Second, at an intermediate level – particularly in an operational context – ensuring sustainability (measured through wellbeing, satisfaction and elimination of work pressure) through increasing autonomy is critical. It was not so much the continuity of work, but the ability to plan, which is the most important criterion for satisfaction, wellbeing and reduced pressure among those who participated in the survey.

Third, concerns for the future are fundamental as far as sustainability is concerned. Addressing this requires macro level policy solutions. The more uncertainties there are, the more stressed and pressurised the people working in the creative industries feel. It is evident, therefore, that people in the creative industries on the one hand are typical entrepreneurs who organise their own work schedule and are less attracted by being employed in an employee relationship than by independence. On the other hand, they also have a greater need for stability than concepts such as 'new independents' have so far been able to give them.

What does sustainable creative work look like?

We conclude by asking what sustainability in creative work might look like: what is the profile of the people who currently appear to be working sustainably in Vienna's creative industries? The results of this survey suggest that the 'sustainable creative worker' can be described more or less as follows. Sustainable workers are more likely to be men than women. They are either very young (21-25 year-olds) or of fairly mature years (over 55) and are likely to live in a joint property with a partner.

They work for the Austrian Broadcasting Corporation or in IT or in advertising and are mainly employees, although they occasionally run their own companies. They earn at least €24,000 net per annum and have extensive freedom to make decisions in their work. They have a whole range of coping strategies for counteracting work pressures both through professional networks and privately. Moreover, they have few concerns about the future. More than other people, they can imagine themselves always working in the creative industries.

© *Sybille Reidl, Helene Schiffbänker and Hubert Eichmann, 2006*

REFERENCES

Casey, B. H. (1999) 'Employment and Skills in the Cultural Sector' in *Cultural Competence. New Technologies, Culture and Employment*, eds. Oesterreichische Kulturdokumentation, Vienna: Oesterr. Kulturdomumentation

DCMS, Creative Industries Mapping Document (2001). Retrieved July 27, 2002 from http://www.culture.gov.uk/creative/creative_industries.html

Eichmann, H., S. Reidl, H. Schiffbänker & M. Zingele (2005) *Branchenanalysen zu Arbeit und Beschäftigung in Wiener Creative Industries*. Retrieved June 2, 2006 from http://www.forba.at/kreativbranchen-wien

European Commission (1998) *Culture, the cultural industries and employment*, Brussels

Gottschall, K. & S. Betzelt (2001) *Alleindienstleister im Berufsfeld Kultur – Versuch einer erwerbssoziologischen Konzeptualisierung*, Zentrum für Sozialpolitik-Arbeitspapier 18/2001. Retrieved June 2, 2006 from http://www.zes.uni-bremen.de

Kalmár, M., G. Kernbeiss & U. Lehner (2005) *Kreativwirtschaft: Nutzt Tirol seine Chancen?*, Innsbruck: WAW

KMU Forschung Austria & IKM (2003) *Erster Österreichischer Kreativwirtschaftsbericht*. Retrieved May 19, 2005 from http://www.creativwirtschaft.at

KMU Forschung Austria & IKM (2006) *Zweiter Österreichischer Kreativwirtschaftsbericht*. Retrieved July 7, 2006 from http://www.creativwirtschaft.at

Kulturdokumentation, Mediacult & WIFO (2004) *Untersuchung des ökonomischen Potenzials der 'Creative Industries' in Wien*. Retrieved August, 25, 2004 from http://www.creativeindustries.at

Lechner, D & T. Phillip (2006) *Kreativwirtschaft in der Stadtregion Linz*. Retrieved July 7, 2006 from http://www.tmg.at/1055_DEU_HTML.php

Pongratz, H. J. & G. Voß (2003) *Arbeitskraftunternehmer: Erwerbsorientierungen in entgrenzten Arbeitsformen*, Berlin: Ed. Sigma

Reidl, S. & F. Steyer (2006) *Zwischen Unabhängigkeit und Zukunftsangst. Quantitative Ergebnisse zur Arbeit in den Wiener Creative Industries*. Retrieved June 2, 2006 from www.forba.at/kreativbranchen-wien

Schiffbänker, H. & E. Mayerhofer (2003) *Künstlerische Dienstleistungen im Dritten Sektor. Teil 1: Ausgangslage: Kunst, Kultur, Beschäftigung*. Retrieved, June 10, 2006 from www.equal-artworks.at

Sunset in the West:

outsourcing editorial work from the UK to India - a case study of the impact on workers

Simone Dahlmann
Ursula Huws

Simone Dahlmann *is a research fellow at Analytica and at the Working Lives Research Institute at London Metropolitan University where she also teaches social research methods.*
Ursula Huws *is professor of International Labour Studies at the Working Lives Research Institute at London Metropolitan University in the UK and the director of Analytica.*

ABSTRACT

This paper presents a case study carried out in a large academic publishing and printing house. Interviews were carried out in both locations with senior and middle management, workers and trade unionsto gain their perspectives on the outsourcing of typesetting and editorial work from the UK to India. In Britain, 'working in publishing' traditionally represented a prestigious and highly sought-after career for graduates with high skills, both generic and occupation-specific. This paper explores the shock experienced by these workers when faced with the prospect of losing their jobs to the Indian labour market and argues that the outsourcing of skilled work in an increasingly globalised labour market introduces new forms of precariousness even to highly qualified workers with diverse skills. However the study also finds that the workers in India who are taking over these tasks are not experiencing the benefits previously enjoyed by their British counterparts. On the contrary, on the evidence of this case study, their jobs too are highly insecure. It concludes that the qualitative effects of offshore outsourcing on employment are more important than quantitative impacts.

'Let's face it. We have to accept that publishing is now a sunset labour market in Britain'.

This astonishing statement was made in 2003, not by the boss of a transnational multimedia empire but by a trade union representative in the country that produced Shakespeare, Jane Austen and the first printed books and newspapers in what is now the dominant global language. He was being interviewed as part of a case study on the relocation of skilled editorial work from England to India by a large and highly regarded academic publisher. The impact of that relocation on the British workforce and on their Indian counterparts is the topic of this article.

The relocation of telemediated work

The case study presented in this paper was carried out as part of the larger EMERGENCE group of projects. EMERGENCE (the acronym stands for 'estimation and mapping of employment relocation in a global economy in the new communications environment') was initially funded by the European Commission in 2000 with the aim of mapping and measuring the relocation of telemediated work[1] around the globe. In the first phase of its work, the project carried out a survey of nearly 8,000 employers across the (then) 15 European Union Member States plus the three largest of the states that joined the EU in the subsequent wave of expansion (Hungary, Poland and the Czech Republic). A parallel survey was also carried out in Australia, involving 1,000 employers.

The survey, some of whose results are summarised in Table 1, found that a wide range of business services were being relocated using telecommunications links, either on an outsourced basis or by companies setting up remote back offices. In the 18 European countries, seven per cent of the establishments interviewed had established remote back offices in other regions and around one in ten made use of teleworkers to deliver work from multiple locations. These were, however, strongly outnumbered by those who *outsourced* information work, either to individual freelancers (11 per cent) or to companies (43 per cent). Whilst most of the companies to which work was outsourced were in the same region or another region in the same country, a significant number were based abroad. In all, nearly six per cent of all the companies sampled outsourced at least one business service to another country using a telecommunications link. Around one company in five was involved in *supplying* outsourced services to customer organisations.

Table 1: Employers' use of remote telemediated work in Europe, 2000

	%
Any remote telemediated work	49
Within the organisation (in-house)	
Employees working in remote back offices	6.8
Multilocational teleworking employees	9.9
Home-based teleworking employees	1.4
Employees working in third-party premises	0.9
Purchasers of outsourced telemediated services	
Any 'e-outsourcing' (using telecommunications for delivery)	43.0
'eLancers' (freelancers using telecommunications for delivery)	11.4
'eOutsourcing' within own region	34.5
'eOutsourcing' to other region in same country	18.3
'eOutsourcing to another country	5.3
Suppliers of outsourced telemediated services	21.0

Source: EMERGENCE European Employer Survey, 2000 (IES/NOP) Weighted figures; per cent of establishments with >50 employees in EU (15) plus Hungary, Poland and Czech Republic. Weighted base: 7305 cases

What were they outsourcing? The unit of analysis developed for use in this survey was

---

[1]   The term 'telemediated work' refers to work that can be digitised and transmitted over a telecommunications link to a remote destination.

The spark in the engine: creative workers in a global economy

the 'generic business function'. Seven of these business functions were identified: creative and content-generating activities including research and development and design; software development and support (conceptually speaking software development is a sub-category of design but was deemed to be sufficiently well-defined and economically important to treat separately); data entry and typing (the routinised low-skill part of content-generation); management functions (including human resource management and the training of workers as well as logistics management); financial functions; sales activities, and customer service (which included the provision of advice and information to the public as well as after-sales support). There was of course some overlap between these categories and they were not exhaustive but they did provide a more stable and internationally comparable unit of analysis than the highly-problematic 'sector' or the rapidly-changing and culturally specific 'occupation' which were the alternative available units of classification.

The two groups of activities of most interest in this context are 'creative and content-generating functions' and 'software development and support'. Interestingly enough, these were also the two functions most likely to be outsourced. Nearly 30 per cent of the employers in the survey outsourced software development and IT support, and nearly 20 per cent outsourced design and creative work, whereas every other function was outsourced by less than 10 per cent of the sample[2] (Huws and O'Regan, 2001). Some of this outsourcing was to locations outside Europe but much of it was supplied by companies based within the EU. Around one company in fourteen in the sample was involved in the supply of outsourced creative work, and one in sixteen in software supply. However instances of outsourced creative and IT work tended to involve smaller numbers of workers than lower-skilled activities such as data entry or customer service.

In the next stage of the research, in-depth case studies were carried out to explore the dynamics of this relocation of work and its impact on workers. In 2001 the EMERGENCE team carried out 62 case studies of organisations that had relocated work to another region or country using a telecommunications link for delivery of the work. Each case involved two separate investigations: one at the 'source' (the place from which the work originated) and one at the 'destination' (the place to which it was moved) and, occasionally, also further investigations at intermediate steps along the value chain. Of these cases (broadly reflecting the survey results) 14 involved 'software development and support'and ten involved 'creative and content-generating functions'. The latter included the movement of work between a Benelux country and Southeast Asia by a children's book publisher, a firm of architects based in a Scandinavian country whose design processes were distributed between Spain, Latin America and East Asia, and a company in Western Europe whose website design was outsourced, first to Poland and then, in a second step, to designers in Siberia, as well as a number of cases where creative work was outsourced or relocated within Europe (Flecker & Kirschenhofer, 2002).

It was clear from the results of this research and from the results of EMERGENCE

---

2   Analysed another way (taking account of the fact that many establishments were involved in multiple outsourced arrangements), of all cases of outsourcing, 38.9 per cent per cent involved software development and 27.3 per cent involved creative functions (Huws and O'Regan, 2001:34).

sister projects in Australia and Canada that the case studies carried out in 2001 reflected a particular moment in a rapidly-evolving reshuffling of the international division of labour. Early drivers of 'offshoring' (as it has come to be known) on the demand side included the skill shortages in routine programming created in Europe, the USA and other developed economies during the late 1990s by the rapid expansion of the internet, the 'millenium bug' and the conversion of European currencies to the euro (Huws, 2003). On the supply side, the collapse of the import substitution policies of economies like India and Brazil had made available on the global market a large supply of well-trained computer science graduates[3]. China had embraced the market economy (obliging Vietnam to do likewise) and the transitional economies of Central and Eastern Europe were also opening up their markets rapidly (Mako and Keszi, 2002). Although the EMERGENCE survey results suggested that the search for scarce skills was the most important driver of relocation in 2000[4] (Huws and O'Regan, 2001), the bursting of the dot.com bubble and the consequent pressure on costs, we hypothesised, might lead to a shift in employers' strategies, with the search for low cost taking over as the dominant driver.

To investigate this hypothesis and explore further the impacts of offshore outsourcing on workers at the 'destination' as well as the 'source', funding was obtained in 2001 from the European Commission's Europeaid programme to carry out further case studies in Asia using the same methodology. In 2003, 59 case studies were carried out in India, Indonesia, the Philippines, Sri Lanka, Thailand, Malaysia and Vietnam. In order to study the relocations in full, these involved supplementary investigations at 'sources' or 'destinations' in Australia, Austria, Belgium, Canada, Finland, France, Germany, Luxembourg, Norway, Sweden, the UK and the USA as well as Hong Kong, and Singapore. As in the earlier EMERGENCE case studies, the largest group of cases (17) involved software development and support. However there were a number of cases involving high-skilled creative work. The functions involved included architectural drawing, graphic design, web design, research and development for three-dimensional modelling, detail design and the development of specialist products for the financial industry. Also in this category was the case study of specialised editorial work presented here (Huws and Flecker, 2004).

---

3   Before India loosened its trade regulations in 1992, these had largely been made available to employers in the UK and US through the mechanism of 'body shopping' whereby planeloads of Indian software engineers were sent to London or New York to work on temporary assignments (e.g. in the lead-up to the 'Big Bang' of 1986 when the London Stock Exchange went electronic) under employment contracts with their Indian employers. Tata Consultancy Services (TCS), the largest of the pre-1992 body-shoppers, used the client relationships built up during this period to launch itself subsequently as an offshore outsourcing supplier, as did several other major Indian players in the sector (interviews by Ursula Huws, Swasti Mitter and Sujata Gothaskhar carried out as part of the *Telework and Teletrade in India and Malaysia* project, 1996-7)

4   In the 2000 EMERGENCE employer survey, in each case where outsourcing took place, respondents were asked why they had chosen that particular supplier. Of the 4,154 reasons given in total, the largest number (22.9 per cent) were classifiable under the heading 'technical expertise and/or the right software/skills'; this was followed (at 12.6 per cent) by 'low cost/most competitive tender'. In descending order, the next most important reasons were 'good reputation/market leaders' (12.3 per cent), 'reliability/good quality/good attitude/creativity' (11.9 per cent) and 'longstanding relationship/strategic alliance/partnership' (9.1 per cent).

The Indian context

After the relaxation of its trade in 1992, India became the most prominent destination for outsourcing of data entry, software development and other back office jobs. The statistics are notoriously unreliable (Huws, Flecker & Dahlmann, 2004; Van Welsum, 2005) but most commentators agree that by the end of the 1990s it was the leading Asian supplier of business services (McCarthy, Belanger & Orlov 2003 I). However this outsourcing had its roots in a much older trend. The UK publishing industry, for instance, had been sending typesetting and printing work to former colonies like Singapore, Hong Kong and Malta since the 1960s. The difference in the 1990s was the ability to use information and communications technologies (ICTs) for very fast and cheap delivery of work which previously had to be physically transported (Huws, 1996). India's assets were a large English-speaking population, well-trained IT specialists and well-educated graduates available to work in skilled jobs for low wages. Other advantages in the 1990s came from the rapid improvements in India's telecommunications infrastructure and time zone differences that made it possible to process work overnight and increase the speed of service to clients in Europe and the USA. All the evidence suggested that Indian companies were diversifying and moving up the value chain rapidly, extending the range of tasks assigned to their employees. It was predicted in 2003 that architecture and law companies would follow the financial and IT sectors into outsourcing (McCarthy, Belanger & Orlov 2003) and in the same year, the *Economist* reported, that financial research & analysis and desk-top publishing for banks and law firms was following back office work, cheque processing and data entry to India (the Economist February 2003).

The UK context

The case study must also be set in the context of broader trends in the British printing and publishing industries which have since the 1970s experienced a process of more or less continuous restructuring, partly because of a series of mergers, resulting in ever-larger global media conglomerates and partly as a result of technological change. During the 1980s, like severalother industries in Britain, publishing became extensively casualised (Huws, 1988). Many companies downsized their in-house workforce and substituted self-employed workers for permanent staff. There was a major expansion in the use of editorial home-based freelance work. Studies by Stanworth & Stanworth (1995, 1997) documented the way that large numbers of formerly in-house editors and proof-readers in the UK book publishing industry had become self-employed freelancers, often still working for their previous employers. In the post-war period editorial work was seen as elite work, requiring at the very least a good university degree in English and often, also, specialist subject knowledge, as well as technical knowledge of the requirements of specific printing processes and some aesthetic or creative ability. It was typically done by people who saw themselves as intellectuals, often women who found it easier to enter than other, more competitive media industries such as television and advertising. The relatively low pay in the sector was offset by such (often illusory) advantages as meeting famous authors and becoming an insider in an intriguing 'world of letters'. In their study of freelancers, Stanworth and Stanworth (2007) showed that this reality was eroding under the pressures of casualisation. They concluded that the managerial impetus for creating a larger home-based freelance editorial staff was not just to reduce office overheads and cut costs but also to match staffing levels with peaks and troughs in demand, rendering the work very precarious and subject to unpredictable swings between 'feast' and 'famine'.

From the workers' perspective, publishing remained an attractive industry to work in, being associated with creativity and fame by association and seen as a route into a career 'in the media'. Thus college leavers and young graduates still competed to enter it, and were at least partially equipped to do so by an explosion in media studies degrees introduced during the expansion of higher education in Britain during the 1980s and 1990s. This fortified the trend towards a relocated, home-based freelance editorial workforce as these young people represented a continuous stream of available workers willing to sacrifice job security and benefits such as sick pay, holiday pay and pensions to their career ambitions. Further substantiation of this trend can be seen in the membership of the National Union of Journalists (NUJ) which represents the largest number of editorial workers in the UK publishing industry. By the mid 1980s, a third of the union's overall membership was self-employed, and the union's Books Branch had to set up a separate Freelance Section to represent their interests in the book publishing sector.

The fact that most of the workers in this case study chose to go freelance rather than accept deskilled work within the company suggests that this trend continues, with an ever-expanding swarm of freelancers competing for what may well turn out to be a dwindling supply of work. As one union member put it,

'If you are made redundant in publishing, you are basically given the choice of "go freelance or leave the industry".' (Interview with Jenny Vaughan, member of the Freelance Industrial Council of the NUJ, 2004)

The UK case study company

The case study company is one of the oldest and largest publishers and printers in the UK, publishing over 2000 academic and educational books and 150 journals a year. As the printing and publishing house of a British university, with a subsidy for its work, the company traditionally enjoyed charitable status, giving it certain tax advantages. At the time of our research, in 2003, it employed around 800 staff in the UK, divided more or less equally between its publishing and printing divisions.

Towards the end of the 1990s the company decided to restructure. Its subsidised, charitable status was coming to an end and, under a new CEO, the management decided it needed to become more strategic and competitive. The company's performance was benchmarked against other printers and publishers and this exercise uncovered relative underperformance in many areas. On the advice of an external consultant, it was decided to outsource the most labour-intensive part of the production, the typesetting, to India. A few years later, two further steps were taken. First, the reading department was downsized substantially, leaving many readers and copy-editors without jobs. The editorial work that had previously been done in the

UK was now moved to India. Second, a second Indian supplier was brought in. In an attempt to minimise the risks involved in dependence on a single supplier, the UK company's strategy was to divide the work between two different Indian offshore suppliers, each of whom were assigned to work on a number of journals and a few books. The underlying rationale was to relocate the work to the second offshore supplier if there were quality concerns with the work of the first. At the time of our research, for every three journals being sent for processing to the first supplier, approximately four were going to the second.

Back in the UK, the reading section was dismantled, and replaced by a new, digital services department. Sixty workers from the reading and origination area were faced with the choice of voluntary redundancy or redeployment. Because accepting redeployment meant being retrained in a range of IT skills and taking on work that was much more standardised and low-skilled than what they were used to, most of the readers and copy-editors accepted voluntary redundancy.

The Indian case study company

It was the first of the two Indian case study companies that formed the focus of our research. This was a new start-up company formed in 1996. The two founders had previously worked together in a typesetting machinery manufacturing company. Having
observed first-hand the growth of offshored typesetting in India, they decided to use their existing networks to establish a position in this market. They gained their first two contracts – of which one was for the UK case study company – by personal recommendation and were only able to deliver the work by outsourcing to another company in another part of India. In the words of the Executive Director,
'We didn't have a clue in this business. We didn't even know how to price the orders and quote for them. Because of my relationship with those customers they told me how the publishing industry model works and how to price.'
The company quickly built up its own staff, growing by about 60% per annum, and by 2003 was employing over 100 people and had acquired ISO 9001 certification[5]. UK customers accounted for 60% of its business. In the early stages, this growth required an investment in training staff to use the proprietary software of the UK client case study company. The company did not only grow numerically but also moved up the value chain, expanding from doing typesetting to copy-editing, proof-reading and preparing journal articles for online publication. Interviewees at the company expressed confidence in the high quality of their work, spoke of the customer's satisfaction with it and their pride in the contribution they had made to helping this customer 'grow its business'.

Interestingly, when they were interviewed for this case study, it became clear that they did not know of the existence of the second Indian company to which increasing amounts of 'their' work was being transferred and were confident that the future they faced was one of continuing growth.

---

5   An internationally recognised quality standard.

The UK story

In the UK, the case study involved unstructured qualitative interviews, on average around 60 minutes in length, with seven respondents from senior management, middle management, workers and the trade union.

The UK workers' perspective

All the copy-editors and readers in the company had undergone a traditional three- year apprenticeship, and most readers had been employed with the case company for many years. The reading department monitored the quality of work through proof-reading and copy-editing and supervised other processes, for example ensuring that deadlines were met. At the time of our interview, this quality monitoring process was being phased out in the UK, as part of the shift of responsibility to India. The 'second proofs' (the second stage of proof-reading) were still being checked in the UK company but soon all reading and copy-editing work would be in the hands of the offshore suppliers.

The UK workers remained very sceptical about Indian proof-reading and copy-editing standards and expected a drop, pointing to previous experiences of spelling mistakes, errors in proper names and confusions between English and American usage. Workers described their feelings of resentment and shock when they were told about the redundancies. One interviewee remembers:

"It sounded so impossible, reading being done in India. I guess we always thought we were doing a privileged job that could not be done anywhere else, especially not by non-native speakers.'

Although most workers were offered the opportunity to be redeployed, 40 readers and copy-editors instantly accepted the voluntary redundancy package[6]; one reader remarked:

"In this area people are in their 40s and 50s, they have no IT skills and are used to reading; there was no appeal in retraining to work with computers.'

Most of those who accepted voluntary redundancy planned to move into the precarious field of freelancing.

The experience of negotiating the change had left them feeling powerless, and, on the whole, disillusioned with their trade union. Once it became evident that management had made up their minds 'there was nothing we could do' . This feeling of powerlessness had generated resentment and frustration even amongst those who had not accepted redundancy. As one worker put it:

'Are we safe now or will there be more redundancies in the near future? We feel we were kept in suspense a long time when we didn't know if we'd have jobs.'

The fact that so many readers accepted voluntary redundancy created a shortfall of available workers. The company's solution was to bring in Indian workers to 'kill two birds with one stone' by simultaneously training the Indian workers and complementing the depleted workforce. Unsurprisingly, this created a real clash of interests. Workers who were asked to train their Indian counterparts wanted to go on strike and approached their trade union

---

6   In making this choice they were not behaving irrationally. Another study of the printing and publishing sector found very low levels of job satisfaction among proof-readers retrained to work on database management (Vendramin, Valenduc, Richardson, Carre et al 2000).

with this in mind. However the trade union refused to support this plan and informed them that they were legally obliged to follow the management's orders. The workers experienced this as another 'slap in the face', as one reader put it, giving this as the main reason for deciding to take up freelance work.

A strong concern about quality emerged throughout the interviews; readers were very clear that they expected a steep drop in the quality of services offered by the case company and also felt that their management did not take this concern seriously because they were entirely driven by costs savings rather than customer satisfaction. This is reflected in the words of one copy-editor:

'Quality issues which used to be paramount no longer are; until customers complain, quality will drop'

Apart from general quality issues, workers expressed worries about the image of particular journals which they believe had set very high quality standards in the past. They doubted whether their Indian counterparts could keep these standards up.

'Being a graduate does not necessarily mean they're good at proof-reading I know there still will be mistakes, I am English that's why I don't get it wrong; my superiors don't want to see that – they think it will work because it is available.'

Despite their disillusioning experiences, workers still had a strong pride in their work and identification with the brand. There was considerable prestige attached to working for a traditional, academic publisher. Working morale was perceived to have been high amongst readers and copy-editors, but was now being replaced with feelings of frustration and disorientation. Interviewees remarked that there had always has been a very low staff turnover and most employees 'used to stay on average twenty years'. They reported that they had heard there was a high turnover in India in the reading department, with people staying for a maximum of three years. This gave them reason to doubt that workers there identify with the company's brand name.

'I am worried about the future, quality, the company's reputation and what our customers think about us.'

The UK management's perspective

The management's rationale for outsourcing was described as arising from necessity rather than choice. General market pressure was driving outsourcing to India in a bid to cut production costs. One manager said:

'People here are resentful, they feel that we are transferring their jobs to India. What they don't understand is that the real story is that this is something we had to do to offer competitive products.'

There was a strong belief that the redundancies had been approached and executed in a scrupulously fair manner and that the message was communicated carefully and transparently. One manager remarked:

'If you cut back in a humane way, if you are not greedy as a company about how quickly you want to cut down, people will understand,'

India was chosen because of the CEO's personal experience of working and travelling there. The main motives were to 'save on production costs' and gain access to a more flexible labour market. The management belief that the UK workforce needs to become more flexible is mirrored in the introduction of performance measures and greater-transparency 'to motivate employees'. This notion of greater flexibility is a critical one: it was believed that relaxed labour laws in India and less workers' protection enable companies to turn work around much more quickly. As one manager said:

'People in India are more flexible in what they will do. If you say to them "I'll pay you so much for so many hours work but I'll tell you what I want you to do over the next 8 to 12 hours", they'll say "fine". Here in this country there is more of a culture of saying 'No, that is not what I was contracted to do" and I'd rather sit and do what I know well and not take any risks and follow my usual routines". That means that over the years, because of union demands, the ordinary workforce has become accustomed to a quality of life which is well beyond the quality of life experienced in the rest of the world, so they became price uncompetitive. Politically that is a problem for us.'

A strong underlying worry about declining quality emerged throughout the interviews, where concerns were expressed very strongly and clearly by workers, although the management was more cautious. Quality checks (at the time of our interviews, only second proofs were being checked in the UK) were disclosing major problems. It seemed likely that the handover process would take longer than originally anticipated. Despite training, quality was worse than expected although one manager insisted that the company recognised the learning curve their Indian colleagues were on and believed that with continuous training and feedback performance would improve. There was however, a considerable sense of pessimism and 'what if it won't work?'. One manager said:

'We've told our suppliers that their performance has to improve and that is about all we can do for the time being.'

Moreover, he added, if the relocation to India fails, there will always be other countries to consider. This manager also insisted that the company had not abandoned its UK workforce but was building a new skills base there, although he admitted that it would be unpopular because the work was so standardised:

'they won't like it so much as it is more boring than the work they used to do'.

Adding,

'There is a lot of resentment among our workforce but they will get used to their new jobs'

The UK Trade Union perspective

A trade union was actively involved in the negotiation around the voluntary redundancies, having been approached by the case company's senior management at a 'fairly early stage', (compared with other UK organisations planning to downsize; UK law requires companies to notify the union in advance if more than 20 redundancies are planned).

The initial intention was to make 60 people redundant over a three year period. A voluntary redundancy package was on offer with the option of taking up redeployment. The union representative recalls a series of 'heated, serious arguments' at the first meetings between the workforce and management. As already noted, the situation escalated when it was announced that six Indian workers would be trained within the reading department, mainly by workers who would eventually lose their jobs to India. Workers approached the trade union declaring that they would strike over this decision. The union strongly objected, making it clear that they would not support any strike action effectively saying:' You've got to do this, it's an order'. Both the management and the trade union representative admitted that this was a significant moment causing 'a lot of resentment and bitterness'. After this escalation workers seemed to come to terms with the finality of the management's intentions and an atmosphere of resignation spread, summed up in the words ' We might as well get the best deal of out this' .

Asked for a response to the company's argument that the UK workforce lacked flexibility, the union representative, somewhat surprisingly, appeared to agree with it. *'If the workers I am representing hear me say that, they'll wonder why I'm not part of the management. But I do think that as a workforce these people "unlearned" to appreciate their jobs and are less willing to try new things.'* Adding to that, he admitted that their union power did not really impact on the company's decision to relocate and pointed out that a more effective way to avoid redundancies would have been to find ways, possibly through worker consultation with management and trade unions, to make this workforce more flexible. But in his view there was no longer any scope for trying anything like that.

From the union perspective, it was felt that the situation was very clear: the number
of redundancies was not drastic and the management had quickly accepted a 'generous
redundancy package' with 18 months' salary being paid out. For the few workers who opted to be retrained, it was negotiated that none would be employed on worse terms than those specified in their existing contracts – especially important for the readers and copy-editors who would be moving to less-skilled work. His conclusion was stark:
'This is the reality trade unions have to live with. 'Let's face it, we have to accept that publishing is now a sunset labour market in Britain'.

The Indian Story

Five semi-structured interviews, each approximately one hour in length, were carried out with managers and employees in the Indian 'destination' company. There was no trade union presence in the company.

Most of its employees are women aged between 24 and 28. Roughly half are married and some also have children. Most are graduates and some have a technical background, with qualifications in IT or printing technology; others have a degree in the humanities. All members of the copy-editing team have postgraduate qualifications, either an M Phil or a PhD.

Although low by European standards[7], remuneration in the offshoring sector

---

7   According to one of our respondents the cost per 1,000 characters for processing an electronic file

(known in India as the Business Process Outsourcing, or BPO, sector) is well above the levels paid in other local industries so it is not difficult to attract educated English-speaking graduates. The company claims to follow a policy of hiring employees from lower and middle income families in the belief that in doing so it is contributing to wealth building in Indian society.

However these relatively high pay levels place workers above the salary ceiling of-fering working hours protection and overtime pay for weekend and evening work. This means that little extra compensation is provided for late and weekend work. The need to work anti-social hours is especially off-putting for women. As the company's HR manager put it,

'We would like to hire a few more men. One of the problems that we face is that many of the women don't want to work over the weekends. They may be ready to work on Saturdays, but certainly not on Sundays, especially the married women, with family and children. Many of the employees depend on public transport for commuting and are particularly reluctant to stay late in the evening.'

The 'flexibility' of the Indian workforce which figured so prominently in the UK inter-views is experienced on the ground as highly problematic. The average time schedule for a particular job is three or four days, but may be as little as 24 hours and is never longer than a week. Whilst the typesetting work done by the company usually allows some leeway, nearly all the editorial work coming from the case study company is 'rush jobs'. Nevertheless, because it is more profitable than typesetting, the company continues to seek out this work. In the director's view, the last-minute nature of the work is inevitable.

'This is the nature of the publishing industry. All the time lost in earlier stages like receiving manuscripts and so on has to be made up for during this period'.

However a middle manager said that he thought the outsourcing arrangement made it easier for the UK managers to get away with incompetent management practices, leaving things until the last minute or failing to give clear instructions, in the knowl-edge that these inadequacies would be invisible to their British colleagues and that the Indian outsourcers would have to 'pick up the pieces'. 'Flexibility' in Britain translates into management challenges as well as stress for workers in India.

'For the rush jobs, work allocation among the employees so that there is a more or less equitable workload is the challenge ... Most of the time, the rush jobs are entrusted to a single group who have to co-ordinate the work amongst them-selves ... there is a higher degree of monitoring for these jobs.'

Because so many steps are involved, the knock-on effect of compressing the schedule for any particular journal issue is considerable. During the short period of time allowed for any given job, a large number of separate tasks have to be carried out. Once the go-ahead is given, the papers and manuscripts are downloaded from the client site through FTP (file transfer protocol); these manuscripts are then distributed to a four-member team of readers for pre-production preparation (which normally takes about two days). The readers check the documents for missing pages, artwork graphics and other details

---

in India was around £7-8 sterling in 2003, compared with a lowest quote of £12 in the UK. Comparable costs in the USA were $25-32 US as compared with around $18 per 1,000 characters in India. Copy- editing is the proc-ess that generates the highest added value in the business.

as well as checking the readability of the document for typing and coding. Dealing with any missing items or inconsistencies requires liaison with the client.

The manuscript then goes into production. In the first step (coding) the document is formatted to produce galleys which are checked against the original manuscript in a proof-reading step. The mistakes found during the proof-reading are corrected in the next step by a team of four people. After these corrections, the manuscript may be sent back to the client or processed further. In the next step, the manuscripts are put into the appropriate house style for the specific journal.

Next comes the pagination of the whole journal issue, following which the table of contents is produced and a final check of the style (including hyphenation) is carried out. A further quality check is then carried out by a group of four senior people before the issue is uploaded to the client site by FTP. If any of the authors want additional corrections to be made, these too are carried out by the Indian company before the journal is finally printed. Each step is monitored using workflow software.

This is exacting, painstaking work, requiring a range of different specialist skills and knowledge, the ability to make judgements about the use of language and an eye for detail. Having to do it under pressure makes it stressful, a stress which may be increased by the knowledge that the speed at which the work is carried out is being closely monitored. Burnout and high staff turnover are not unexpected in such circumstances.

Despite their general statements of confidence in the future growth of their company, it is clear that some clouds hang over the future of its relationship with the case study company in the UK. With the trend towards more online publishing, the UK company has reduced its dependence on the proprietary software in which the Indian company has invested so much staff training effort and is moving towards the use of standard off-the-shelf publishing software packages. This has eroded their competitive advantage. Although it does make it easier for them to approach other clients in the publishing industry, it also poses a threat: any company can now move its business easily from one vendor to another, since the underlying technologies are the same. The only recourse left to the company in this scenario is to continuously strive to reduce costs, improve quality and efficiency and introduce better work processes. This puts constant pressure on the workforce to meet ever more exacting standards.

Although the UK company had not informed them that they had already shifted much of their business to a rival company in another part of India (or, indeed, that they were also investigating outsourcing some work to China), this company had noticed a reduction in the flow of work. As one manager put it:

'Though in the normal business itself, there are some variations in the number of pages received for working, over the last few months the quantum of work from this source has also been decreasing … It has made the employees nervous and they are feeling insecure and worried about their future.'

The response has been to search actively for new business. The company still expects to expand its operations in the near future. They are targeting new customers in Europe and the USA and have also approached Australian companies for outsourcing contracts.

Even it they are successful in this aim, however, given the competitiveness of the market, it is not at all clear whether this will necessarily result in sustainable employment.

Conclusions

Most of the literature on the employment effects of offshore outsourcing (e.g. Bardhan & Kroll, 2003, Norwood, et al 2006, Sako, 2005, Pain & van Welsum, 2004, van Welsum & Reif, 2006, UNIFI, 2002) has focused on the numbers of jobs affected, reflecting public panics about the mass migration of employment from the developed economies of the North to the global South.

This case study, along with many others carried out by the EMERGENCE team (Flecker & Kirschenhofer, 2002, Huws and Flecker, 2004) suggests that the qualitative impacts on work, and on workers' security may in fact be much greater than the quantitative effects. To take the example of the English-language academic publishing industry, there is every likelihood that it will continue its exponential growth. In the words of one market survey of Scientific, Technical and Medical (STM) publishing:

'The niche nature of the market and the rapid growth in the budgets of academic
libraries have combined to make scientific publishing the fastest growing
subsector of the media industry over the past 15 years. Moreover, the STM
market is quite insensitive to the ups and downs of the economy and therefore
a stable and reliable field for long-term investments.' (versita.com, undated)

This suggests a net worldwide growth in jobs, a growth which may well more than compensate numerically in any given European country for jobs relocated to other parts of the world (Huws, 2004). As the trade union officer interviewed in the UK observed, the actual number of jobs lost in this relocation was not huge and it seems likely that most of the workers displaced found themselves some sort of alternative employment, albeit more precarious, as freelance proof-readers or editors. Nevertheless, major damage was done: to their pride in their work, their trust in their employer, their confidence in their trade union, their self-respect, their sense of their worth on the labour market, the security with which they could look forward to the future and (in their view) also to the quality of the brand which they had devoted decades of their working lives to building up.

Their experiences could be multiplied across an industry which in the 20th century was one of a very few that offered satisfying work to well-educated women and men who wanted some connection with the world of ideas whilst still earning a modest living, people who were prepared to sacrifice high wages for the sake of doing a worthwhile job with intrinsic rewards. Their shock and disappointment stands in for a broader disenchantment; their new precariousness symbolises that of many. Several of our respondents clearly saw themselves as representing the tip of an iceberg. As one put it,

"If reading can be done in India, why not database management and spreadsheet
handling?'

It could be argued that they represented a labour elite, late survivers of a privileged layer that waxed fat on the remains of the British Empire. If the highly educated young women in India who are now doing their former work enjoyed the prestige and security that publishing work seemed to offer at its best in the UK inthe 20th century, then this could indeed be seen as a kind of poetic justice. The reality revealed by this case study, however, suggests that the new precariousness has not only been exported along with the jobs but magnified in the process. The introduction of generic software and standardised processes, in combination with the outsourcing relationship, has reduced the mutual commitment of the parties, forcing suppliers to compete against many others in a globalised market for increasingly standardised skills, where both their performance and their prices can be continuously compared with those of their competitors. The pressures are passed down the line with the 'crunch' falling on the workers who are unlucky enough to be squeezed closest to the deadline, and furthest from the centres of power. These stresses are evidenced in dramatically higher rates of staff turnover in the new Indian workforce (with a typical tenure of less than three years) compared with the older UK workforce (with a typical tenure of over 20 years).

Although a literature on globalisation, company strategies and offshoring is now emerging, few studies have taken a qualitative approach and even fewer have placed the study of outsourcing within a context of other factors taking place within organisations enabling workers's perceptions of precariousness to be studied (Benson & Littler 2002). There is, however, an extensive body of research linking the concept of job precariousness to the effects of redundancies and unemployment on workers (Frechet, Langlois & Bernier 1992). Research looking at job precariousness also illustrates the psychosocial impacts on workers in situations of growing employment insecurities (Malenfant, LaRue, Mercier and Vezina 2002). Fear of losing one's job, a lack of coping strategies, financial instability and adverse health effects may all be outcomes of insecure work situations. A review of studies (Quinlan, Mayhew & Bohle 2001), linking precarious working conditions to occupational health and safety found that precarious employment was associated with a deterioration in occupational health and safety in terms of injury rates, disease risk and hazard exposures. The same review identified a negative association between occupational health and safety and companies that are involved in outsourcing and organisational downsizing. Such heightened job insecurities interact with the already greater sense of precariousness experienced by most part-time, freelance and other contractual work contributing a further source of stress. Whether workers remain in employment or go freelance, it seems that there is no escape from these pressures.

Requirements for flexibility and adaptability can be factors closely linked to the precarisation of work. From the employer's perspective, flexibility offers a way to adapt to an increasingly unstable economic environment. For the workers, on the other hand, the requirement to be more flexible may weaken contractual and other employment conditions. The search for flexibility emerged as a prime motive to outsource to India in this case study company.

Added to these interlinked effects is another: the impact of changes in skill requirements. For the minority of UK workers in this case study who chose not to take voluntary redundancy, the only other choice was to accept much more standardised, lower status work. Adjusting to these new skills meant a development, which, according to these interviewees, felt very alien to them compared with the work they were used to. A subtle process of deskilling can be observed as new job requirements sidestep the existing skills base in favour of a new one. In this process, the old skills are devalued and workers feel that they are becoming more interchangeable. Even if they do not fall into objective definitions of precariousness (e.g. because they still have full-time permanent jobs) the subjective experience is nevertheless one of replaceability. The knowledge that the job might go offshore hangs like a sword of Damocles over their heads even if the threat is never realised. It may therefore be more useful to see the impact of offshore outsourcing not so much as the displacement of jobs but as rendering them more precarious. In other words offshoring's primary impact on labour is to discipline it rather than eliminate it altogether.

This case study also raises large questions about the role of trade unions in representing their members whose jobs are affected by offshore outsourcing. The interview accounts painted an ambiguous picture: on the one hand, the trade union had provided professional support in negotiating redundancy packages that were reasonably generous (by British standards); on the other it had refused to support the workers in their dispute with management. Although it was evident that there were broader concerns within the union about the increasing numbers of local job losses to India, an effective strategy on how to counter them had not yet been visualised. The editorial workers interviewed made it clear that they wanted more support than they had been offered to help them come to terms with their new condition, support that they felt should have been offered by both management and trade union.

We can conclude that trade unions need to develop strategies that will enable them to transcend national borders as easily as their employers. If not, as the sun sets on their traditional fields of negotiation, there is a danger that they could become increasingly marginal.

© *Simone Dahlmann and Ursula Huws, 2006*

REFERENCES

Bardhan, A.D. and C. Kroll (2003) *The New Wave of Outsourcing*, Berkeley Ca: Fisher Center for Real Estate and Urban Economics, University of California

Benson, J. & Littler, C (2002) *Outsourcing and workforce reductions: an empirical study of Australian organizations*, Asia Pacific Business Review, 8,3, 16-30

The Economist, 'Outsourcing to India: Backroom deals', 2003, 22-28t February:86-89.

Flecker, J. & Kirschenhofer, S. (2002) *Jobs on the Move: European Case studies in relocating eWork*, IES Report 386, Brighton: Institute for Employment Studies

Frechet, G., Langlois, S. and Bernier, M. (1992), Transition in the labour market – a longitudinal perspective, *Industrial Relations Journal*, 47:79-99

Huws, U. & O'Regan, S. (2001) *eWork in Europe: The EMERGENCE 18-Country Employer Survey*, IES Report 380, Brighton: Institute for Employment Studies

Huws, U. (2003) *When Work Takes Flight: Research Results from the EMERGENCE Project*, IES Report 397, Brighton: Institute for Employment Studies

Huws, U.,S. Dahlmann and J. Flecker (2004) *Status Report on Outsourcing of ICT-enabled Services in the EU*, Dublin: European Monitoring Centre on Change of the European Foundation for the Improvement of Living and Working Conditions

Huws, U. (1988), 'Remote Possibilities: Some difficulties in the analysis and quantification of telework in the UK. In: Korte, W.B., Robinson, S. and Steinle, W.J. (eds), *Telework: Present situation and future development of a new form of work organization*, Amsterdam: Elsevier Science

Malenfant, R., LaRue, A., Mercier, L. & Vezina, M (2002), Job precariousness, work relations and social integration, *Nouvelles pratiques socials*, 15:11-130.

McCarthy, J.C, Belanger, N. & Orlov, L.M. (2003), *Unlocking The Savings In Offshore*, Cambridge Ma: Forrester Research Report

Norwood, J., C. Carson, M. Deese, N .J. Johnson, F. S. Reeder, J.E.Rolph & S. Schwab (2006)*Offshoring: an Elusive Phenomenon*, Washington D.C.: National Academy of Public Administration

Quinlan, M, Mayhe, C & Bohle, P (2001) 'The global expansion of precarious employment, work disorganization, and consequences for occupational health: a review of recent research', *International journal of health services*, 31, 2:335-414

Sako, M (2005) *Outsourcing and Offshoring: Key Trends and Issues*, Oxford: Said Business School

Stanworth, C. & Stanworth, J. 'The Self-Employed without employees – Autonomous or Atypical?' *Industrial Relations Journal*, 1995, 26:3:221-229

Stanworth, C. & Stanworth, J. Managing an externalised workforce: freelance labour-use in the UK book publishing industry. *Industrial Relations Journal*, 1997, 28,1:43 – 54.

UNIFI (2002) *Globalisation and the trade union movement -What is the true cost of outsourcing?* London: UNIFI

Pain, N. and D. van Welsum (2004) *International Production, Relocation and Exports of Services*, Paris: OECD

Parker, A (2004) *Two-speed Europe: Why 1 Million Jobs will Move Offshore*, Cambridbge Ma: Forrester Research

Van Welsum, D. and X Reif (2006) *The Share of Employment Potentially Affected by Offshoring: an Empirical Investigation*, Paris: OECD

Vendramin, P, Valenduc, G., Richardson, R., Carre, D, et al (2000). *Flexible work practices and communications technology*, Brussels: European Commission

Versita.com (undated) *STM Publishing Industry and Market*. Retrieved on November 5, 2006 from http://versita.com/UserFiles/File/STM Publishing Industry and Market.pdf

ACKNOWLEDGEMENTS

We would like to thank Rajendra Bandi and Vasanthi Srinivasan at the Indian Institute of Management in Bangalore, India for carrying out the research in India for this case study. The Asian EMERGENCE project, within whose scope this research was carried out, was funded by the European Commission's Europeaid Programme (Asia IT@C Programme). Ursula Huws directed the project in her capacity as an Associate Fellow of the Institute for Employment Studies, in Brighton, UK. Further information about the EMERGENCE project can be found on http://www.emergence.nu

'Suits' and 'creatives':
managerial control, the expropriation of fun and the manufacture of consent

Bob Hughes

Bob Hughes *is a senior lecturer in Interactive Media in the Publishing Department at Oxford Brookes University in Oxford, UK.*

ABSTRACT

Human skill poses a perennial problem to capitalist enterprises. This paper suggests that they have discovered, in the concept of 'creativity', a new weapon in the war on skill which simultaneously generates consent, sanctifies the use of inexperienced and expendable labour, and gives the manager even more power to control the worker while acting out the role of parent and protector. Creativity (as understood by modern managers) is an ineffable quality which 'we know when we see' – i.e. its existence and value are in the gift of the (managerial) beholder. Helpless and powerless, it is especially apt to be found amongst the young and innocent. This paper draws on Michael Burawoy's study of 'Manufacturing Consent' in an engineering shop in the 1970s, and the author's own experience of working as a 'creative' in advertising agencies in the 1970s and 1980s.

In not much more than 50 years, the word 'creative' has become transformed from a fragile attribute of small children and poets into a mighty 'engine of economic growth'. How has this happened? Indeed, *what* has happened?

The fashionable orthodoxy, proclaimed for example by John Howkins (2001) and Richard Florida (2002), is that the 'creative industries' are an evolutionary step onward from the 'old' sweat- and skill-based industries, and we need 'new rules for a new economy'. But if we look at the scientific literature on creativity, and listen to what so-called 'creative types' actually say about their work, it is hard to find a clear basis for this separation.

In my own time as a 'creative' in advertising (during the 1970s and 1980s) the term was a bone of contention. It had apparently entered usage in the late 1950s. Today, advertising is seen as one of the first of the 'creative industries', but the new label was not accepted there without question and is still not used there without heavy irony. A famously creative ad-man, David Ogilvy, detested the term. He spoke (and his work still speaks) for a great many 'creatives' when he wrote:

The so-called Creative Revolution usually ascribed to Bill Bernbach (founder of Doyle, Dane, Bernbach – DDB) and myself in the fifties could equally well have been ascribed to N. W. Ayer and Young and Rubicam in the thirties ... Creativity strikes me as a high-falutin' word for the work I have to do between now and Tuesday.' (Ogilvy, 1983)

As for the scientific literature on creativity, this tends to support Ogilvy's view that it does not differ greatly from other kinds of work; definitions of creativity, for example as offered by Mihalyi Csikszentmihalyi (1975), overlap so extensively with the definitions of skill, for example, as offered by Charles More (1980), that they might as well be considered part of the same phenomenon. Moreover, major developments in mind science of the past quarter-century indicate that the separation of intellectual from manual activity (the 'Cartesian split') is largely bogus. A succession of works, for example by Richard Gregory (1981, 1998), Francisco Varela (1992), Antonio Damasio (1994) and Joseph Ledoux (1998) have led as it were to a 'resurrection of the body' in mind-science: thought and physicality are inseparable. It is all work, after all, and all attempts to differentiate it and attach different values to its different varieties require serious explanation.

Coercive cultures

In 1974 the sociologist Michael Burawoy took a job as a machine operator at a Chicago engineering works, and noticed that the labour process he was part of was not entirely organised on the strict Taylorist lines he had anticipated. It gradually dawned on him that the piece-rate system was organised as a sort of game (called 'making out'[1]) and this, rather than the larger realities of profit and exploitation, dominated the social milieu of the workplace. Making out provided engrossing moment-by-moment challenges and satisfactions for the worker; it underpinned the social status system and fuelled conversation within the plant and outside it, creating what Burawoy termed a 'coercive culture' where it was impossible to critique one's work except in the relatively trivial terms of the game. The vertical conflicts between management and workers had been successfully 'lateralised' into worker/worker rivalry. A game, says Burawoy, generates its own needs and means of satisfying them, which, although not primary, become a prime focus of concern, and so come to seem 'natural and inevitable. Alternatives are eliminated or cast as Utopian' (Burawoy, 1979:93).

The insights he came away with seem to shed much-needed analytical light on the so-called creative economy, offering a radical re-interpretation of 'creative' as an addictive new game for workers (and also consumers) to play, 'manufacturing consent' (as Burawoy puts it) to their own exploitation. The crux of the matter is that effective exploitation is not just a matter of maximizing control and eliminating uncertainty; on the contrary: 'securing worker cooperation rests on a minimal uncertainty, the possibility that the workers will assert some control over the labor process' (Burawoy, p 87).

'Creative', I suggest, works for capital in exactly this way. In the workplace (if not in science) it is above all else a *contested* term which creates a highly-exploitable 'zone of uncertainty'. The contest is not just over the meaning of the word, but whether what the worker has done is, indeed, creative or not – i.e., is valuable or worthless. The old economy's skilled worker could settle the matter with a micrometer-gauge, to

---

1   'Making out' meant producing enough items above the normalised ('100 per cent') output rate below which the basic wage was paid, in order to start clocking up modest bonuses on the piece-rate system – but without exceeding the 140 per cent upper output limit agreed between the union and the management.

show that the work was indeed correct to within so many thousandths of an inch. The new-style creative worker never knows whether his or her work is worthwhile or not until the boss, or the client, or a sufficiently large and powerful group of peers, declares it so.

Rewarding: the 'work' of recognition

The power of the word 'creative' is pretty well summed up in that expression so loved by managers: 'I'll know it when I see it' (or as they still say in the original creative industry, advertising, 'the man from Del Monte, he say "yes"!'). Indeed, one could go so far as to say that the rise of the concept of a 'creative industry' is a particularly clear expression of capitalism's preference, not for creating value, but for *bestowing* value on things simply by *recognising* them (and then, as a reward for this kindly act, taking *ownership* of them).

I am not being flippant. The calligrapher Edward Johnston (who invented modern sans-serif type for London Transport in the early 1900s, so that people 'could see where they were going') believed that 'appreciation, or rather "to see that a thing is good" (v Genesis) is the final creative act; in fact, that a thing is not completely created until it has been appreciated' (Johnston 1959:256). Recognition bestows value and therefore embodies power: a kind of act of love which, when turned into a cash value, easily becomes a kind of rape.

This is consistent with the simultaneous rise of the importance of intellectual property (IP). Indeed, Howkins (2001) defines 'creative industry' as one that creates intellectual property. Perhaps it is all really part of what Vananda Shiva (in *Biopiracy*, 1998, cf Bowring, 2003) has called 'the second coming of Columbus': the 'discovery' and annexation not only of other people's lands, rivers and forests, but also of their plants, animals, knowledge and genes.

This means that 'creative' has exceptional disciplinary force. It touches very deeply on what it means to be a human being. The British psychologist Liam Hudson noted in 1966: 'In some circles "creative" does duty as a word of general approbation – meaning, approximately, "good"'(Vernon 1970:217). But 'creative' can be a much more potent compliment than mere 'good', and 'uncreative' a much more devastating verdict than 'bad'.

Be that as it may, this paper proposes that 'creativity' is an important new area of capitalist mischief-making; turning work into a game, the better to divide people, galvanise consumption, and secure consent. I want to elaborate this proposition firstly by examining the managerial history of the 'c-word', followed by a short account of its impact in my own experience as a 'creative worker' (as a copywriter in an assortment of UK advertising agencies in the 1970s and 1980s).

Creativity as a Cold War recruit: against boredom and the Soviet Union

Scientific interest in creativity (in the sense of getting new ideas) began in the late 19th century, for example with the mathematician Henri Poincaré's influential 'Foundations of Science' (1908, quoted in Vernon,1970). But, apart from some very rare occurrences[2], the world of business and politics took no interest in the concept until the start of the Cold War. It happened quite abruptly, in the USA, in 1950. Hudson expressed a commonly-held view in 1966, that the cause was:

---

2   For example in 1923, Herbert Hess's 'Creative salesmanship: scientific ideas for salesmen, salesman-agers and sales administrators'.

'a diffuse cultural ground-swell, elevating the scientist from the status of technician to that of culture hero; and a more specific concern on the part of the American nation (i.e. the USA) with the state of their armaments industry.' (1966, quoted in Vernon 1970: 218)

A key event was J.P. Guilford's presidential address to the American Psychological Association (APA) in 1950, promoting creativity as a strategic national asset. An early 'creativity sceptic', Robert Weisberg (1986), observed that Guilford was operating outside the academic mainstream on so-called 'creativity testing'. During the Second World War he had been Director of Psychological Research at the Santa Ana Army Air Base, working on the selection and ranking of aircrew trainees. His address to the APA caught the military-industrial establishment in a moment of excitement and anxiety following its successes with the Atomic Bomb, radar etc., afraid that the flow of scientific goodies might dry up. The anxiety became public hysteria in 1957, when Soviet engineers launched the first man-made satellite, Sputnik. Writing in 1958 (as the 'missile-gap' obsession was taking shape), Guilford explicitly linked the need for research into creativity with the USA's

'mortal struggle for survival of our way of life in the world. The military aspect of this struggle, with its race to develop new weapons and new strategies, has called for a stepped-up rate of invention.' (Traits of Creativity, 1959, quoted in Vernon 1970:167)

Guilford planted two other important seeds: the idea that 'creative' would be important for maintaining consumption (as in 'creative pastimes' etc. to fight 'boredom arising from increased leisure time'); and the 'divergent thinking' model of creativity, with its emphasis on 'flexibility' and prejudice against 'linear' thinking. The 'myth of divergent thinking' was demolished early on by well-designed and successfully-replicated experiments – for example Dunnette, Campbell and Jastaad's examination and demolition of brainstorming in 1963 – one of many such experiments described by Weisberg (1986, p62). Despite this, divergent thinking became part of the management gospel and still turns up in new forms in new personality tests, for example in Fiona Patterson's 'Innovation Potential Indicator' (IPI-Howkins 2001, p16) – a psychometric test currently in favour in the UK – which appears to offer employers a way of sorting the easily-bored, 'innovation oriented' and potentially 'creative' recruit from the dull, introverted, inflexible types. The 'anti-boredom' role seems to have succeeded in a way Guilford didn't perhaps anticipate: in helping to create a strong general prejudice against ways of life that are stable and predictable, to tar-and-feather forces that strive to introduce some stability into people's lives such as traditional trade unions, and central planning, and to establish the idea of precariousness as both exciting and necessary.

So, 'creativity' went mainstream, with US government funds for research, and cheered on by popular journalism. This version of creativity, which we might call the Guilford Strain, rapidly escaped into the corporate environment.

This 'explosion of creativity' seems to have had two phases: from the mid 1950s till the mid 1980s, there was a fairly distinct 'creative heartland' consisting of the advertising agencies (which also started calling themselves an 'industry' at some point during this period) and parts of the media; and 'creative hobbies' such as painting by numbers or rug-making from kits. In the second phase, 'creative' radiated into almost every aspect of life until (as Rob Pope puts it, in his very rich and detailed account): 'nowadays we can apparently "create" everything from "the right image" to "job opportunities" and "a market"' (Pope, 2003:40). The latter phase coincides closely with three other important phenomena: the collapse of the Soviet Union, the surge of globalisation and offshoring, and the invasion of all industries by electronics. Indeed, since the mid 1980s 'creative' and 'technology' have come to seem entirely natural companions, with the indicative slogan 'unleash your creativity' appearing on advertisements for all manner of personal computer products and peripherals.

Yet there is evidence that all this talk of 'creativity' is not (Florida notwithstanding) matched by any increased, subjective sense of creativity in the workplace. On the contrary, Ewart Keep has found that, in UK National Skills Surveys, the number of employees reporting 'a great deal of choice' over the way they worked fell from 52 per cent in 1986 to 39 per cent in 2001. Keep observes: 'the opportunities for displaying creativity at work appear to be shrinking rather than expanding' (Keep, 2002).

Electronics have been used across the whole spectrum of industry to augment the sales effort – by allowing incremental, sales-oriented improvements to and accelerated obsolescence of previously stable technologies – so it could be said that the technology has allowed advertising to invade everything that moves.

From armaments to advertising: creativity becomes the new Calvinism

Why should advertising, of all businesses, have been the one that first latched on to 'creative', and even made it its own? Why not an industry that actually creates something? This apparent paradox is consistent with Baran and Sweezy's (1966) account of the vital role played by the sales effort in modern capitalism. It also fits with and supports a view that in some circumstances capitalism is less concerned with production *per se*, or profit, than it is with power. What more natural way to neutralise a dangerously capable workforce than by siphoning off its most articulate and inventive members? Furthermore:

'The greatest damage done by advertising is precisely that it incessantly demonstrates the prostitution of men and women who lend their intellects, their voices, their artistic skills to purposes in which they themselves do not believe, and that it teaches [in the words of Leo Marx] "the essential meaninglessness of all creations of the mind: words, images, and ideas". The real danger from advertising is that it helps to shatter and ultimately destroy our most precious non-material possessions: the confidence in the existence of meaningful purposes of human activity and respect for the integrity of man.' (Baran & Sweezy 1966, quoted by Robert McChesney and John Bellamy Foster, 2003)

How is the trick achieved? Modern management demands 'excellence' and the desired, excellent individuals must be contradictory types: creative thinkers whose rebellious, disrespectful energies must both constantly excite and never upset the corporate applecart. This creative stereotype (which no human being can fulfil for long without coming to harm) has become a sort of storm-trooper for labour and management policy since 1950. Where and when was it forged?

One can see it taking shape in the work of the 'creativity gurus', like ad man Alex Osborne, who seized on Guilford's 'divergent thinking' and developed it in yet more management-friendly (and even more scientifically suspect) directions.

Osborne (the 'O' in advertising agency BBD&O), added an important twist to creativity with his idea of 'brainstorming' (1959), which rapidly became a management-training industry in its own right. Whereas Guilford was interested in *discovering* creative individuals, Osborne (and subsequent rivals, like Edward de Bono with his 'Lateral thinking' and W. J. J. Gordon with his 'synectics') insisted that *anybody* could be creative – *provided* they submitted to the rules of the game. Thus, brainstorming introduced a Calvinistic element: in principle, anyone *could be* one of the elect, but nobody could be sure that they *actually were* of the elect, until the 'day of revelation' (the brainstorming session itself). And on that day, it would be up to the manager, or the group, to decide who was creative and who was not.

The elements of game-playing and submission to ritual and quasi-paternal authority helped foster the idea of work as compulsory fun for infantilised workers, with a gangsterish presumption against those experienced workers who 'knew too much' to join in the fun, or to sustain a convincing pretence of doing so.

The 'creativity training industry' continues to flourish in the consumer economies. Anna Craft (an educationist) describes a recent shift of focus onto 'everyday creativity' by (for example) the UK's National Advisory Committee for Creative and Cultural Education (NACCCE), which advocates teaching all workers how to be 'creative' (Anna Craft, 2003). Which might be interpreted as a way of saying 'teaching workers to enjoy whatever work they're given': a cheap alternative to the Government's failed 'high-skill, high-value economy' project (Lloyd & Payne 2002; Keep, 2002, Bolton 2004). And this is linked to a boom in motivational courses and training in general, which increasingly cover newly-defined 'skills', such as team-working, 'motivation'[3], and even 'creativity'.

My own passage from skilled work to 'creative' work

I joined my first advertising agency as a trainee copywriter in 1976. I had been trying to make a living as a calligrapher and signwriter and learned about advertising whilst helping a commercial artist friend to do 'finished art' (camera-ready artwork) for local advertising agencies. 'Finished art' deserves a mention: it was perhaps a good example of the persistence, or re-creation, of skill in a notionally deskilled industry. Hand lettering had been a core skill in commercial art, but it had largely been replaced by new technologies including Letraset dry-transfer lettering, the IBM 'golfball' typesetter, and 'bromides' (quick photographic reduction/enlargement systems for line and halftone artwork). However, the new technologies gave rise to new and interesting skills – 'bashing down Letraset' required a well-evolved technique involving adhesive tape, an expensive, coated art-board known as 'CS10' and a surgeon's scalpel. Artwork was assembled with Cow Gum on CS10, with a neat paper cover, and the stamp of the relevant trade union, the NGA (National Graphical Association), on the back. If

---

3   For example, see Sharon Bolton 'Conceptual Confusions: Emotion Work as Skilled Work', in Warhurst, Grugulis & Keep, 2004

there was no NGA stamp, the ad could not run because the printing industry was a 'closed shop' in which only trade union labour could be employed for such tasks.

This was generally agreed to be 'skilled work'. It was explicitly *not* what the advertising agencies would call 'creative' work (and we never used the word) yet it had all the features of creative work, as described for example by Mihalyi Csikszentmihalyi (1975), in terms of knowledge, skill, control and risk-taking, and the subjective pleasure of doing the job. The finished piece was always a delight to the appreciative eye. We often remarked that it had much greater aesthetic merit than the ad itself (more often than not, a scene of retail carnage announcing 'Prices slashed!' or 'Massive savings!'). We took care that things were trimmed straight and clean with no nasty scabs of extruded Cow Gum. The process camera wouldn't have minded, but we were judged by humans and did things properly. It seemed sad that so few people ever saw our work. In an earlier generation people would have seen it all the time: we would have been up on step-ladders, doing it in public, earning small amounts of admiration but, of course, less money. On the other hand, we were not responsible for the ads – we just did the artwork – which was comforting.

When I moved from this role to within the advertising agency I found myself embroiled in a welter of undeclared, laterally-displaced conflicts. I learned that I was a 'creative', my boss was the 'creative director'[4], and I was part of a 'creative team'. It was difficult to establish trust with one's fellow team members because nobody knew for sure what anyone else was earning, and there was continuous rivalry between the various creative teams – mostly over who got to work on the prestige accounts and new business pitches. But some trust was achieved – largely I think through the intense, rich and often hilarious discussions we had, in the necessary search for agreement and clear criteria in the tricky matters of expression and design.

A creative team consisted of a copywriter and a 'visualiser' – later on the title of this job changed to 'art director' – and perhaps a junior or two, depending on the volume of work on that team' accounts. A busy retail account might keep a number of visualisers squeaking away with their Magic Markers, while the copywriter agonised over alternative ways of saying 'prices slashed'. The visualisers had generally done some sort of art school training but the copywriters had no training at all (and received none, apart from occasional peer comment). But training was, for some reason, an alien concept: this was a game in which one supposedly won or failed on one's one merits, and indeed, progression could be rapid. It was less obvious what happened to people who did not progress – although I do remember an inconclusive conversation once that began 'I wonder what happens to old copywriters?'.

Each creative team took its instructions from an account executive, who had access to The Client. Account executives were always known as 'suits'. The suit would prepare a written brief for each job, which the creative director would check and perhaps send back for revision before passing it on to the team, who might also challenge it. The relationship between creatives and suits was plagued by mutual distrust, incomprehension,

---

4   He had resolved to become an ad-man after seeing the 1948 Cary Grant film 'Mr Blandings Builds His Dream House' – in which the hero saves the day by recognising the perfect copy-line for Wham Ham, when his cook declares: 'Mister – if you ain't eatin' Wham you ain't eatin' ham!'

fear, and contempt – although occasionally friendships would develop, giving rise to the possibility that the new grouping might defect and set up an agency of its own, taking its clients and a few favoured colleagues with it.

After approval by the client, the team's visuals and copy (known as 'concepts') went to a place called 'production', where the creatives' rough efforts were translated into precise, visual specifications for the guidance of the finished artists, typesetters, illustrators, photographers, printers etc who had to turn our concepts into something that could be physically produced and would look OK. Production work was strictly segregated from creative work. It was skilled in the traditional sense: you could assess it by objective criteria (at the most basic level, whether the type fitted or not). Production people were sometimes unionised and always went home at 5.30 pm or got paid overtime. Creatives were not unionised – indeed, the idea seemed alien – and stayed at work till 6.00 pm or later and never claimed overtime. Looked at logically, production workers had the better deal – but they were very clearly a disparaged class, subservient to the creative department, which was where the fun was, apparently.

Discretion, and the disciplinary uses of creative fun

In the 'new economy', there has been quite general recognition of the phenomenon of 'work disguised as fun' (e.g., Ross, 2004). The general idea is that if workers can be persuaded that they are enjoying themselves, and have special privileges that other workers don't have, they will be content with lower wages. This is probably true (as it was true in the creative department) but there is an additional dimension: the power-assymetries that lurk in the grey, undefined area where the perks of the jobs blend into 'pilferage and the fiddle' (Ditton, 1977).

Creatives had a range of privileges. The most important privilege was a certain, circumscribed freedom to do what you had always wanted to do: drawing or writing – plus other activities that helped you get better at it: arguing, looking through portfolios of photographs, viewing showreels. This freedom blended imperceptibly into debatable areas: wandering off to the shops for the afternoon, ostensibly to look at 'the product' through the eyes of 'the target market'; spending half the morning in a café because 'the ideas flowed better' that way; in some cases, drinking four or five pints of Guinness at lunchtime because 'I write my best ads when I'm drunk'.

These privileges perhaps created what Ditton calls 'a hedonistic surplus' (a sense of having been rewarded over and above the value of the time stolen from the company); more importantly, they were indeterminate in the same way as the privileges of the rural poor during the period of the enclosures: an action tolerated as mere pilferage one day could be punished as theft the next. They were always available for managerial challenge, and so worked ultimately to the disadvantage of the employee.

A fascinating paper by Michel Anteby (Anteby, 2003) discusses the practice of *perruque* (literally, 'the wig': making things for personal use in the firm's time with the firm's materials) in a French aerospace factory. This is another category of 'indeterminate privilege' very prevalent in the advertising agency – and very definitely nearer to the larceny end of the pilferage/theft spectrum. Anteby observes that *perruque* was beneficial to the company as well as the workers – for example, improving social cohesion, signalling trust and status, and forging useful friendship- and knowledge-networks that supplemented the narrower, less responsive formal company structure. In the advertising agency *perruque* activities ranged from the theft of art materials and 'doing foreigners' (private freelance jobs, possibly for other agencies) to the design of elaborate leaving and birthday cards and a sort of currency in favours of this kind. In one agency where I worked, there was a brief craze for making scurrilous but unattributable audio tapes about the detested creative director. These were produced in an ingenious if laborious way: the message was carefully written out backwards so that it could then be read backwards (with some difficulty and helpless hilarity) into a tape-recorder. The tape was then reversed for playback by careful splicing, and left lying around in the boardroom. This sounds like an act of rebellion but if it was, it had little effect. We all felt a great thrill of childish guilt and glee, but the creative director stayed put.

The 'great advertising' game

In Burawoy's machine shop, life was dominated and shaped by the game of 'making out'. In the creative department, the equivalent obsession was the constant desire to do 'great ads' – which is to say, ads that you would be proud to say you'd worked on, and which would get you a job in a 'good' advertising agency. A 'good' advertising agency was one where, it was assumed, your creativity would at last be recognised, encouraged and rewarded.

In Britain in the late 1970s 'great ads' included a famous series of surreal poster ads done for Benson and Hedges cigarettes by Collett, Dickenson and Pearce (CDP); David Abbott's ads for Volvo cars and Parker pens; and the Cadbury's Smash Martians. These were the ads our friends and family thought of, when 'advertising' was mentioned. Then, as now, 'great ads' were an infinitesimal fraction of all advertising – but we somehow believed that we could and should be doing ads like these. People would throw endless energy into any project that offered the chance of producing ads that would 'look good in the book' (the personal portfolio that was a passport to a good agency) and by the time I left the world of ad agencies in the mid 1980s competition for creative jobs was so intense that young and no doubt very talented graduates would work for nothing as 'interns', just so that they could 'build up a book' and say they'd worked for Saatchi and Saatchi, DDB, BBH, JWT or another of the big names in the business.

Every week we pored over the new issue of the advertising magazine *Campaign* to see who had won what accounts and awards and who had done which great ads in which agencies and speculate on the chances of getting a job there. Successful teams were represented in a remarkably formulaic and consistent way, which I am quite amazed to find is still going strong 30 years on. A typical article features a photograph of two bored-looking men staring scornfully at the reader from a risky-looking back alley. One wears a suit; the other some exclusive-looking casual attire. In the accompanying text, they speak of their steely commitment to producing 'great advertising' and their contempt for the mediocrity, complacency, failure to take risks and lazy thinking that are vitiating the industry and endangering its survival.

The suits were generally thought to be conspiring to prevent the creatives from doing great work. They would insist on cramming extra items into an ad – sabotaging its elegant, forceful message – or allow the client to modify a cleverly-wrought headline, or come up with inconvenient facts that needed to be mentioned in the ad, undermining the whole, daring proposition or ditch the 'creative' campaign we'd worked on in favour of a bold-and-bloody price offer. Alternatively they would sidle up to us with a sad little brief with no budget and a confused rag-bag of products and ask us to 'do something creative' with it or, even worse, 'jazz it up a bit' – betraying the full, horrifying extent of their incomprehension. They thought creativity was something we could just sprinkle on the product, like fairy dust.

Viewed as a game system, there was a huge amount going on here – much more than in the relatively straightforward machine-shop where Burawoy worked. Indeed, the 'suits and creatives' division seemed to allow management to run two different and sometimes mutually conflicting games simultaneously on the same problems – an outrageous waste of human talent, but clearly a sound business proposition when talented workers can be persuaded to give so much of their time for nothing, and every producer of goods or services in the economy is obliged to advertise to the limit, or perish.

'Speciation' and the internal market

Burawoy examines the role of the internal market in jobs in helping to maintain consent. In his machine shop this took the form of an evolving system of job differentiation, pay differentials and incentives for long service, which kept skilled workers from leaving and reduced the scope for industrial action. In the advertising agencies (and apparently in more modern 'creative industries') the internal market was very different.

A striking feature of ad land's internal market was a sort of 'speciation': two quite separate populations of workers ('suits' and 'creatives') that had become so different at the genetic level they could no longer interbreed. It was very rare indeed for a suit to transfer to creative work, or *vice versa*. Both were exploited. But there were also power assymetries between the two groups. The suits included the senior managers, account-handlers, researchers, planners, media-buyers and public relations people, and it was quite common for individuals to move up or across the food-chain from any of these quite different starting points. Suits might also 'move over to the client side' (or 'come in from the client side') i.e. go and work for a client company, for instance as their marketing manager. Among the creatives, there was almost no internal career progression. In my experience it was rare for someone to start as a junior and then work their way up to team-head, let alone creative director or managing director. The general idea was that you would 'get your book together', 'build up a showreel' and then jump ship to another (better) agency. Appointments were nearly always made from outside, with as much of a fanfare as possible and an eye to the agency's prestige. A new junior team joining the agency would be described as 'young, raw talent' and perhaps 'hungry for awards' (an implied threat to the complacent natives) When making senior appointments, notoriety, fame and exoticness all seemed to be important criteria. And while it could be an excellent move for a suit to 'move to the client side', it was career suicide for a creative to do the same thing: in-house creatives were assumed to be very inferior life forms with hopelessly low creative standards and skills.

There were further species-barriers within the creative department itself. There was one between writers and art directors, and a massive one between the creatives and the production people. It was most unusual for an art director to switch to writing or vice-versa – and a severe breach of etiquette when a writer attempted to produce his or her own visuals. Likewise, it was very rarely that someone from 'production' progressed to the creative department, and it would have been an outrage for a production layout artist to be asked to do a visual.

These demarcations were not the idea of any trade union, and no shop steward could have enforced them as successfully. They operated at such a deep level of the culture that they did not even need to be mentioned. They meant that quite simple jobs could become much more complicated and take much longer than they need have done. In pre-War times (before the creative department existed) the writer's copy would go straight to a 'commercial artist', who would do all the visual design work from 'the creative bit' through to the final type specification. In my day, all 'concepts' had to pass through the intermediation of an art director, whether talented, talentless, literate or illiterate, who would strain to impart some creative magic to the subject matter, whether it was wanted or not.

The worst asymmetry was the asymmetry of truth-telling. For example, the suit could be fairly candid about the merits of the product being advertised: he or she could decide not to sell it on its merits and go on price instead. The creative however had to find or create some merit in even the most dismal offering, even if the client candidly admitted the product was 'crap' – and to do that you had to enter into the delusion heart and soul on a daily basis, and come up with something that, even for five minutes, seemed 'great'. The sack awaited anyone who admitted 'this is the best we could come up with'. And to get promoted, to get onto the good accounts, to get your next job, you always had to appear to be loving your work, to be proud of the ads in your portfolio (and in many cases, to pretend that they were your own) and to sincerely believe that the work you were doing right now was the best fun and the most interesting challenge you'd ever had in your life.

The rise of the creative illusion

Richard Florida in his *Rise of the Creative Class* paints an optimistic picture of a new kind of worker, emerging in all areas of life, who is for some unexplained reason 'no longer satisfied' with the regimented, predictable lives people led until as recently as 50 years ago. The reader is coerced into the vision by incessant use of the first person plural: 'we pack every second full of creative stimuli' (p14); 'we trade job security for autonomy' (p13), 'we progress from job to job with amazingly little concern or effort' (p7). He defines 'creative' largely by lifestyle, and this brings all manner of other workers into the creative fold: lawyers and accountants (those who mix work and play; wear no tie, work in the café), hairdressers, restaurateurs (who love cooking). To what extent are these workers like the 'creatives' in advertising: insecure workers putting on the bravest possible face; in effect, commodifying themselves?

It is obviously not the case that all members of this new, creative class really are nurturing their creativity and feeling fulfilled every second of the day. The hard data on earnings (for example in Benner, 2002:203-233) show that the creative classes have been sold a pup: old, boring job progression and security till retirement have been traded for a quick buck in your late twenties, and the 'fun' of 'walking a lifelong tightrope' (Benner *et al*, 1999). What Florida is describing could equally be construed as a nightmare, where ever more people are making ever more frantic efforts to present a carefree, in-control, autonomous appearance to their apparently carefree, in-control, autonomous friends and colleagues. This may be the inevitable consequence of fixation on the *products* of creativity, and failing to pay attention to the *experience* of creativity.

Thus, the word 'creative' has been purloined by capital, but in a rather silly and one hopes ultimately futile way. It has got the label but not the real thing. The actual experience of creativity either happens or does not happen according to its own rules, which are increasingly well understood (and, increasingly, understood by workers themselves). It absolutely demands the very conditions that capital seems most intent on eliminating: physical and emotional security, abundant knowledge of task and context, accumulated facility at deploying that knowledge, freedom to apply it as one sees fit, an interesting challenge to apply it to, and, usually, a keen-eyed, good-humoured audience for one's efforts. Just about everything one can think of that has value, in whatever sense, comes into being that way – be it a theory of matter, a TV ad, or an earthenware pot – so that all well made things are a kind of challenge to capitalism, insofar as they demonstrate to human beings what human beings can do when they have the chance.

A creative economy would be a good idea

The proper response to the idea of a 'creative economy' is probably Ghandi's, apropos Western Civilisation: 'it would be a good idea'. And it isn't impossible to imagine what a creative economy might be like: we cherish what's left of economies that relied more on human creativity than ours does. The beauty of a hand built wall or street, or a farm wagon, or piece of furniture is as much a physical experience as a visual one. Well laid out typography and beautifully lit photographs are pretty good, too – the tragedy being not that 'creatives' spend so much time fussing over these things, but that these things can only be done, in the present economy, in special ghettos that are increasingly segregated from everyday life, and dedicated to the furtherance of waste.

They are all intimations, however, of a world in which human life and activity might be a wonderful addition to the environment.

© *Bob Hughes, 2006*

REFERENCES

Anteby, M. (2003) 'The moralities of poaching – manufacturing personal artifacts on the factory floor', Ethnography 4(2): 217-239
Baran, P. A. & P. M. Sweezy (1966) *Monopoly capital. An essay on the American economic and social order*, New York; London: Monthly Review Press
Benner, C. (2002) *Work in the New Economy – Flexible Labor Markets in Silicon Valley*, Oxford:Blackwell

Benner, C, B. Brownstein & A.B. Dean (1999) *Walking the Lifelong Tightrope: Negotiating Work in the New Economy*, San Jose, Ca: Working Partnerships USA. Retrieved on July 11, 2006 from http://www.wpusa.org/publications/indiex.pl?pub=tightrope

Bolton, S. (2004) 'Conceptual Confusions: Emotion Work as Skilled Work', *The Skills that Matter*, eds. C. Warhurst, I. Grugulis and E. Keep, Basingstoke: Palgrave Macmillan

Bowring, Finn (2003) 'Manufacturing Scarcity: food biotechnology and the life-sciences industry', *Capital and Class* 79:107-144

Burawoy, M. (1979) *Manufacturing consent: changes in the labor process under monopoly capitalism*, Chicago; London: University of Chicago Press

Craft, A. (2003) 'The Limits to Creativity in Education: Dilemmas for the Educator', *British Journal of Educational Studies*, 51(2): 113-127.

Csikszentmihalyi, M. (1975) *Beyond boredom and anxiety: the experience of play in work and games*, San Francisco; London: Jossey-Bass

Damasio, A. R. (1994) *Descartes' error: emotion, reason and the human brain*, London: Picador

Ditton, J. (1977) 'Perks, pilferage, and the fiddle: The historical structure of invisible wages', *Theory and Society* 4(1): 39-71.

Florida Richard, L. (2002) *The rise of the creative class: and how it's transforming work, leisure, community and everyday life*, New York: Basic Books

Gregory, R. L. (1981) *Mind in science: a history of explanations in psychology and physics*, London: Weidenfeld and Nicolson

Gregory, R. L. (1998) *Eye and brain: the psychology of seeing*, Oxford: Oxford University Press

Howkins, J. (2001) *The creative economy: how people make money from ideas*, London: Allen Lane

Johnston, P. (1959) *Edward Johnston*, London: Faber and Faber

Keep, D. E. (2002) 'ICT and its Impact on Skills and Creativity – Transformatory Catalyst or Dependent Variable?'. Retrieved on July 11, 2006 from http://www.terra-2000.org/Terra-2002/Pages/abstract_prague.htm.

LeDoux, J. E. (1998) *The emotional brain: the mysterious underpinnings of emotional life*, New York: Simon & Schuster

Lloyd, C. & J. Payne (2002) 'On the 'Political Economy of Skill': Assessing the Possibilities for a Viable High Skills Project in the United Kingdom', *New Political Economy* 7(3): 367-395

McChesney, R. & J. B. Foster (2003) 'The Commercial Tidal Wave', *Monthly Review* 54(10)

More, C. (1980) *Skill and the English working class, 1870-1914*, London: Croom Helm

Ogilvy, D. (1983) *Ogilvy on advertising*, London: Pan.

Pope, R. (2005) *Creativity: theory, history, practice*, Abingdon, Oxfordshire; New York, NY: Routledge

Ross, A. (2004) *No-collar: the humane workplace and its hidden costs*, Philadeplphia Pa: Temple University Press

Varela Francisco, J., E. Thompson, et al. (1991) *The Embodied mind: cognitive science and human experience*, Cambridge MA:The MIT Press

Vernon Philip, E. (1970) *Creativity. Selected R"eadings*, Harmondsworth: Penguin Books

Warhurst, C., I. Grugulis, et al. (2004) *The skills that matter*, Basingstoke: Palgrave Macmillan

Weisberg, R. W. (1986) *Creativity: genius and other myths*, New York: W.H. Freeman

Make like a man:

the demands of creative work, gender and the management of everyday life

Bettina-Johanna Krings

Bettina-Johanna Krings *is a senior researcher at the Institute for Technology Assessment and Systems Analysis (ITAS) Forschungszentrum at the University of Karlsruhe in Germany.*

ABSTRACT

Drawing on a study in the multimedia sector in Stuttgart, Germany, this paper argues that the living and working conditions of women have adapted strongly to the traditional breadwinner concept and that this change has major consequences for general social and cultural development. The study concludes that a historical shift from 'maternal spaces' to the breadwinner model is a sign of deep changes in the reproductive sphere. It analyses the temporal organisation of work-life balance and finds that, although women have gained access to some highly-skilled positions in the labour market which have granted them new forms of autonomy and independence, they have also been exposed to new forms of stress. These pressures are experienced in a range of different ways both by childless women and those with children, leading to a variety of strategies for managing daily life, each of which entails some losses, as well as gains. Although a critique of the modernisation of working cultures has been opened up, this paper argues that in order to explain the societal impacts of these changes there is a need for further exploration of both the perception and the quality of the losses experienced by women in these change processes.

This paper draws on the results of a study of living and working conditions in the multimedia sector in the Stuttgart region of Germany, carried out by the Institute for Technology Assessment and Systems Analysis (ITAS) on behalf of the Baden-Württemberg Ministry of Social Matters, completed in 2003[1]. The study aimed to evaluate the changes in this sector from a gender theory perspective.

Initially, three assumptions were made. The first was that changes in the structure of work in this sector, which employs a high proportion of women, would reduce the social pressure on women trying to balance the demands of job and family. The second was that, because working conditions in this sector appeared to be 'knowledge-marked' (Funder 2005, Priddat 2001) rather than 'gender-marked'[2], the increased importance of knowledge as a production factor would have a compensatory impact on gender relations within the workplace, reducing gender segregation. The third assumption was that the 'work anytime, anywhere' hype surrounding the new tech-

---

1   Cf. Krings, B.-J.: Wandel der Arbeits- und Lebensbedingungen im Multimediabereich aus der Genderperspektive, Wissenschaftliche Berichte FZKA 6892, Karlsruhe 2003.
2   In other words, the division of work was not so much based on a traditional pattern of gender segregation as on a functional separation of tasks based on specific skill-sets.

nologies would create opportunities for workers to reorganise their work flexibly in time and space under their own control.

All these assumptions were confirmed to some extent by the study. However there was no evidence of the development of new models of work or of changes in temporal or spatial flexibility. On the contrary, the pressure of the demands of their work had obliged most of the women to develop individual action strategies which overspilled into the private sphere[3]. It was also noteworthy that whilst the daily management of the conflicting demands of work and home life played a central role in the working lives of women in the multimedia sector, for men there had been little significant change. An important methodological tool used in analysing these strategies was the German concept of *Allgemeine Lebensführung*. This can be loosely translated into English as 'individual conduct of life' or 'design of life' or 'life plan' but its meaning encompasses not only how personal behaviour and lifestyle may be objectively described but also how this life is subjectively constructed. For conceptual clarity, the word (which is defined more fully below) has been left in its original German in this paper.

The results of the study add weight to the thesis that working conditions in this sector have a strong impact on the *Allgemeine Lebensführung.* of women. The decision whether or not to start a family is only one example of this. Individual strategies can be considered as a rationalisation of the whole of daily life. Job, family, partnership and individual personal needs all have to be managed in a highly rational and functional way. The cumulative effect of these individual strategies seems likely to bring about unexpected consequences at a societal level.

After looking at the specific work conditions in the multimedia sector, this paper goes on to outline the theoretical and methodical framework of the study before presenting a classification of the action strategies of the men and women who were interviewed and finally discussing some of the implications of the results for further research.

Women working in the multimedia sector

The study drew strongly on a previous study of the multimedia sector carried out in the same region by Gerhard Fuchs and Hans-Georg Wolf[4]. The term 'multimedia' is used broadly, to refer not only to particular technologies or products, but to all those parts of the IT sector that are involved in producing the knowledge and broad applications incorporated into multimedia products and processes. Besides the technical constituents of digital media, such as sound, film, graphics, and text, it also encompasses associated activities involved in 'networking, integration, and interactivity'(Fuchs & Wolf 2000:11).

---

3   In industrial sociology, the blurring of the boundaries between work and life has generated a large literature (see Voß 1998, Minssen 1999, Kratzer 2003). Some recent studies have suggested that this blurring can be noted on all social levels and in temporal, spatial and gender-specific dimensions (survey: Gottschall & Voß 2005).
4   The project *Regional Renewal by Multimedia* (REMM) by the Academy for Technology Assessment in Baden-Württemberg, completed in 1997, carried out a range of surveys in order to find out the conditions under which regional multimedia industry clusters are established in the region and how this development is supported by regional actors (cf. Fuchs &Wolf 1998a, 2000).

The German state of Baden-Württemberg, in which Stuttgart lies[5], has a broad representation of employers involved in both the production and the application of information technologies. Fuchs and Wolf have divided the sector into three categories. The *core subsector* comprises firms, which are directly involved in the production of multimedia applications. Examples of this are internet companies or producers of CD-ROM. The second group, referred to as the *first periphery*, involves the production of information and communication technologies and the generation of content. This is a large group and includes telecommunications, advertising, software production and graphic design firms. Some traditional industries (such as publishing) also belong to this group. The third group, referred to as the *second periphery* includes most other sectors, including the public sector, there being almost no sectors in the economy that do not use some application of information and communication technologies (Fuchs & Wolf 2000:12).

Fuchs and Wolf show that the boundaries between these subsectors are open; information and communication technologies are used as multifunctional technologies across all economic sectors and therefore the term 'multimedia' cannot be used with any precision to define a particular sector.

In Stuttgart, as in Germany as whole, the proportion of women in the *core subsector* is extremely low, as is generally the case in informatics in Germany.[6] In the *first periphery,* however, the proportion of female employees is much higher, especially in advertising, graphic design and media content. With a few prominent exceptions, in the Stuttgart region this subsector is characterised by a large number of small and medium sized firms[7] which, under the pressure of technological change, have undergone a series of changes in working conditions over the last fifteen years. This organisational restructuring has, however, introduced forms of temporal flexibility and project-oriented as well as team-oriented work, which has made them particularly attractive for women.

During the 1980s and 1990s a large research literature on working conditions in the IT sector[8] in Germany concluded that it would become a major employer of skilled women (Boß &Roth 1992). There were several reasons for this (Boes & Trinks 2005:283). First, the switch to a strong customer orientation changes core competences, with social competences and teamwork (thought to be more feminine in character) gaining in importance, whilst the number of purely technical tasks (more likely to be found amongst men) decreases in many jobs. Second, organisational structures, such as flat hierarchies, informalised career paths, and open enterprise cultures offer increased scope for individual and creative actions and, hence, improved professional opportunities for women (whose career paths have traditionally been regarded as less continuous than men's). Third, the promotion of women is often highlighted in corporate strategies, which emphasise the sector's needs for performance, creativity, and qualifications and push for the integration of women, giving a high profile to issues likework-life balance and the promotion of

---

5   In the state of Baden-Württemberg the Stuttgart region (aprox. 3, 52 firms per 100,000 inhabitants) has the highest density of firms in the multimedia sector, mostly located in urban areas (see Fuchs &Wolf 2000:16).
6   The extremely low proportion of women in the core subsector of the multimedia sector is remarkable. Even young girls show a low interest in studying technologies, informatics and natural sciences (Zwick & Renn 2000).
7   A study shows that over 70 per cent of firms in the region have less than 20 employees (Menez et al. 2001).
8   Generally defined in terms of the interaction between computer and telecommunications technologies

women. Finally, there are significant numbers of women in managerial positions in this sector, especially in the middle levels where the number of women with responsibility for personnel is above the average across the whole economy (Funder 2005).

The assumption was that these conditions would increase the employment of women in this sector. However the employment rates of women have actually decreased slightly in recent years, in absolute terms. But, unlike other knowledge-based sectors, multimedia still offers attractive work opportunities to women who are attracted to a flexible and creative working environment.

After the 2000 stock exchange crash, the multimedia sector in the region entered a phase of economic crisis and stagnation. Stuttgart, with its high concentration of multi-media firms, was hit particularly hard, especially the small firms. The drop in sales resulting from the general decline of the local economy heightened competitiveness, which led to a dramatic fall in product prices, especially for software companies. Economic decline shook the prevailing enterprise culture and put downward pressure on the working conditions, with the scrapping of a number of social integration measures that had been introduced during the 1990s. From the employers' point of view, the sector was undergoing a process of 'normalisation' (Boes & Trinks 2005:288).

The methodological and theoretical approach of the study

Methodologically the study was based on the concept of the *Alltägliche Lebensführung* developed in the late 1980s by sociologists at the University of Munich in Germany to analyse how peoples' daily lives both change and are changed by the increasing flexibilisation of organisational patterns (Jurczyk & Rerrich 1993, 1995). The concept differentiates analytically between the temporal, spatial, rational and emotional aspects of a person's organisational self management in order to analyse how work structures interact with aspects of daily life such as partnerships, family life and social and cultural activities. Individual strategies are regarded as an active system that reveals how work and life are socially constructed in industrialised societies and what temporal, social and emotional resources are available within a society (Voß 1995:34). Because these strategies are formed in reaction to existing frameworks, they cannot be regarded as the simple result of individual agency but must be seen in both their objective and subjective dimensions; and not just as the results of individual psychological disposition but as a sociological reconstruction of societal reality (Oevermann et al. 1978, Wohlrab-Sahr 1993).

The methodological tool used to analyse these strategies for living was the development of typologies that make it possible both to compare and amplify individual perspectives whilst simultaneously putting them together to form a larger picture that can be evaluated in terms of its general structure. Thus both the subjective and objective logics of daily life can be identified separately and compared enabling conclusions to be drawn at a societal level (Wohlrab-Sahr 1993).[9]

These typologies were evaluated from the perspective of gender research which (in contrast with feminist research) focuses primarily on a comparison between men and

---

9   In order to ensure the comparability between the types, the construction of the case studies was subdivided into common aspects so that general conclusions about changes in working and living conditions could be formulated.

women (Becker-Schmidt & Bilden 1995). Because the study found that the tensions and ambiguities within individual *Allgemeine Lebensführugn* were significantly greater for women than for men, this paper focuses mainly on the contradictions in women's practices of day-to-day life management, especially in adapting to the breadwinner model. The ambiguity of women's' *Allgemeine Lebensführung* necessitates a clear methodological instrument to analyse the social and cultural changes in the daily organisation of the productive and reproductive spheres to ensure that the researcher's own preconceptions do not influence how the interview material is interpreted (Harding 1990).

Twenty open interviews were conducted with sixteen women and four men aged between 20 and 45. All worked full time in the multimedia sector, with work ranging from creative activities to management. The sample included people with and without partners and with and without children. Generally it was much more difficult to find women with children than without. The interview questions addressed five broad themes: the work situation; the living situation; strategies of day-to-day organisation and self-management; the problems encountered and costs incurred in the day-to-day organisation of life and values, visions and individual expectations.

The male interviewees formed a comparison group within a sample featuring the different levels of meaning of the female strategies. Although the men showed a generally open minded attitude towards family life, work life balance and future perspectives, they had not concretised this in relation to their own temporal and spatial flexibility and could therefore be said to represent the 'breadwinner model' in their *Allgemeine Lebensführung*.

Labour as the *leitmotif* of a subjective lifestyle

It is characteristic of the multimedia sector that the job is the dominant constitutive element of both male and female *Allgemeine Lebensführung* In every case, it was work structures that made up the central *leitmotif* of *Allgemeine Lebensführun* even amongst women with children. For instance, one respondent who had originally decided to take a 'nursing break' by reducing her working hours for three years after the birth of her son, quickly went back to full-time employment because she could not bring this way of life into line with her concept of herself as a woman. Despite this dominance of work in their lives, individual strategies varied according to family background, individual orientations, and value structures as well as their particular circumstances. No strategy was easy, however. Each one took a heavy toll on both psychic and material resources to make it work.

In the interpretation of the interviews, a four-fold typology emerged. These four ideal types can be found in all the case studies in various forms and represent prototypes for the management of work and life. The distinction between the types is constructive, since there are parallels and overlaps between all these *Allgemeine Lebensführung*. These types have been named 'Control', 'Discipline', 'Individual Freedom'and 'Stringency'. The first three of these, and especially 'individual freedom', have also been identified in other comparable studies carried out in different working contexts (cf. Wohlrab-Sahr 1993, Behringer 1998, Manske 2003).

Control

The *control* type subjects the rhythm of general life entirely to the structures of work. The prototype of this action strategy is a female interviewee, who identifies strongly with her company and work conditions[10] and who had decided at an early stage to pursue a successful career and not to have children. She reduces the risk of having to deal with unexpected contingencies to a minimum by rigid control strategies.

'It's a case of "either/or", I do not think that you can love your work and still have children, to be honest. I believe that one thing always suffers and if so, I wanted to make the right choice. Either I want to be a real mother or I want to commit myself to work and as I think that I am not really predestined for being a mother, it was clear relatively early ... that my priority lies somewhere else.'

Deciding early on that she was not a born mother, this respondent chose to concentrate fully on her job. She made this clear to her partner before they married; 'this was clear before anything else was clear', and now he sees 'how much stress a child causes'. Although she knows that this is an 'egotistic' attitude, she feels she contributes to supporting families that 'give birth to children' through her 'high taxes'.

This respondent works in a very structured manner. Trained as a saleswoman, she describes how familiar the company's processes are to her and how she has them 'under control'. Her work is often very hectic, and one of the reasons she likes to work in the evening is that it is quiet at this time when customers do not call and she can work calmly. She speaks of the 'terror of availability' which in her opinion has increased considerably with email.

She thinks that lack of time is the biggest problem she faces. In her job, she is constantly confronted with stress and time pressure which she tries to circumvent by extending her working hours. Outside work, she tries to 'reduce the stress' by doing sports and refloxology massage with a colleague at least once a week. She knows that she must take care of herself if she wishes to spend her remaining working time in an acceptable state of health so she tries to avoid always giving her job top priority. But stress is 'always there', including at home, where there is always 'something to iron and to wash and to clean'.

This respondent has always been the decision-maker in her private life, where it is important to her to stay in control of the household and her social environment. She concedes that she is rather 'dogged' in household matters, much more 'materialistic' than her partner, and with a need to be 'perfect'. As a result, she has more 'problems' than he has. But, she says, they both try to negotiate compromises.

In her life, this respondent is stressed to a very high degree. Her physical and psychic well-being and her private life are affected by her stress at work. She knows this and tries to counteract it pragmatically, with more or less success. Her inner state, however, is mostly 'nervous' and 'tense'. Still, her stress in the job appears to be at a fixed level that she cannot and does not seem to wish to change. Nevertheless, she says she feels 'satisfied in her job' and 'happy in her partnership'.

---

10   This respondent was a 36-year old woman (I 16), married with no children, working as an industrial sales representative in a marketing agency (cf. Sample Krings 2003).

Although she reflects very little about her life, she sometimes admits to wondering whether she is repeating her father's life pattern without seeing any possible way of changing this.

'I cannot tell you, I don't know whether I think about it ... Of course, I sometimes think about whether it is really my pattern to repeat what my father did. He grafted away all his life and died at the age of 50. Of course, I have to say clearly no, but I do not know, how I can avoid it. It could only be avoided by working in another sector ...'

She knows that a large part of her 'self-confidence and personal happiness' are derived from her work, and she does not want to and cannot do without it but it nevertheless does not give her a sense of fulfilment. Nevertheless, the creative part of her work makes her feel very happy and she enjoys the feeling of completing a project successfully. She looks forward to material security and a guaranteed income in her old age and she is realistic and matter-of-fact in realising that this means that she will have to work for a very long time.

Here, the strategy of control creates a rigid framework of values and routines that protects and structures her way of life and her security. She reacts inflexibly and in a closed manner to any unforeseeable event. She lives with an obsessive feeling of responsibility from which she cannot escape. She has internalised the traditionally 'male' role and oriented her vital processes towards 'control' and 'efficiency'. She is aware of the price she pays – her health, but uses the same efficient strategies to ensure that this too remains under control.

Discipline

In contrast to the control type, the *discipline* type tries to remain open to demands from all sides. Although work still plays a dominant role, this type claims to have integrated it with other aspects of life. A woman manager provides an example of this prototype[11].

Unlike the control type, she perceives the processes of life not as a threat but as a design challenge that necessitates clear decisions and self-discipline in everyday life. Before becoming a mother this respondent worked twelve hours a day with 'at least' four evening meetings per week, and also went into her office for several hours on Saturdays and Sundays. Since the birth of her son, she has given up weekend work, but is still working 'more than 100 per cent' (she estimated that she worked 140 per cent of the official working week). This 'unpaid additional work' is done with pleasure, as she 'enjoys working' and work has become part of her identity. This respondent selected her apartment to ensure that she could get to work in less than ten minutes and has fixed the start of her working day to fit in with her family obligations.

This respondent and her husband (who also works full time) have organised their child care: three days a week with a childminder, with a relative standing in on the other working days. There is close contact both with the respondent's parents-in-law and with her own parents.

---

11   This 39-year old respondent (I 7) works in a management position in an editorial department. She is married, and has a son (cf. Sample Krings 2003).

This respondent takes prime responsibility for the household but her husband takes care of visits to the shops, dry cleaning and shoe repairer on working days and does most of the laundry. She 'organises' the household, anticipating what work will be needed and delegating parts of it. She also does the weekend shopping, cooking and cleaning of the apartment.

The overall organisation of everyday life is determined very much by the demands of work. Her conception of the job involved a blurring of the two spheres, but she tries to counteract this establishing a strict separation of work and family. She says that she organises family-related tasks so that 'the job does not suffer - this cannot be'. Phone conversations with her husband about the practicalities of household organisation are limited to 'a matter of twenty to thirty seconds'. She avoids longer private calls because they would distract her too much from her work.

Her son is so well adapted to this tightly-organised everyday life that even when he is sick, the time is 'chosen so smartly' that it happens at the weekend or during the holidays.

> *'Well, I have to knock on wood – one, two, three – he is a very healthy child, and when he has fallen sick this has fortunately been during my holidays or at the weekend, he has … sometimes, I think he realises it … it is just (she laughs) it sounds strange, but it is just … it fits, and so far, no serious accident has occurred. I mean, I have always been able to organise something.'*

She considers her marriage to be 'stable'; with serious disputes only occurring when 'everything is about to collapse at home' and the stress of the job takes its toll. She attributes her ability to combine her professional and private lives so well to the quality of their partnership and to her own self-discipline.

Contrasting herself with her own parents, who have their own company and are 'very busy', she says she does not want her child to 'just live alongside' but considers it very important to achieve a harmonisation of job and family. Her idea of being a 'good mother' involves trying to create an 'ideal world' during the time she spends with her son: 'during this short time, these two or three hours in the evening'. For her, it is most important that her son feels that his parents are always 'there for him' although she does not have as much time for him as other mothers. She is convinced that he benefits from his parents' lifestyle.

To meet these high demands, her life is characterised by strict discipline, which results in permanent stress of the highest order. Pains she experiences in her back and jaw may well be interpreted as a consequence of her need to 'clench her teeth' and to carry 'loads that are too high'.

She presents herself as a woman who has to 'hold her ground' in life. Her roles as a mother and partner have been subordinated to this conviction which, nevertheless, coexists with traditional value structures expressed in a feeling of responsibility for the wellbeing of those around her. Like the control prototype, she concedes that the job has priority in her life, but she also feels committed to 'female values'. Enormous personal effort is required to meet these exacting standards and her life is only made possible by strong personal discipline, organisation, and integration of the social environment into the planning process. The strategy of disciplining general life is the only means by which continuity between the different areas of life can be achieved.

Sometimes, this respondent dreams of living an entirely different life.

*'I could tell you a dream (she laughs), something I really … I would like to give up
      everything in Germany and move to the South of France. But this is something
      I said ten, fifteen years ago, I always said "this is what I would like to do when
      I'm fifty". Then I will do this: I will cut all ties and open a little bistro, and do a
      bit of bed and breakfast (she laughs) … Yes, because I think that this is some-
      thing completely different, but whether I will really do so… it is just a vision.'*

Individual Freedom

For the *individual freedom* type the subjective power of being able to design both one's
own life and the social process is the most important priority. For this, work is an absolute necessity to gain access to social resources which are achieved through individual
effort rather than social affiliation by birth or gender.

The focus is on the person's own competence and the internal urge to take life actively into her own hands. Her life is characterised by openness, courage, and the ability
to plan. This attitude is very frequently found in young people, although our prototype
for this type was thirty three years old, a childless freelance graphic designer, living
with her partner in a shared apartment[12].

She organises her time flexibly, at least when she is working directly for own clients
(a minority of her contracts) and likes to organise her days freely, doing housework or
going for a walk in between work tasks. Her professional workload varies considerably.
*'Totally, totally different, sometimes I have to refuse contracts for months and can
      hardly manage and I work during the weekends and on holidays and so on.
      But sometimes nobody calls.'*
Often the work extends into the evening and weekends. Sometimes she works at her office
during the day and then at home in the evening for her 'private customers' where she feels
she has to meet their needs in a very flexible and willing manner. Whilst recognising the
stress they cause, she regards these pressures as 'normal' and typical of this type of work
which she says she can handle because she knows that the stress is always ' limited in time'.
For her, this is the big difference between her situation and that of an employee.

She finds it difficult to say no to offers of contracts because she fears that if she does
so she will not be asked again, so she tries to meet all demands, saying that her 'pain
threshold is very high as far as stress is concerned'.

During the course of their relationship, she and her partner have evolved a flexible
division of labour in which individual needs are prioritised, and organisation does not
take up much space in her life. She tries actively to resist overly high demands and pre-
fers to spend her free time in private activities saying that 'personal contacts are most
important'. She likes eating out and going to the cinema and does sports three times
a week but the rhythm is dependent on her work situation. She does not make rigid
divisions between work and non-work activities or pursue any specific activities at the
weekends, which are also subject to the rhythm of her work.
*'No, actually, the weekend… Actually, it's the same as during the week, except, that,
      when I am booked, I sleep longer at the weekend and go shopping and have*

---

12   The prototype of this action strategy is a 33-year old (I 6) freelance graphic artist without children,
who lives with her partner in a shared apartment (cf. Sample Krings 2003:52 ff.).

a long breakfast and go downtown, but, since I have breaks sometimes, I some-
times also do such things during the week. And then, at the weekend there is
no big difference.'

Whilst believing that the challenges in her life are 'in the usual range' she distinguishes
between those that are caused by work-related stress and those that are part of the normal processes of life. She tries to handle the former pragmatically, saying that she is able
to work well under pressure. For help with the latter she turns to her friends and family,
with her father playing an important role. She presents herself as a 'master of the art of
living' who has succeeded in developing a successful life plan despite the ups and downs
in her life. However she also knows that her independent and flexible life has its price.
Although she acquired clear orientations and 'moral conceptions' from her parents, she is
trying to free herself from the 'standards, conventions, and education' of her past. She at-
tributes the differences between herself and her parents to the new opportunities offered
by modern life:

'Well, they also might have had the possibility, but they simply set other priorities,
but they were also under the supervision of their parents and, of course, they
experienced other things, such as war, when they were children, and so on,
but… God knows, things were different in those days, I mean, they did not
think for long about whether they wanted children or not; they married and just
had children. I mean, today, the problems are completely different, and prob-
ably when you have children you will also ask questions like: when you have
children, how will you organise your work?, this was not a question in the past.
That's why … the decision today is not always easy.'

She would not consider giving up her 'freedom', which is the *leitmotif* of her life and what
makes her different from her parents. Her most basic orientation is towards the possibility of saying 'yes or no'.

This respondent regards the changes that have taken place in the gender order as
positive because men have been relieved of their economic responsibility and women are
able to make independent decisions. She emphasises her individual sphere of responsibility although it is important to her that she and her partner plan their life jointly. She has
put off the decision whether to start a family, finding it hard to decide whether to have
children which she associates with giving up her autonomy, feeling 'a large uncertainty',
because she does not wish to entirely 'dispense with her life' and is afraid that the primary
care of the child will 'stick' with her. The lack of models is important here; she does not
know any woman who is able to combine both areas in a way that does not forced her to
give something up. She does not, however, regard such dilemmas politically, as aspects of
gender inequality. On the contrary, for her, everything is a matter of individual decision.

Stringency

The *stringency* type is characterised by rationality in general life[13]. Here, the prototype is
a male company director. Divorced, with two children from his former marriage, he now

---

13   This prototype is represented by a male interviewee (interview no. 10), who has founded his own
enterprise together with partners, a consulting company for digital communication strategies and technologies.
The respondent owns the majority of the enterprise and is its general director. Divorced, he lives with a new
partner and has two children from his previous marriage (cf. Sample in Krings 2003:52 ff.).

lives with a new partner. This respondent is someone who regards self-confidence and competence as crucial for success in life. He has a wide range of responsibilities for the running and strategic development of the company.

'Well, I am so lucky that we entered the market successfully with hardly any prepara-
tion. In principle, I am involved in individual projects. But most of my present
tasks very, very much focus on the vision of the company. As we have made
such a good start that secures us and allows to think further and not only about
the daily business, I can leave aside the daily business to a large extent and can
care about the vision of the company, the future of the company, and I can initi-
ate the necessary steps.'

Trust and openness are integrated into a stringent concept of work which he expects his employees to share. Compulsory working hours for all employees in the company is from 9 30 am to 6 pm. As a rule, he stops work at 7 pm but may work until 10 pm or later if a project schedule requires it. He does not consider that his position as director puts him in a special position but expects his employees (all of whom work full time) to show equal dedication and identification with the company.

Regarding himself as a 'career changer' he selects his staff on the basis of social skills and human competences rather than formal qualifications, qualities which he thinks he can judge on the basis of his experience and personal judgement.

Since the break-up of his marriage, which he attributes to a neglect of his family, his role as a father has acquired a new importance in his life. With relatively frequent contact with his children (an arrangement he says he has worked hard for), he makes an effort to live a 'piece of everyday life' with them, to take an interest in school matters, to go to parent-teacher conferences, and to be available as a 'contact partner'.

'In fact, it is rather normal. Actually, I'm not the "event person", who looks for high-level
experience and where every day, cake is served on the table ... No, it's really
normal, they are with me and I read or do something different, and the children
also do something.'

However this process is still incomplete. His new partner works full-time. They spend the time with his children together and also go on holidays together and the situation is not easy for either of them and often leads to conflict. He recognises that it is difficult for his partner to accept his children, but thinks that 'many steps' have already been made in a positive direction. Meanwhile, he tries to 'drive on two tracks' and to make time for his relationship with his partner who has asked him to change his gender-specific conception of his role and to take on some household responsibilities and play a more active role in the partnership. He has ventured on these new processes and considers himself to be 'on the way'.

This respondent's certainty and commitment are very striking. He appears to be in command, and very much at home, when he is talking about his sector or his company and it is here, at work, that he feels himself to be creative. In his non-working life, however, he is less certain, and was clearly challenged personally during the crisis of his divorce. When asked how much he identifies with his father's life, he is reluctant to answer, saying that he considers this issue to be too intimate. He concedes, however, that he is slowly starting to 'think about it'.

'I have contact … Yes, yes, I have contact. Not too much, at the moment, I have contact with my father, with my brothers and sisters.'

In response to the question 'do you have the impression that your life is similar to your father's?' he answered,

'This is an exciting question, yes. An exciting question, and I am slowly starting to think about it. It is striking in many ways, but in the end, no, I believe, no, really not.'

For him, the job is the place where decisions are made, plans developed, and competences formed. Vital process, which are threatening when they cannot be calculated or manipulated, have to be rationalised, processed and integrated into this stringent professional concept in order to achieve a successful *Allgemeine Lebensführung*.

The contradictions of dealing with a work-oriented life

It is clear that, albeit in different ways, work is the central reference point in all these strategies, especially for women in the multimedia sector who identify with their fathers and see labour as the means of realising their own life models. The very different strategies of control, discipline, individual freedom, and stringency can be observed both for women and men but represent a much greater change of cultural and social patterns for the women, who have to overcoming their uneasiness with traditional patterns of femininity in adapting to a conception of labour that has traditionally been very masculine. Trying to reconcile high performance delivery at work with continuity in private life leads to considerable ambivalence and high friction losses for these women. Although they insist that children, partnerships and the social environment ultimately matter more to them than their jobs, their subjective identity formation nevertheless takes place mainly through work.

The most extreme is the *control* type in which not only are work processes themselves, and the working day itself, strictly regimented, but this control also extends to the vital and emotional processes of life. From an early age, general life is subjected to the standardised requirements of the job and decisions are made against open life processes in order to avoid unpredictable events.

The *discipline* type can be seen as representing the 'perfect woman', who 'manages' job, family, and partnership whilst still keeping her spirits high. Her way of life can only be safeguarded through tight organisational regulation and a disciplined time regime that encompasses the whole social environment, not just work, requiring strong individual effort .

For the *individual freedom* type, success or failure is attributed entirely to the individual's own efforts and individuality plays the dominant role in both work and private life. For this type it is also important to be able to control vital processes.

Although the *stringency* type is found to some extent in all the case studies, it is particularly common amongst men, whose attitude to success contrasts with that of the women interviewed. Whereas most women attribute their success to 'having been lucky' in their professional careers, for the men, success is something they are entitled to, so long as they pursue their goals with sufficient consistency.

With a few exceptions, the lives studied here can be described as 'strategic' in the sense that life is subjected to a purpose- and target-oriented perspective, which enhances 'the long-term tendency towards a growing rationalisation and self-discipline of the actors in society' (Kleemann et al. 1999:17). Because the change has taken place within a single generation, this tendency is particularly visible for the female interviewees, for whom it entails both gains and losses.

The main gain, which by all the women interviewed aspired to, may be described as 'access to social resources'. This access offers life models of individual autonomy guaranteed by economic independence and recognition as full members of society. Because men's and women's lives are interlinked, the uneasiness of these women with traditional gender roles affects both sexes, and their deviation from traditional roles affects many aspects of life including partnerships, education and the general design of life (Becker-Schmidt 1995).

The main losses can be seen in the need to adopt inflexible and rigid lifestyles. The domination of daily life by the structures of work had resulted in a suppression of vital processes for nearly all the women interviewed (the two exceptions, interestingly, were both women with children). The ability to maintain a successful lifestyle in the face of this pressure depends very strongly on the psychic dispositions and living conditions of the women. Achieving a sustainable work-life balance requires detachment from the original family, the development of life visions outside of the job, and stable emotional relationship structures. For the women interviewed, adopting the traditionally male labour model is rarely a matter for reflection and is generally seen as the only possible way of life.

These women regard 'performance' and 'efficiency' as the decisive factors in their professional careers and refuse to see themselves as women who are discriminated against or to see gender equality demands as relevant to their situations. Personal commitment and dedication are what matters for career development, in their view. No reattachment to or orientation towards traditional 'maternal worlds' was observed in any case study.

On the contrary, it is clear that everyday life is shaped by the structures of work, with time pressure, stress, and internalised feelings of tension spilling over into private life. To cope with these, it seems that aspects of 'efficiency' and 'quality assurance' have also started to enter general life, although the background of general tension makes it difficult to see the ways in which this leads to the control of relationship structures and the rationalisation of emotions. Relationships with partners and children are subjected to the breathless dictates of work demands and vital processes like ageing, individual affections, personal needs or events like illness or death among friends or family become threatening because they might shake the belief that everything is under individual control. Leisure and chances to stop and think are driven out by 'time pressure' and 'haste' resulting in some cases in morbid stress phenomena. A 'separated life' (Beck-Gernsheim 1993), a life based on labour, is not conflict-free, but gives rise to ways of life that must be assessed very differently from their traditional counterparts.

The vitality of work – preliminary conclusions

In order to be successful at work, these interviewees had to engage in a 'permanent balancing act' (Hielscher/Hildebrandt 1999) which made huge demands in terms of expertise, willpower, and individual time management. Work-related skills alone are not enough to meet these demands; the challenges of work have to be met with both 'body and soul'.[14] This balancing act affects both men and women, who increasingly have to align their personal lives with the demands made on them by their employers, developing, as we have seen, a variety of strategies to achieve this. Whether the arrangements that result are considered to be enriching or burdensome can only be assessed within the context of each individual life.

The strategies of control and discipline illustrate the submission of living processes to the primacy of labour. The biological and social rhythms of life, the transmission of traditions, periods of rest and a huge range of non-market activities, such as gardening, intellectual activities or care for others, disappear under the relentless demands of the working day, leaving little or no time for social and political commitment, music or creative activities. Detached from many possibilities of life, these respondents have developed time regimes that reflect their compulsion (see also Boes & Baukrowitz 2002, Boes & Trinks 2005, Kahlert & Kajatin 2004). The losses entailed in these processes are perceived and processed in a variety of ways but they are rarely, if ever, attributed to the conflicting social conditions under which these women live.

These findings confirm those from other studies within German industrial sociology, which have concluded that post-Taylorist business strategies are deeply ambivalent. On the one hand the new working conditions of the kind found in the multimedia sector offer workers autonomous working conditions with a considerable degree of independence. On the other, these conditions often result in an internalisation of the company's objectives and a self-economisation of the workforce.[15] These 'bindings' directly influence their social and cultural references at several levels (Jürgens 2003, 2005).

There is an agreement between industrial sociology and feminist literature that the restructuring of work impacts the private sphere[16]. Polarisation around the issue of children is one clear indicator of this. In Germany in the past three decades, the proportion of lifestyles without children (at 65.3 per cent) has clearly overtaken those with children (at 33.9 per cent) (Manske 2003:141). This applies to both women and men but, as demonstrated in our study, it is the lives of working women that are especially affected by this.

'What this means […] is obvious for men, who concentrate their social activities mainly on their professional careers. They are in danger of being caught in a

---

14   Sometimes described as the 'subjective dimension of work', this development combines two ways of using personnel resources: an increased use of subjective achievements in the organisation of work at the company; and extended access to the subjective potentials of working people (Baethge 1991, Kleemann, Matuschek, Voß 1999).

15   The term 'workforce entrepreneur' has been coined to describes the phenomenon whereby employees assume responsiblity for the results of their activities and reaching their objectives, having to translate requirements into decisions and work processes and take responsibility if the goals are not met. Elements of the role of the entrepreneur are transferred to the employees; self-control, self-economisation, and identification with the company become central (Voß, Pongratz 1998, Voß 2002, Pongratz, Voß 2003). For an overview of feminist criticism of this approach see Aulenbacher, 2005.

16   Gender research has observed the development of new lines of differentiation among employees in such new work cultures. Whereas gender is relativised in the case of young, qualified women without children, other women - mainly due to the reduction of social security offered by the state – are exposed more than ever to the double burden of family and job. Strong integration into labour structures magnifies the impact of unforeseen occurrences. As a result, criteria such as the age of employees gain in importance (Aulenbacher 2005).

rationalisation trap: the lack of mental, emotional, and sensory experience
that is gained in the psycho-social field of household and private supplies
[...] may freeze the lively capacity for work.' (Becker-Schmidt 2003:105)

It is clear that women in highly skilled professions have gained social recognition, economic independence, and social autonomy and these have had an immediate effect on the structures of their sexual relationships, on lifestyles and on women's broader social relationships. However a look at the other side of this coin discloses states of deep exhaustion, permanent hurry, and feelings of loss, suggesting that the price of this successful professional integration is a sacrifice of the 'lively' areas of private life.

From the perspective of gender research, this raises questions about gender and the new work cultures. Women have been integrated successfully into certain sectors of qualified employment, especially highly-skilled services where they have a strong presence, at least below the management level (Nickel 2004, Lohr & Nickel 2005, Manske 2003, Kocyba 2005) and have repeatedly demonstrated their willingness to adapt to company requirements for high flexibility and mobility and adjust their lives to meet these demands. This does not only apply in the IT sector, but also in other service companies such as banks and consultancies where women have been relatively well positioned since the mid 1990s. These jobs have not only given them economic security but have also opened up opportunities for self-realisation and professional self-development, as is demonstrated in the cases presented here. Communicative, creative, and expressive aspects of work have gained in importance compared with traditional job cultures[17].

But, despite the positive features of these developments, there is a need for careful study at an individual level of how these losses are perceived by the women affected and what impact they have had on their daily lives. This study suggests that the gains and losses resulting from changing working and living conditions are complex and ambiguous and will have to be analysed in a way that makes visible the contradictory social relationships that lead to these gains, losses and paradoxes. What is clear is that they are experienced with 'mixed feelings' (Becker-Schmidt 2003:118).

The study also supplies some evidence of a tendency towards rationalising the private world, observed in a more acute form in a US study by Arlie Russell Hochschild who found that the office is increasingly being perceived as 'home' whilst the home is experienced as a place where work is always waiting (Russell Hochschild 2006)[18]. It can be concluded that a highly effective work culture has given rise to an internalised compulsion to work more efficiently and permanently and produced a situation in which the reproductive sphere becomes a threat to the capacity to work in this way (Voß 2003:331, Oechsle 2006).

---

17   Kocyba points out that dependent labour 'sells' its own work capacity (and not the product of the work). 'For the seller in this workforce, this means that, whatever the activity he is asked to do may look like, he can hardly understand it as a self-realisation in the sense of reaching the targets set by himself' (Kocyba 2005:141).
18   Russell Hochschild also mentions the 'double socialisation' (Becker-Schmidt) of women in the company she studied. This is typified by a high commitment that is not usually gratified, 'whereas men with their experienced refusal of requirements possibly may not make a career, but still get a safe employment and/or may be with the family or think of leisure time, if they wish' (Aulenbacher 2005:51).

Here, as gender research has pointed out, it is relevant to look at the relationship between the productive and reproductive spheres in society which, though separated, are still inter-related in terms of how they are recognised or devalued. In this study, a strong orientation towards the father's life model was associated with a lack of social recognition of maternal worlds, demonstrating that there is a lack of models in which the life and work of working men and women are in balance[19].

It was also observable that the decision not to have children does not release women from the simultaneous experience of both gains and losses in their lives. This ambivalence between conflicting value spheres (care, nurture, and social integration on the one hand, and autonomy and independence on the other) constitutes a 'rationalisation of female behaviour in the private sphere' (Illouz 2006:51).[20] As illustrated in this study, these rationalisations are derived from a range of different individual needs and attitudes. Nevertheless, it is obvious that the integration of women into this type of market-oriented labour is in clear conflict with private life, which, at a societal level, has the task of maintaining and renewing not only the workforce, but human life itself. So far, very little scholarly attention has been paid to what this means concretely for the individual or for society as a whole. This omission is dangerous, because a new balance between life and work is necessary to address a range of urgent social problems, including the creation of jobs, the globalisation of labour and, at least in Germany, the falling birth-rate. The social integration of maternal worlds into the lifestyles of both men and women is a necessary precondition for this.

'When looking for tasks to keep the work of women and men lively, strong visions are needed. Work cannot only be found in the sphere of necessity. It contributes to celebration, to strengthening relationships, to hospitality and to enjoying nice things. This has to be included in life.' (Becker-Schmidt 2003:128ff)

© *Bettina-Johanna Krings, 2006*

REFERENCES

Allmendinger, J. & A. Podsiadlowski, (2001) 'Segregation in Organisationen und Arbeitsgruppen', Heintz, B. (ed.) *Geschlechtersoziologie*, Wiesbaden: Westdeutscher Verlag:276-307

Alltägliche Lebensführung (ed.) (1995) *Alltägliche Lebensführung. Arrangements zwischen Traditionalität und Modernisierung*, Redaktion: W. Kuderas, S. Dietmaier, & S. Opladen: Leske & Budrich

Aulenbacher, B. (2005) 'Subjektivierung von Arbeit. Ein hegemonialer industriesoziologischer Topos und was die feministische Arbeitsforschung und Gesellschaftsanalyse dazu zu sagen haben', Lohr, K & H. Nickel, *Subjektivierung von Arbeit – Riskante Chancen*, Münster: Westfälisches Dampfboot:34-64

Baethge, M. (1991) 'Arbeit, Vergesellschaftung, Identität – Zur zunehmenden normativen Subjektivierung der Arbeit', *Soziale Welt*, H 42/1991:6–19

Baukrowitz, A.& A.Boes (2002) *Arbeitsbeziehungen in der IT-Industrie. Erosion oder Innovation der Mitbestimmung?*, Berlin: edition Sigma 55 Jg.:10-18

Baukrowitz, A. & A. Boes(1996) 'Arbeit in der 'Informationsgesellschaft' – einige Überlegungen aus einer (fast schon) ungewohnten Perspektive', Schmiede, R. (ed.) *Virtuelle Arbeitswelte*, Berlin: edition

---

19   The discussion of work-life balance covers a number of issues, including the working time regime, family research, family policy, future work models and other related issues (cf. Oechsle 2006, Metz-Göckel 2004).

20   This rationalisation represents a process of clearance and disclosure of personal values and preferences. 'What do I want? What do I need? Am I adventurous or do I need security?' This process is successful when the women observe themselves, control their emotions, assess their decisions, and take the direction selected. In this way, numerous life models are generated, which end up becoming cultural forces of change' (Illouz, 2006).

Baukrowitz, A., A.Boes & B. Eckhardt(1998) 'Veränderungstendenzen der Arbeit im Übergang zur Informationsgesellschaft – Befunde und Defizite der Forschung', *Enquete-Kommission Zukunft der Medien*, a.a.O:13–170

Baukrowitz, A. & A.Boes (2001) 'Bewegung in den Arbeitsbeziehungen – Das wandlungsfähige deutsche System passt unterschiedlich gut', *Die Mitbestimmung*, H 6:42–45

Bechmann, G. G. Frederick & B-J. Krings (1999) *Information Society, Work and the Generation of New Forms of Social Exclusion (SOWING)*, Regional Report for Germany, Karlsruhe: Forschungszentrum Karlsruhe

Bechmann, G. G. Frederick & B-J. Krings (2001) *Information Society, Work and the Generation of New Forms of Social Exclusion (SOWING)*, Final National Report, Germany, Karlsruhe: Forschungszentrum Karlsruhe

Beck, U. (1986) *Die Risikogesellschaft*, Frankfurt/M.: Suhrkamp

Beck-Gernsheim, E. (1993) *Das halbierte Leben*, Frankfurt/M.: Fischer

Becker-Schmidt, R. (1995) 'Von Jungen, die keine Mädchen und von Mädchen, die gerne Jungen sein wollten. Geschlechtsspezifische Umwege auf der Suche nach Identität', in: Becker-Schmidt, R. & G-A. Knapp (eds.) *Das Geschlechterverhältnis als Gegenstand der Sozialwissenschaften*, Frankfurt/M./New York: Campus, S. 220-246

Becker-Schmidt, R. (2003) 'Umbrüche in Arbeitsbiographien von Frauen: Regionale Konstellationen und globale Entwicklungen', in: Knapp, G-A. & A.Wetter(eds.) *Achsen der Differenz. Gesellschaftstheorie und feministische Kritik II*, Münster: Westfälisches Dampfboot:101-132.

Behringer, L. (1998) *Lebensführung als Identitätsarbeit. Der Mensch im Chaos des modernen Alltags*, Frankfurt/M.; New York: Campus

Boes, A. (1996) 'Formierung und Emanzipation. Zur Dialektik der Arbeit in der "Informationsgesellschaft"', Schmiede, R. (eds.) *Virtuelle Arbeitswelten. Arbeit, Produktion und Subjekt in der 'Informationsgesellschaft'*, Berlin: edition Sigma:159-178

Boes, A & K. Trinks (2005) 'Interessen und Interessenhandeln von IT-Beschäftigten in der Genderperspektive', Funder, M.,S. Dörhöfer & C. Rauch (eds.) *Jenseits der Geschlechterdifferenz? Geschlechterverhältnisse in der Informations- und Wissensgesellschaft*, München und Mering: Rainer Hampp Verlag:284-304

Boß, C. & V. Roth (1992) *Die Zukunft der DV-Berufe*, Opladen: Westdeutscher Verlag

Castells, M. (1996) *The Rise of the Network Society*, Malden, USA; Oxford,UK: Blackwell

Datenreport (2002) *Zahlenreport für die Bundesrepublik Deutschland*, Bonn: Bundeszentrale für politische Bildung

Fuchs, G & H.G.Wolf (1998a) *Multimedia Unternehmen in Baden-Württemberg: Erfahrungen, Erfolgsbedingungen und Erwartungen*, Arbeitsbericht Nr. 128 der Akademie für Technikfolgenabschätzung in Baden-Württemberg, Stuttgart

Fuchs, G.& H.G.Wolf (2000) *Regionale Erneuerung durch Multimedia?*, Baden-Baden: Nomos

Funder, M. (2005) 'Gendered Management? Geschlecht und Management in wissensbasierten Organisationen', in: Funder, M., S. Dörhöfer & C. Rauch, (eds.) *Jenseits der Geschlechterdifferenz? Geschlechterverhältnisse in der Informations- und Wissensgesellschaft*, München & Mering: Rainer Hampp Verlag:97-122

Gottschall, K. & G.G.Voß (2005*) Entgrenzung von Arbeit und Leben. Zum Wandel der Beziehung von Erwerbstätigkeit und Privatsphäre im Alltag*, München: Rainer Hampp Verlag

Harding, S. (1990) *Feministische Wissenschaftstheorie. Zum Verhältnis von Wissenschaft und sozialem Geschlecht*, Hamburg: Argument-Verlag

Hielscher, V. & E. Hildebrandt (1999) *Zeit für Lebensqualität. Auswirkungen verkürzter und flexibilisierter Arbeitszeiten auf die Lebensführung*, Berlin: edition sigma

Illouz, E. (2006) *Gefühle in Zeiten den Kapitalismus*, Frankfurt/M.: Suhrkamp

Jürgens, K. (2003) 'Die Schimäre der Vereinbarkeit. Familienleben und flexibilisierte Arbeitszeiten', *Zeitschrift für Soziologie der Erziehung und Sozialisation*, 23 (3):251-267

Jürgens, K. (2005) 'Kein Ende von Arbeitszeit und Familie', *Arbeitszeit – Familienzeit – Lebenszeit. Zeitschrift für Familienforschung*, Sonderheft 5, Wiesbaden:165-183

Jurcyk, K.& M. Rerrich (eds.) (1993) *Die Arbeit des Alltags. Beiträge zu einer Soziologie der all-*

täglichen Lebensführung, Freiburg, Br.: Herder

Kahlert, H & C. Kajatin (eds.) (2004) *Arbeit und Vernetzung im Informationszeitalter*, Frankfurt, M.; New York: Campus

Kleemann, F., I. Matuschek & G.G. Voß (1999) *Zur Subjektivierung von Arbeit*, Veröffentlichung der Querschnittsgruppe Arbeit&Ökologie beim Wissenschaftszentrum Berlin:99–512

Kocyba, H. (2005) 'Selbstverwirklichung im Unternehmen – Chance als Anerkennungsfalle?', Funder, M., S. Dörhöfer, S & C. Rauch. (eds) *Jenseits der Geschlechterdifferenz? Geschlechterverhältnisse in der Informations- und Wissensgesellschaft*, München & Mering: Rainer Hampp Verlag:139-153

Kratzer, N. (2003) *Arbeitskraft in Entgrenzung. Grenzenlose Anforderungen, erweiterte Spielräume, begrenzte Ressourcen*, Berlin: edition Sigma

Krings, B-J. (2003) *Wandel der Arbeits- und Lebensbedingungen im Multimediabereich aus der Gender-perspektive*, Wissenschaftliche Berichte FZKA 6892, Karlsruhe: Forschungszentrum Karlsruhe

Lohr, K. & H.M. Nickel(2005) 'Subjektivierung von Arbeit – Riskante Chancen', in: Lohr, K.& H.M. Nickel(eds.) *Subjektivierung von Arbeit – Riskante Chancen*, Münster: Westfälisches Dampfboot: 207-232

Manske, A. (2003) 'Web Worker. Arrangements der Sphären im Spannungsfeld von Vereinnahmung und Ergänzung', Gottschall, K. & G.G. Voß (eds.) *Entgrenzung von Arbeit und Leben*, München & Mering: Rainer Hampp Verlag, S. 261-282, 2. Auflage 2005

Manske, A. (2003) 'Arbeits- und Lebensarrangements in der Multimediabranche unter Vermark-tlichungsdruck – Rationalisierungspotenzial für den Markterfolg?', Kuhlmann, E. & S. Betzelt(eds.) *Geschlechterverhältnisse im Dienstleistungssektor. Dynamiken, Differenzierungen und neue Horizonte*, Baden-Baden: Nomos:133-146

Menez, R., I. Munder, I. & K.Töpsch (2001) *Qualifizierung und Personaleinsatz in der IT-Branche*, Auswertung der Online-Studie BIT-S, Arbeitsbericht der Akademie für Technikfolgenabschätzung Nr. 200, Stuttgart

Metz-Göckel, S. (2004) 'Wenn die Arbeit die Familie frisst: Work Life Balance ein Genderproblem?', Kastner, M. (ed.) *Die Zukunft der Work Life Balance. Wie lassen sich Beruf und Familie, Arbeit und Freizeit miteinander vereinbaren?*, Kröning: Asanger, S. 107-139

Minssen, H. (ed.) (1999) *Begrenzte Entgrenzungen. Wandlungen von Organisation und Arbeit*, Berlin: edition Sigma

Nickel, H. M. (2004) Zukunft der Arbeit aus feministischer Perspektive', in: Baatz, D., C. Rudolph, C. & A. Satilmis (eds.) *Hauptsache Arbeit? Feministische Perspektiven auf den Wandel von Arbeit*, Münster: Westfälisches Dampfboot:242-254

Nordhause-Janz, J & D. Rehfeld (1999) 'Informations- und Kommunikationswirtschaft Nordr-hein-Westfalen', *Institut Arbeit und Technik* (ed.), Graue Reihe des Instituts Arbeit und Technik, Band 1. Gelsenkirchen

Oechsle, M. (2006) *Deutschland in der Zeitfalle? Zur Rezeption von Arlie Russel Hochschilds 'Keine Zeit' in Deutschland*, Einleitung in Russell Hochschild a.a.O.:VII-XIX

Oevermann, U. (1978) *Probleme der Professionalisierung in der berufsmäßigen Anwendung sozial-wissenschaftlicher Kompetenz*, Frankfurt/ M. (unpublished manuscript)

Pongratz,H. J. & G.G. Voß (2003) *Arbeitskraftunternehmer. Erwerbsorientierungen in entgrenzten Arbeitsformen*, Berlin: edition Sigma

Priddat, B. (2001) *Frauen als virtuelle Unternehmerinnen: hyper organisations of work, life and household*, Ein Beitrag zur Geschlechterfrage der New Economy, Witten: Verlag Witten

Russell Hochschild, A. (2002) *Keine Zeit. Wenn die Firma zum Zuhause wird und zu Hause nur Arbeit wartet*, Wiesbaden: VS-Verlag, 2. edition 2006

Voß, G.G. (1991) *Lebensführung als Arbeit. Über die Autonomie der Person im Alltag der Gesells-chaft*, Stuttgart: Enke

Voß, G.G. (1998) 'Die Entgrenzung von Arbeit und Arbeitskraft. Eine subjektorientierte Interpre-tation des Wandels der Arbeit', *Mitteilungen aus der Arbeits- und Berufsforschung*, 31 (3):473-487

Voß, G.G. (2003) 'Entgrenzte Arbeit – Gestresste Familien', in: *Zeitschrift für Familienforschung*, 15. Jg., H 3/2003:329-335

Voß, G.G.& H.J.Pongratz (1998) 'Der Arbeitskraftunternehmer. Eine neue Grundform der Ware Arbeitskraft?', in: *Kölner Zeitschrift für Soziologie und Sozialpsychologie*, Jg. 50, H1:131–158

Wohlrab-Sahr, M. (1993) *Biographische Unsicherheit. Formen weiblicher Identität in der 'reflexiven Moderne': Das Beispiel der Zeitarbeiterinnen*, Opladen: Leske + Budrich

Zwick, M.& O. Renn (2000) *Die Attraktivität von technischen und ingenieurswissenschaftlichen Fächern bei der Studien- und Berufswahl junger Frauen und Männer*, Stuttgart: Akademie für Technikfolgenabschätzung in Baden-Württemberg

ACKNOWLEDGEMENTS

I would like to thank Linda Nierling (ITAS), the anonymous peer reviewers, and Ursula Huws for their extremely constructive comments on the first draft of this paper.

Who are the fairest?
ethnic segmentation in London's media production

Ashika Thanki
Steve Jefferys

Ashika Thanki *is a researcher currently employed as a*
fieldworker by the Red Cross
Steve Jefferys *is professor of European Labour Studies and direc-*
tor of the Working LIves Research Institute at London Metropoli-
tan University

ABSTRACT

London is a global media city where over 30 per cent of the workforce is from black
and ethnic minorities. Yet only seven per cent of those in media production come from
these minorities, and they are concentrated in lower level and non-mainstream jobs. The
authors argue that the anachronistic survival of institutional racism is not simply about
the survival of a discriminatory 'monoculture'. While racism is enabled by the major
casualisation of the industry, it is also functional, helping to defend a stable process of
elite formation and defence in a key area of capitalist ideological production. This racism
is about power and the authors' research into why ethnic minority professionals quit London's media production sector also explains how this power imbalance deters resistance.

Labour markets in the audio-visual industries are not a pretty sight. Structured
around an over-supply of nearly all kinds of often interchangeable and adaptable
skills, they are closer to the casual labour pools formerly foudn on London's now gentrified docks than to a market in the sense of independent buyers negotiating terms
with independent but potentially unionised sellers.

While the British Broadcasting Corporation (BBC) remains aloof, with its strongly Oxbridge[1] elite management and public service tradition offering some employment protection to a privileged few, in the rest of the audio-visual sector, recruitment,
training opportunities, progression and promotion are almost completely casualised.
Extreme flexibility rhymes with extreme informality. And what the research reported
below points to are some of the more poignant effects of this casualisation: the use
made of this power to discriminate against the 'other'. This 'other' may be any person
who does not come from the same elite background, but there is evidence that the
'other' who is denied equality in mainstream cultural production is non-white. White
workers appeared to be systematically treated in a less unfair manner than black. This

---

1   'Oxbridge' is a term used in Britain to refer jointly to the elite universities of Oxford and Cambridge.

is important since, while under-representation of minorities cements social injustice in labour markets generally, in the media industries it can also undermine the development of social cohesion.

The processes of elite formation and defence against the minorities described here are not a simple British 'exception'. In France in the summer of 2006 columns of newsprint were devoted to commenting upon the use by one TV Channel of a solitary temporary black-skinned news anchorman in front of the cameras. This paper, focusing on the world's second global media city, London (Krätke 2003), raises questions about why ethnic equality should be developing so slowly within the power structures and fluid labour markets of cultural production.

Cultural production through the audio-visual sector and its media outputs is central to the ways in which contemporary capitalist power is legitimated (Habermas 1989, Chomsky 2003, Harvey 2006). Power is made to appear rational and hence legitimate in part through its tolerance and encouragement of a variety of media outputs, and in part through its structural dominance over the content of what is produced.

It is true that there is a huge range of choice in the societies of signs in which we now live (Lash & Urry 1994). Yet, simultaneously, cultural production appears to be increasingly concentrated in enormous global media groups that operate as networks of business units and imprint massively on the processes of globalisation (Krätke 2003). This dualism also covers a paradox. On the one hand media capital*ism* embraces competition and variety; on the other hand, individual media capital*ists* prefer to act as a 'we' consciously shaping their own class evolution and interests.

As Castells (2000) argues, elites do form and reproduce global networks, but the evidence we present here suggests that they do so under specific constraints of time, space and location, and for specific purposes. In cultural production in particular, whose commodities derive in greater measure from human creativity, the more the sway of the American variety of capitalism giving primacy to external financial markets (Whitley 1999), the more important are these constraints. In each global media city the elite formation process seeks to control the external market by limiting full participation in the sector to chosen insiders. The selected insiders receive a degree of protection from the ravages of the market place and, in exchange, generally exercise self-control or self-censorship in delivering acceptable cultural products. Purposeful choice is thus exercised in elite recruitment and network formation.

The result of these choices, as Campion's recent industry review and interviews with 102 UK programme makers argues, is that since the 1980s, while there are many more women than before in media production, for ethnic minorities there was 'disappointing' progress:

'Although... the presence on screen of people from some ethnic minorities increased between 1993 and 2003, the increases were almost entirely due to their appearance in incidental roles. The total volume of (and spend on) television programmes defined as "multicultural" dropped substantially between 1998 and 2002 across all the terrestrial channels.' (Campion, 2005:4)

Despite a well-presented, rational case for involving ethnic minority people at all levels and in all professions in media production in order to develop informed and balanced messages (Harrison & Woods 2000) and a huge range of initiatives aiming to promote 'cultural diversity', a process of elite defence appears to take precedence over equal opportunities.

The rational case for diversity creates yards of written guides to good human resource management practice. In the wake of the McPherson Report (1999), the BBC even went so far as to set minority recruitment targets. But elite defence is relatively simple in the context of a casualised sector structured around informal personal contacts. The ideological ramparts at the heart of the audio-visual industries are thus successfully defended by the talented 'us' against the unknown and evidently less-talented 'other'. Casualisation provides a highly effective method of ensuring that 'insider networking' works to reproduce rather than revolutionise the ranks of cultural production workers.

Campion argues that the elite defence mechanism in cultural production should be described as an excluding and discriminating 'monoculture' rather than as 'institutional racism':

'I feel that to call it institutional racism is to limit our understanding of it. What exists is a very strong industry monoculture which excludes and discriminates against all sorts of difference in subtle and often, on a personal level, unintended ways. The cumulative impact of the sort of day to day marginalisation described above means that few people who come from a different background or bring a different perspective remain and rise through the industry. The ones least likely to do so are those who are perceived as most different and made to feel most different.' (Campion, 2005:93)

However, as the research described below outlines, the consequences of this 'monoculture' are very real for whole groups of people who are defined by the elite in terms of their 'otherness'. Racism cannot therefore be properly understood as simply historical xenophobia, or minorities reduced to being a mere sub-set of victims of a general cultural exclusion. Rather, racism is about social relations within contemporary economic and political structures (Balibar & Wallerstein 1991, Solomos 2003), and hence it is about power. It is a social relationship like those of class and gender that embodies the power relations of both domination and subordination. But what is specific about it is that it simultaneously constructs an 'inferior other' (De Rudder *et al*, 2000). Racism may be based on colour and physical features or on culture, nationality and way of life, but acts, institutions and industries become racist when they explicitly or implicitly deny equality by insisting on or reproducing the superiority of a particular culture (Parekh 2000).

If the mechanisms in place within an industry, such as its casual labour market, interact to ensure that the superiority of a particular culture survives, then this can properly be described as 'institutional' racism. Our argument, drawn from research into why white majority and ethnic minority professionals leave the sector in London (Thanki & Jefferys, 2005), is that within cultural production this institutional racism is functional for both elite defence and the ideological legitimation and reinforcement of global market capital relations.

We first describe the audio visual sector in London, illustrating the ethnic division of labour. Then we evidence some experiences of that segmentation. Finally we return to the discussion concerning the rationality of racism in cultural production.

London: a global media city

London is a major centre of global media production. In 2004, of the roughly 160,000 UK media workers whose employers identified them in a national Skillset (2005) census, over half worked in the city. Skillset is a recently created organisation with responsibility for skills and training in the broadcasting, film, video, interactive media (electronic games, offline multimedia and web and internet) and photo imaging subsectors. The largest of these subsectors in London is interactive media, employing around 23,900 people. Broadcast TV is the second largest of these subsectors in London, employing around 12,300 people. A further 10,000 work in broadcast radio.

Freelancing is a highly significant and growing working trend within the audio visual industries. Skillset's census confirms that at least a quarter of London's media labour force on any one day work as freelancers. But other Skillset research into working patterns within the audio visual industries suggests that around another 26,000 freelancers were active in London's workforce but not recorded as working on census day. This suggests that the total audio visual workforce in London is approaching 100,000 of whom some 45,000 are freelance.

Table 1 shows the 2004 London total employment (employees and freelancers) by industry sector and the reported distribution by gender and by ethnicity.

Table 1: Employment in London's Audio Visual Industries by sector, 2004

Sector	Total employed	Women %	BME %
Web and Internet	20,100	33	10
Broadcast Television	12,300	50	9
Broadcast Radio	10,000	49	8
Independent Production (Television)	8,200	43	5
Cable and Satellite Television	5,300	57	5
Post Production	4,500	27	5
Commercials Production	2,500	32	3
Offline Multimedia	2,400	29	1
Facilities (Studio/Equipment Hire)	2,100	24	6
Animation	1,400	43	7
Electronic Games	1,400	7	3
Corporate Production	1,100	36	5
Other	1,000	40	6
Digital Special Effects*	600	na	na
Film Distribution*	500	na	na
Processing Laboratories*	400	na	na
Total (and weighted averages)	73,700	39	7

Source: Skillset (2005). *gender and ethnicity breakdown not acailable. All figures are rounded to the nearest 100. Cinema exhibition, photo imaging and performance are excluded.

The seven per cent estimate of Black and minority ethnic (BME) people working in the London media industries on census day 2004 is in line with the eight per cent UK national BME labour force participation rate, but very low compared to the 32 per cent BME share of the whole working age population in London. There is thus a very considerable under-representation of non-white workers within the audio visual industries in London by comparison with their presence in the capital city. The 39 per cent of women in the sector, by contrast, is more closely in line with the 44 per cent women's share of the London working age labour force in 2004 (ONS 2005). 'Monoculturalism' does not appear quite as fairly distributed across those at risk of discrimination as Campion (2005) suggests. If employment in the audio visual industries is examined by occupational area rather than industry, the picture changes again.

Table 2: Employment in London's Audio Visual Industries by occupation, 2004

Sector	Total employed	BME %
Production	8,800	7
Producing	7,700	9
Journalism & Sport	5,200	7
Television Broadcasting	5,100	5
Post-Production	4,700	5
Radio Broadcasting	2,800	1
Broadcast Engineering	1,800	12
Runner	1,700	5
Studio Operations	1,300	5
Art & Design	1,300	3
Camera	1,200	3
Sound	1,000	8
Lighting	800	3
Library/Archives	700	7
Programme Distribution	600	3
Film Distribution	500	na*
Processing Laboratories	400	na*
2D/3D Computer Animation	300	-
Special Physical Effects	300	-
Make Up & Hairdressing	200	6
Costume/Wardrobe	200	4
All other occupational groups**	21,000	7
Total (and weighted averages)	73,900	7

Source: Skillset (2005). *no breakdown available; ** includes finance, general management, HR, IT, premises operations, press & PR, sales & marketing, secretarial/admin. -= less than 50. All figures are rounded to the nearest 100.

The data are less complete than they are for the head-count, in some instances because 'occupation' is less clearly defined in small companies. For London, Skillset's data shows that the greatest presence of ethnic minorities is in journalism and sport (16 per cent) and in broadcast engineering (12 per cent) while their presence in other occupational groups falls within a range of one to eight per cent. The data available are shown in Table 2.

These figures throw up many questions about discrimination and segmentation. Why should the highest BME proportion by a long way (16 per cent) be in media journalism and sport? Does this reflect the well-established anti-racist campaigning of the National Union of Journalists? Is there a racial stereotyping taking place with the concentration of BME workers in sports-related media activities? How can we explain the differences between the BME proportions in sound (eight per cent) compared with camera (three per cent) when the numbers involved are virtually identical? Is this also related to stereotyping, pay and/or training? Why should the web and internet industries have the highest overall proportion (ten per cent) of BME workers? Could it be because their employees are effectively 'invisible'? Why do TV and radio broadcasting – although still low, at nine and eight per cent respectively, - appear better than the other subsectors? Does this reflect the role of public regulation and of effective training mechanisms in ensuring the recruitment and retention of BME staff? Or could it be an effect of the fact that these sectors are relatively well unionised?

Further work is required to interpret these data fully, but the very variety of the distribution they reveal appears once again to refute Campion's 'monocultural' thesis. An active process of recruitment and selection is working more clearly against BME people in certain occupations than in others, raising several questions about the denial of racism implicit within the notion of a general discriminatory culture that affects all, and all equally.

Research findings

The questions posed by the Skillset data within a major mature and growing London industry led to the research described here. We were commissioned by Ofcom, the regulator of the UK communications sector, to find out why ethnic minority workers quit London's audio visual industries. In the course of our research we interviewed 31 current or former workers in the audio visual industries about how they entered the industry, and about their working lives and experiences within it, and why they finally left. Half of these were ethnic minority and half ethnic majority workers, and all were still active in other labour markets.

Two potentially contradictory factors framed people's experiences: the audio visual industries provide very challenging, creative and often rewarding work, making them high-profile and attractive to many outsiders; but the whole sector is also extremely competitive and structurally insecure with a strong dependence upon freelancers and some very poorly paid workers.

Entry into the sector is difficult. Having 'contacts' helps significantly in securing that first job or a promotion. A growing 'contract culture' has increased feelings of job insecurity and workers are often compelled to work freelance because so few staff jobs are available. This often has the effect of placing still more weight on the role of internal industry networking, from which minority workers are often excluded. A mixed race interviewee who had left the sector argued that:

'A lot of middle class white people have links into the media which they can tap,
you know – Mummy, Daddy, Auntie ... somebody might work somewhere,
know somebody – do you know what I mean?'

The particularly strong dependence upon informal networking and freelancing still present a number of specific obstacles and barriers to working class people and particularly those from minority ethnic backgrounds. Together these create a web of indirect racism that is dense enough to 'push' many of these professionals to quit as the audio visual industries are predominantly middle-class and their senior posts are still largely run by a largely white 'old boy' Oxbridge network. Another mixed race interviewee commented,

'[The] employers essentially employ people like themselves [white, male]...This is not
necessary just by race but also by class and gender and there has to be some
exceptional reasons why you then employ somebody who is not like you,'

'Outsiders' often report they are not listened to because the higher, more powerful and influential tiers of the media hierarchy are disproportionately filled by white upper middle class people. A Caribbean leaver in his 30s made the point that

'Even if the subject matter is an issue that is relevant to minorities within this country, whether it is comedy or drama or documentary, who is the executive
on this programme? Who is the series producer? Who is the director...[It's]
a very hard and fast white middle-class industry...They feel that it is their
natural right to run the media.'

We would not disagree with Campion (2005) that disabled workers, women and those who do not come from upper class elite education often experience discrimination. But to pretend that what is happening to BME professionals is on a par with the experiences faced by other individuals who are not white, male and elite educated, and is not racism is to fail to see the power relations at work within white-black stereotyping discrimination. This 'monocultural' critique thus misjudges racism's extent, depth and structuring consequences, as can be seen where positive discrimination was taken and then stalled.

Special training schemes aimed at encouraging ethnic minorities to enter the industry were introduced from the early 1990s and did have some short-term effects, particularly where funding was available to secure a post for periods of more than a year. These schemes brought some improvements. One mixed race leaver in his late 40s, talking about his career in broadcasting since the early 1990s, observed:

'When I first joined the [broadcaster]...the only Asians were women who came at
night [to clean] and the only blacks were in the canteen. You might have seen
that one person – that black man in the news, a reporter – but very, very few
non-whites otherwise.'

As Tables 1 and 2 indicate, the situation has improved since then. But the training schemes were only put in place in the BBC and some other large companies, and are now being wound down in the face of demands for improved financial performance and the political shift to an emphasis on labour market 'diversity' rather than labour market 'equality'.

The minority ethnic respondents we interviewed also believed it was only those positions at the lower end of the industry hierarchy that were in reality open to minority ethnic people, or very occasionally as one token reporter or commentator in front of the camera, or a single one-off programmes aimed at ethnic niches. So the training programmes had improved BME representation without changing power relations. Black professionals remain outside the elite and hence are generally powerless to ensure that representative recruitment and training and programme selection takes place.

How does the process of network elite formation and its defence against the 'other' take place? Once ethnic minority workers had overcome the obstacles to getting into the sector, they were convinced that the expectations and pressures on them were greater than for white professionals. Although any individual may always consider that they are personally overworked, this view was sufficiently consistent, and generally reported in such a matter of fact way, for it to appear self-evident to many of them. One Pakistani-origin man in his 20s made the point that this was a major reason ethnic minority professionals do not get on in the 'mainstream'. They were accepted in the 'ethnic minority media' area; but outside of that they had to be really exceptional to get treated equally.

Several respondents described the audio visual industries as being 'institutionally racist' with invisible barriers making BME 'normal' career progression an exception. Institutional racism was defined by them as being more than direct discrimination in employment practices or promotion. It included the indirect racism and other prejudices that were embedded in the structures and the culture of the industry.

An Asian leaver in her late 30s described experiencing the impact of institutional racism early on in her career. She felt her ambitions to become a presenter were discouraged on the grounds of her race and gender:

'I was working for local radio and it was all white guys [who] presented all the shows.
I really wanted to have a go at presenting. And they were like "no that is never going to happen for you". He was nice about it but he just said that "you know it is an old boys' network. You are just not going to crack that one".'

Another Asian leaver talked of 'hitting the glass ceiling' when senior programme commissioners were still not willing to listen to her ideas - despite having worked for the main broadcasters and as a freelancer continuously for ten years. An Asian leaver in his 20s described his experience:

'Personally, [I left the] industry because of psychological pressure ... You are in a workplace or you are trying to get into the industry and you are getting discriminated and ... you cannot talk about it because if you do you get blacklisted or probably no one is going to believe you.'

In some rare cases direct racism is used to mark out the insider's territory. Talking of her last job as a runner in a team where she was one of only two ethnic minority staff, one young mixed race leaver reported:

'[A new person was recruited and she was responsible for our contracts]. She decided to remove one of my colleagues because he was too noisy, too loud ... He was African. She decided I was 'too quiet' for television. The rest [of the runners] were [given contracts for different programmes] ... and [they] were white'

Another mixed race leaver described an incident early in his career:

> *'I worked at a radio station. I was covering for a receptionist's break. The marketing manager came in and he said that he didn't want me to cover the break because I didn't project the "collective image of the radio station".'*

How widespread is such race discrimination in this labour market? There can be no definitive answer, but in 2002 a BBC-commissioned survey asked explicitly 'do you think it is harder for people of ethnic minorities to get a job in the media than it is for white people?' As much as one third of the whole (UK-wide) sample agreed. But more than half (54 per cent) of the Black and 57 per cent of the Asian respondents believed it was harder (BBC, 2002).

Insider network defence also operates to defend the ideological line of the dominant elite. An example was what happened after September 11 2001, with several Muslim professionals arguing that they were subsequently treated even more differently. In some cases, Muslim researchers and journalists described being suddenly sought after by editors and commissioners because of a perception that they would possess 'insider' knowledge in all matters relating to Islam, terrorism and Al-Quaeda. For one Muslim journalist 'the phone wouldn't stop ringing'. In others, question marks were now placed over their professional ability to produce programmes on issues relating to or involving Muslims and Islam. One Muslim woman who wore a hijab was directly accused of lacking objectivity:

> *'One editor said to me "I don't believe you have objectivity in the issues you care about". I said "What are those issues?"... She replied "Muslims and Islam"... What she was saying is ridiculous.'*

This evidence again questions the 'monoculture' analysis. Women as a whole are no longer thought to lack the 'objectivity' to report on war or rape. Negative stereotyping is retained for the 'other'.

Another way in which the dominant ideology is defended is through programme stereotyping by the dominant white male elite. Programmes were often regarded as portraying caricatures of minority ethnic people and their lifestyles. An Asian leaver argued:

> *'There are not enough black programmes ... When they do something it is like "Babyfather"[2] or Asian terrorists...or bad characters on "Eastenders"[3]. That is not what our lives are like.'*

What forms do opposition to this experience of direct and indirect racism take? The classic forms of resistance are 'fight' or 'flight'. What our research showed is that the informal structure of the sector first encourages passivity and ultimately pushes the exit or flight strategy to the fore.

For freelancers, the situation is arguably more precarious in an industry where contracts are often awarded through personal contacts. Freelancers, dependent on good references and recommendation from previous clients, fear being considered 'troublemakers'. One Asian leaver felt that challenging the racism that he experienced would only succeed in labelling him and thus become a barrier to working on other projects:

---

2   a BBC series featuring a Black single father..

3   a popular British soap opera.

'I just became very passive about it ... I have seen the consequences of people going to unions and I just feel that mud sticks. It stays with you.'

The reasons for the absence of fight derive largely from the casualised nature of the labour market which generalises the view that resistance could adversely affect workers' careers. Two of the BME leavers we interviewed had directly challenged the racial discrimination that they had experienced and, in both cases, the process of complaint was long-drawn out and neither received support from others in the industry. For both of these leavers, the only official source of support was their union, which helped them both to reach settlements. Both individuals argue that they had been 'branded' and had to continue to field accusations and rumours spread by their previous employers for taking a stand against racial discrimination. This impacted on their ability to find work within the industry and had required them to diversify and 'take flight' into other occupations. But many of the other minority ethnic workers we interviewed expressed fears of being 'singled out' as trouble-makers, as reported above, or even of losing their jobs, especially when the racism came from their managers. When asked whether they believed the unions could help they replied that they had not even considered taking that route. For them the structural imperatives of the media industries meant that 'exit' came before 'voice'.

Is racism functional to cultural production?

This evidence of the ways in which the defence of the ideological values and personnel composition of the dominant white male elite network take place in a major global centre of the audio visual industries such as multi-racial London is instructive. At one level the racism involved is not 'rational' to the capitalist system driving it. Capitalism makes no distinction between the 'white' and the 'brown pound' referred to by some of those we interviewed. If there is a strong enough 'business case for diversity', then 'black' programmes will be made and shown, or support will be given to global broadcasters who deliver political messages confirming (American) capitalist hegemony.

But at another level the continuing racism – and its gender and class aspects – do have a rationality, and one that is particularly crucial to the global media. This rationality arises from the vital importance of this very special commodity, one whose production and distribution technologies are being revolutionised at high speed and with uncertain consequences. The rational reason for excluding or marginalising 'outsiders' in favour of the dominant racial and ideological elite is that this commodity, above all others, requires stability and certainty in its production and consumption. The 'other' must be kept at arm's length for just as long as is needed. And as the 'racialised other' increasingly becomes the 21st century's working class, its representatives remain viewed with suspicion, as 'not one of us'.

Mirror, mirror ... will those who get the fairest treatment remain the fair?

© *Ashika Thanki and Steve Jefferys, 2006*

REFERENCES

Balibar, E. and I.Wallerstein (1991) *Race, Nation, Class,* London: Verso

BBC (2002) *BBC/ICM Race Survey,* London: British Broadcasting Corporation

Campion, Jain M. (2005) *Look Who's Talking: Cultural Diversity, Public Service Broadcasting and the National Conversation,* Oxford: Nuffield College

Castells, M. (2000) *The Rise of the Network Society, The Information Age: Economy, Society and Culture,* Oxford: Blackwell

Chomsky, N. (2002) *Understanding Power: the Indispensable Chomsky,* New York: New Press

De Rudder, V., C. Poiret and F. Vourc'h (2000) *L'inégalité raciste. L'universalité républicaine à l'épreuve,* Paris: Presses Universitaires de France

Habermas, J. (1989) *The Structural Transformation of the Public Sphere: An Inquiry into a Category of Bourgeois Society,* Cambridge, MA: MIT Press.

Harrison J. and L.Woods (2000) 'European Citizenship: can Audio visual policy make a difference?', *Journal of Common Market Studies,* 30:3

Harvey, D. (2006) *Spaces of Global Capitalism: Towards a theory of uneven geographical development,* London: Verso

Krätke, S. (2003) 'Global Media Cities in a Worldwide Urban Network', *European Planning Studies,* MAN 11.6: 605-628

Lash, S. and J.Urry (1994) *Economies of signs and space,* London: Sage

Parekh, B. (2000) *Report of the Commission on the Future of Multi-Ethnic Britain,* London: Runnymede Trust

Macpherson, W. (1999) *The Stephen Lawrence Inquiry,* Cm 4262-1. London: The Stationery Office

ONS (2005) *Region in Figures: London,* 9, Norwich: HMSO

Skillset (2005), *Employment Census 2004: The Results of the Fifth Census of the Audio Visual Industries,* London: Skillset

Solomos, J. (2003) *Race and Racism in Britain,* Basingstoke: Palgrave Macmillan

Thanki, A. and S.Jefferys (2005) *Leaving London's Audio Visual Industries with Regrets: why black and minority ethnic professionals quit,* London: Working Lives Research Institute

Whitley, R. (1999) *Divergent Capitalisms: The Social Structuring and Change of Business Systems,* Oxford: Oxford University Press

Rethinking progressive and conservative values:

Spain's new economy workers and their values

Armando Fernández Steinko

Armando Fernández Steinko is Professor of Sociology at the
Universidad Complutense de Madrid in Spain.

ABSTRACT

Drawing on interviews carried out with workers in the new economy in Madrid, this paper
argues that the dichotomy 'individualism versus collectivism' is inadequate to describe
their value systems. It proposes instead an alternative typology based on distinctions
between 'personal' and 'organic' values and 'diversified' and 'non-diversified' interests.
The development of these values is placed in the context of the specific history of indus-
tralisation in southern Europe, which, along with eastern Europe, differs significantly from
that of the economies of northern Europe which industrialised earlier and whose working
classes developed different models of solidarity.

Some years ago, the communist East German writer Stephan Hermlin, analysing the
failure of socialism in eastern Europe, wrote:

> 'When I was fifty years of age, I made a horrible discovery. Among the sentences
> whose meaning has seemed evident for me for many years was the following:
> "In place of the old bourgeois society, with its classes and class antagonisms,
> we shall have an association in which the free development of all is the con-
> dition for the free development of each". I do not know when I began reading
> this sentence as it is written here. I read it this way because it corresponded
> with my understanding of the world in those days. My astonishment and even
> fright was enormous when I found out, many years later, that this sentence
> from Marx in the Communist Manifesto actually says exactly the opposite,
> that: "the free development of **each** is the condition for the free development
> of **all**".' (Hermlin, 1979:23)

Stephan Hermlin's confusion was, and still is, quite prevalent within the socialist movement. It is not the product of a theoretical misunderstanding, however, but has deeper
roots.

Solidarity, individualism and the transition to capitalism

The deeper explanation for this confusion between individual and collective interests
is the fact, that during the first three quarters of the 20th century, most recruits to socialism could be described as 'new proletarians'- those parts of the population who were
quickly drawn into modern industrial and state capitalist (and in the later period, Fordist) employment in regions that were rural or dominated by traditional industries. This

process was extremely rapid and traumatic in the Mediterranean countries and in eastern Europe (those regions east of the Elbe)[1]. In this context, the dominant values were, and could only be, those that had characterised traditional, pre-capitalist societies: family and community ties based on hierarchical structures. These ties, which remain strong even to this day, were important political and ideological resources that could be counterposed to capitalism and market ideology. But they were (and still are to some extent) based on forms of solidarity that were not democratic but asymmetrical, forms that can best be described as 'organic solidarity'. Within these regions there was a strong collective involvement but also a rather unequal distribution of power, knowledge and authority. Charisma was primarily based on male domination, with an emphasis on the importance of physical strength for obtaining an income, and also on a strong rejection of individualistic attitudes, because these posed a serious risk to the reproduction of the entire social and economic system.

In these regions, many pre-capitalist family and community-based practices survived for a long time, including the extended family form known as *zadruga;* the peasant communities known as *obschtschinas*; and the collective use of land (*the mir* in eastern Europe, or *tierra comunal* in the Mediterranean). This created a socio-economic situation and a system of values in these regions that were quite different from those that prevailed in northern Europe. In the south and the east, this situation endured well into the second half of the 20th century and fed into revolutionary movements, producing the dominant substratum of socialism in Europe during the 20th century.

Both Fordism and state-oriented socialism were able to exploit these ideological and cultural traditions for their own purposes, but they also helped to bolster the authoritarianism and corporatism that arose in Portugal, Spain, Italy and (to some extent) Germany. The huge cultural gaps between east and west and between central and southern Europe, which were systematically exploited for political purposes by the theorists of the cold war, can be partly attributed to this historical and structural social reality. This regional diversity also explains the loss of hegemony within Marxism of the discourse of personal emancipation. It also has something to do with the occupation of this space by political liberalism after 1968, which led to a decline of the left in Europe.

Only a minority within the left tradition insisted on the strategic importance of individual freedom encapsulated in the slogan 'the free development of *each* is the condition for the free development of *all*', a minority that was politically isolated within the large European socialist and communist parties. During the 1980s, this led to an exodus from the revolutionary left to political and economical liberalism.

This trend seems, however, to have halted since the erosion of the Fordist paradigm (see, for example, Bouffartigue, 2004). This aim of this paper is to discuss the meaning of this change and explore the dialectical relationship between individualistic and

---

1   Europe can be divided in the three zones (A, B, and C) depending upon how it made its transition to capitalism, its dominant type of labour and property during the long journey from feudalism to modernity, its family structure and the speed and nature of its industrialisation and urbanisation processes. The core of the A zone is England, Benelux, north east France and parts of Germany. In this zone capitalism arose early but did not generate the most revolutionary workers' movements during the twentieth century because it also created social mobility and rapid productivity growth. The B Zone stretches east of the geographical line going from the Elbe river to the Trieste peninsula and the C Zone includes the regions of the Italian peninsula south of Tuscany, those situated south of the Duero-Ebro river in the Iberian peninsula and some parts of the Balkan peninsula (Steinko, 2004).

collectivist values and its implications for a modern emancipatory perspective. In order to do so, it draws on some empirical research carried out in 2004 amongst employees in the so-called 'new economy' in Spain, as part of a more general study entitled 'the limits of boundaryless work: research on new ways of working' financed by the German Ministry of Science[2].

The study

Between February and June, 2004, in-depth interviews were carried out with ten new media workers in Madrid, two of whom were also active in their trade unions, plus one academic expert on the sector. All but two of these were interviewed twice, with an average total interview time of three hours. Their occupations ranged over a broad field including graphic design, creative direction, body shopping services, network and services management, product distribution, software consultancy, technical consultancy, database administration and programming. Most were somewhat older than the average for the sector, with ages ranging from 28 to 43 and a median age of 37. Three were computer science graduates and one a fine arts graduates, with the remainder having either dropped out of university or not attended university at all. Two still lived with their parents, three were married with children, with the remainder living alone or with partners. Three were working in small firms (20-30 employees) and two in large organisations (a telecommunications company with 5,000 employees and a public research institute with 2,500 employees) with the remainder in firms with 200-300 employees.

Work in the new economy in Spain

For the purposes of this research the 'new economy' was subdivided into three subsectors: multimedia, software development and internet firms[3]. The new economy is supposed to be a trendsetter in the evolution of work within the neo-liberal organisation of work and society. It is a sector that is extremely sensitive to business cycles, stock exchange fluctuations and market competition. It is also subject to rapid changes as a result of mergers, strategic alliances, and speculative takeovers or sales of whole firms or holdings in them. Alternations between periods of boom and bust can radically alter working and living conditions in a matter of months. More than in any other sector, it is in the new economy that boundaryless work and self-exploitation (extra hours, weekend working and almost no regulation of working conditions) are most likely to be found and indeed to be regarded as normal.

---

2   Spread across several institutes, this project whose work had a number of separate components. Its outputs include,*Work within Project Networks,* Freie Universität Berlin – Institut für Allgemeine Betriebswirtschaftslehre (Prof. Dr. Jörg Sydow); *New Forms of Labour and Changes within Gender Arrangements,* Universität Bremen – Zentrum für Sozialpolitik (Prof. Dr. Karin Gottschall); *Firms' Needs for Autonomy and Labour Law Re-regulation: the Case of Salary Regulation,* Universität Oldenburg – Juristisches Seminar (Prof. Dr. Thomas Blanke).; *New Forms of Industrial Relations? Changes in Work,* Ruhr-Universität Bochum-Lehrstuhl Organisationssoziologie und Mitbestimmungsforschung (Prof. Dr. Ludger Pries); *Work Organisation within Knowledge Industries between Autonomy and Linkages,* Soziologisches Forschungsinstitut e.V. Göttingen (SOFI) (Prof. Dr. Michael Schumann/PD Dr. Harald Wolf); *Effects on Social and Work Psychology of New Forms of Contract-Management,* Universität Bremen – Institut für Psychologie und Sozialforschung (Prof. D. Birgit Volmerg).

3   The multimedia sector was coded A, the software development sector B and the internet sector C in this research; these codes can be used to distinguish where the interviewees quoted in this paper worked.

The impacts of these forms of work are especially acute in Spain, which is the OECD country with the longest experience of high unemployment (mainly among people under 35 years of age), the highest proportion of the workforce on temporary work contracts, and one of the lowest levels of social spending in Western Europe.

The prevailing attitude to work in this sector reflects its use of mainly young workers who are perfectly aware of how volatile their working contracts are, and how temporary their economic privileges. They realise the necessity of accepting any work that is available, whatever the personal relations, until they find another job or manage to climb (temporarily) up the firm's hierarchy. Because the welfare state is underdeveloped, the family is the main institution providing social protection and social embeddedness. This is a situation that relies for its support on the values of solidarity between generations, genders and family members with indefinite and temporary labour contracts. Since the work culture is so strongly short term in character, it is very difficult to develop long-term plans for their own lives, to become independent or to 'grow up' as autonomous individuals.

This situation leads to a political crossroads. On the one hand, it can encourage infantilisation – a voluntary assumption of subordinate roles based on asymmetrical power and authority structures. These values tend to generate conservative attitudes even among young people, leading to uncritical acceptance of neo-liberal policies. These asymmetrical power and authority structures are not only present within families but also within most of the firms in the new economy which are typically very small and unprofessionally organised, based on a sort of pioneer mentality, with a company director who acts as a father, concentrates all the power and shows favouritism towards one or another of his children (employees). Family life and firm life are very much linked to each other and this facilitates an overspilling of attitudes from one institution to the other. Protest, trade union activities and rebellion are almost impossible within these spaces, not just because of the objective situation but also because of the personal nature of the relationships.

On the other hand, this situation can also lead to a protest against this state of things and to a more critical and sceptical attitude This does not have to mean a rebellion against the parents' values as it did during the 1968 era; neither does it necessarily result in trade union organisation. More usually it leads to a strong desire to become independent, to refuse identification with the aims of the family/firm and to leave the parental home, even if this means that life will become economically harder and there will be less time for leisure because it is no longer possible to rely on their mothers' cooking and the household chores being done by the parents' domestic workers. The pursuit of personal goals and the development of individual values forms part of such a reaction.

What are the factors that determine which of these options is adopted? The results of this research suggest two groups of closely inter-linked reasons, objective and subjective. Values have a certain autonomy, which means that even when the objective conditions are similar, individual values can vary, as a result of which political attitudes will also be different. Objective conditions also play a determining role (for example whether there is a mortgage to pay, whether the employee has children and a range of other factors which it is beyond the scope of this paper to discuss. Nevertheless, critical attitudes only seem to develop where certain values are in place.

The values of Spanish employees in the new economy

All the interviewees were motivated by the high dynamism of the sector with its culture of constant innovation. They enjoyed the way they were always being presented with new challenges, ranging from cracking secret Microsoft codes or discovering a programming error to the knowledge that their work was from contributing to a television advertising spot that would be seen by millions of people, or a movie that would be premiered with a splash in a prestige cinema. Nevertheless, their values did not fit neatly within conventional schemes, traditionally captured (especially by the left) in the dichotomy between 'individualistic' values on the one hand and 'collective' or 'solidarity' values on the other. Whilst it is undoubtedly the case that the dichotomy between progressive and conservative values still exists as before, the best way to explain it is not in relation to individualism versus collectivism but as a result of other dichotomies such as those between *diversified* and *non diversified* interests, *personal* and *organic* attitudes, and *consumeristic* versus *non-consumeristic* values.

Diversified versus non diversified interests

Within this group of interviewees, the personal factors that seemed to lead to a broader range of interests were age and maturity, marriage or an informal stable relationship and living away from one's parents. However work-related factors also played a part, with professional recognition leading to a broader range of interests. Although they might be very interested in them, this group had a less extreme attachment to work and computers. Compared with those with narrower interests, they had more 'other things' going on in their lives which meant that they had become less exclusively job oriented and developed a more diversified way of thinking and living. Those with diversified values had developed more distance from their work and this had opened up the possibility of formulating a more questioning attitude.

Because the workers are strongly motivated and the work is generally absorbing, not having diversified values has a major effect on political attitudes: the predisposition to endless work does not just grow because of the individual's social and economic ambitions and necessities, but also because of the absence of other things to do. In developing this all-encompassing focus on work, they are playing into the hands of neo-liberalism. This does not mean that employees with diversified interests do not like their jobs; just that they also like to use their time for doing other things and being with other people besides their work mates.

Examples of interviewees with diversified interests include A1[4] who is doing a doctorate in fine arts and desperately wants to find more time to finish it. Because his research topic has nothing to do with computers, he mixes with completely different people in his academic life. A2 has rented a studio to paint in, not only to diversify his sources of income by selling his paintings, but also to have something in his life apart

---

4   Interviewees were coded according to the subsector they worked in.

from work and family. This gives him a more critical and personal perspective on the sector and its rhythms. B3 likes to retreat to his little country house, enjoy nature and do some traditional construction work. C1 says that he would like to have a more intense political and social life and attend book launches, public lectures and other events. In the case of B4 (a woman with a child) the reasons for wanting to diversify her life have more to do with family relationships.

'I love my work, but I have another life apart from it. I like to do things with my boyfriend and I like languages and so on, but I have to discipline myself not to come home too late, not to do just this one thing, but also to spend time with my boyfriend. I am not very sure that it will be always possible to do this. When I was at Arthur Andersen I worked even more than now for less money. There, you really did not have a private life at all; you weren't even supposed to want one. When it reaches that point, you start losing control of the outside world although, in exchange for it, you do get the chance to control another little world .'(B4)

Diversified interests were more evident in the multimedia sector than in software or internet firms. They were also more common among those with artistic skills and jobs involving interaction with clients (A1, A2, B3) than among those with more purely technical skills and occupations (C2). They also seemed to be more prevalent among those who could be defined as 'middle-middle class' than those who were categorised as 'middle-lower class' and were more linked to *less consumeristic* than to *consumeristic* attitudes. B3 used the phrase 'yokel profile' *('perfil paleto')* to describe the unidimensional non-diversified type, which is culturally narrow and almost exclusively interested in technical issues. This is a Spanish expression that sums up a combination of low culture with a way of life that is consumer-oriented (and therefore believed to be a very 'modern') but also very narrow minded and simple.

'I think this yokel profile is much more common in exclusively technical jobs. When people have to travel and to meet with other people from outside their own little world, they should be broader minded and have an opinion about more than just one thing. And this is not a question of being a graduate or not. I once went on a business trip with a younger colleague. She was a telecommunications engineer and had done a masters degree whilst working at Arthur Andersen in the USA but itt was simply impossible to find anything to talk about except computers and computers.' (B3)

Employees with non-diversified interests tend to concentrate almost all their intellectual and time resources on their work, but not all of it. According to recent studies, employees of the Madrid region who have a job (63% of the population of the Madrid region is less than 45 year old[5]) have a 'work hard and play hard mentality'. However, the search for amusement is not so much a sign of diversified interests but of a hedonistic and consumeristic night life (e.g. in bars and discos). It involves going out with money in their pockets with other work mates of the same age, partly to talk about work issues. A strong career orientation and competitive mentality are

---

5   Indicadores municipales de la Comunidad de Madrid (http://www.madrid.org/iestadis/fijas/ estructu/general/otros/ im00_02.htm)

characteristic of this group who also showed a strong interest in the value of money and social climbing. Employees with more diversified interests were usually older, more sceptical towards technology, with a broader and more critical view of the sector in which they worked and more personal opinions about general issues such as society or technology in general, the Iraq war or other topical issues. However, age alone does not provide the only explanation. As one interviewee put it

'There are some 50-year-olds with no diversity at all.' (F1/C3).

Other values must also be taken into account.

Personal versus organic attitudes

Employees whose attitudes are more *personal* tend to develop their own points of view and criteria for making decisions and organising their work and social lives. By contrast, those whose attitudes are classed as more *organic* do not present themselves as assertively and assume the values, aims and rationalities of the institutions they belong to, mainly the family and the firm. Organically oriented attitudes do not necessarily demonstrate more or less social awareness; they simply express a primary orientation towars micro-institutions and a lower capacity for – or a lower interest in – thinking in a broader way and viewing the firm they work or the technology they use in a wider context. Social life and social awareness are present, but their focus is narrowed to the circle of friends and family, to the project team or to the family-firm that employs them. When it comes to solidarity, the 'others' are just the members of this small group, including the family but not larger groups of people or society as a whole. It is not correct to regard them as 'individualists', because they have a strong group spirit. But the collective values they share are of a type that precludes thinking in terms of justice, social contexts or humanity.

Comversely, having more personally oriented values does not necessarily mean holding individualistic or even egotistic attitudes. It describes a capability for seeing things in a more distant way, from a more individually developed personal perspective. Among these interviewees, 'having your own ideas' can mean being able to keep a sense of perspective (both intellectually and in practice) in relation to issues like technology, clients, projects or competitiveness which might otherwise become overwhelming. It enables them to see these as part of a broader (social) system, and not as all-encompassing issues affecting all aspects of their lives, even including their health. This attitude is threatening to employers who do not like their employees to have their own ideas outside the general frame in ways that give them a critical perspective on concepts like competitiveness, modernity or technology. They prefer to define these unilaterally for the whole firm/family. Trade unionists interviewed for this study said that they have constantly to remind the employees who come to them for help that

'You should not forget that the firm, the work and the project are not your children
– that you and your family exist apart from them.' (F1/C3)

In doing so, they are trying to persuade these workers to develop a certain distance from the work and to follow their personal interests and needs and not only those of the firm, the clients or the project. In other words, they are urged to liberate themselves from this kind of organic solidarity that transforms them voluntarily into slaves of their work. These trade unionists describe employees who are strongly conscious of the high unemployment and volatile security in the sector, with many younger people waiting behind them for a chance of a job and are ready to 'give all of themselves' when they are assigned to a project. They do not only do this for objective reasons but also for subjective reasons (C3, C4). The factors that seem, from these interviews, to contribute to ending these organic attitudes include growing older, establishing one's own household, engagement and marriage , each of which stimulates the urge for personal development and the pursuit of individual interests and goals.

The computer industry is certainly full of organic attitudes but the phenomenon is deeper and more general than this: it is part of the south European social system. Because workers typically live with their parents until they are over 30, and because so many firms in this sector are very small and family-like, this kind of attitude spreads from the family to the firm and to work life in general. Employees do not question the decisions of their managers or the meaning of a project they are working on in the same way that they would not question their fathers or their university or technical college teachers. This is the 'plot mentality', the culture of the small community in which everything is assigned its own place, with no scope for questioning the inner rules and hierarchies.

'In technical colleges nobody disputes the opinion of the professor, even when there are unfair things going on, nobody really protests. You have to study too hard to have time to think about general issues. When you complain you have the feeling that you are a black sheep.' (B4)

There is no doubt that there is a relationship between personal attitudes and diversified interests. Diversified interests tend to give employees a broader view of their own lives and make them see their work as only one part of their existence. In this process their preferences become multidimensional instead of one dimensional (Marcuse, 1964). This attitude makes it possible to develop more personal attitudes and to build up a certain distance towards their 'own' firm, project, or even parents. Without at least some element of these values, it is very difficult to develop a critical perspective towards neo-liberalism or the prevailing norms in the new economy. Conversely, the development of such values brings a greater individual maturity, a maturity that makes it possible, for instance, to question government statements on issues such as the war in Iraq.

Conservative versus progressive values

A number of features of work in the new economy lead to a propensity for more individualistic attitudes than are found in Fordist work cultures: salaries and working conditions are negotiated individually; there are extremely high rates of job turnover and movement between firms; and there is a strong emphasis on the importance of personal values and attitudes in this sector. This seems especially to be the case in the software and internet sectors; rather less so in the multimedia sector. It is more prevalent in smaller firms, grappling daily with the hyper-competitive pressures of the market, than in large firms that are global players, where the corporate culture and more regulated work relations often create a feeling of a 'corporate community' which goes beyond the 'plot mentality' of the small, family-like firms.

This individualism, however, is quite unlike the purely individualistic attitudes described in the methodological literature, neoclassical economic models or concepts of liberal citizenship. It coexists with other elements that push towards solidarity which seem to force their way through. Organic attitudes are only one, politically conservative, example of this. One reason for this is that the objective reality of work in the sector is too heavily based on teamwork, social interchange and day-to-day interdependence. Absolute individualistic and competitive attitudes or values that are simply anti-collectivist (in the sense of Walter Lippmann, 1955) are therefore neither functional nor desired by anybody, including the management, since they often go against efficiency, health, organic firm cultures and common sense. An example of this apparently contradictory value trend is the difficulty companies experience in developing coherent incentive policies. On the one hand, they need to establish bonuses for all the employees of the firm linked to global performance because work is more and more collective and impossible to fragment into individual performance achievements. On the other hand, they also want to ensure that there are individual incentives in order to maximise individual performance. Such contradictions are not easily resolved (A2).

But there are also other, more progressive anti-individualistic elements emerging. Spanish and Mediterranean societies contain strong elements of a collectivistic culture that transcends ideological differences and does not exist in the same way in northern and western Europe. There are close interconnections between personal and non-personal relationships and between individual and communal causes and life experiences, even within the competitive new economy sector, especially, and precisely in those firms whose cultures are the least directly linked to multinationals, global players and the 'American style' (B3), in other words in the (mainly Spanish) small and medium sized firms. To those in the transplanted and so-called 'modern management cultures' linked to the core of the neo-liberal culture, trans-national capital and 'one best way' practitioners, such attitudes are 'not very professional'. But the fact is they are one of the bedrocks of the Spanish competitiveness model because they generate considerable flexibility and are very prevalent both at work and within the social system surrounding work (family, friendship and so on). It is therefore not uncommon to see employees not only working well together, helping each other with computer problems outside working hours and sharing 'soft working times', but also co-operating to organise night life, vacations and parties together (A1, B1, B4, C1).

'At work we all share a lot of knowledge among ourselves but not so much with the bosses. There are a lot of email lists, all the time you are asking your work mates questions;, they tell you their opinion, and you do the same. There is a lot of mutual help; the sharing of knowledge is constant. This is very motivating and creates a good atmosphere.' (B4)

This explains why all the interviewees considered the atmosphere to be good or very good where they worked (A1, A2, B4, C1, C2) even though they all also admitted that the stress was enormous. When the atmosphere is regarded as less good (as for B3) this is attributed to the 'narrow-minded' and 'yokel' atmosphere related to a culture dominated by employees with non diversified interests. In a significant number of cases, personal relationships developed at work even lead to engagement and marriage.

What we observe here seems to have not only elements of a traditional way of living and working together based on collectivist values but also a way of life that is distinctively post-Fordist, an expression of a youth culture resulting from the low average age of employees in the sector. Individual attitudes and identities are formed with reference to the peer group, hierarchies are not accepted between people of the same age (although they are when there is an age difference), and there is shared curiosity about discoveries involving complicity within the 'gang', whose members are perceived very differently from 'outsiders'.

> 'When you keep yourself apart from the group and, for example, you do not join in
> a card game, they look at you with mistrust. This means that there is an im-
> plicit drift to come together even outside work. Nevertheless, everybody is
> very discreet about what they earn. In fact they are nice people, but when I
> decide not to go with them, what I want is to have more time for myself, to
> develop other interests and cultivate other relationships outside work...Now
> I am working on a translation of the Communist Manifesto of Karl Marx, I
> am taking out all these horrible Latin American expressions nobody really
> understands; I am looking for examples from our time to explain its meaning
> and so on. I also want to separate those elements, which are not valid any
> more from those which are still very real.' (D2)

The spontaneous rejection of individualistic attitudes does not mean at all that younger people tend, for example, to organise themselves collectively to defend their interests or that they are automatically progressive, anti-war or against neo-liberalism, although it is likely that they could very well become so if political organisations and trade unions manage to find a formula for interesting them in a more intense engagement. It just means that the traditional dialectics of collectivism versus individualism are not suitable for defining their position. Such concepts can even can generate confusion if they are applied in the traditional way to political values following the script that collective values are supposed to be progressive in and of themselves themselves whilst individual values are intrinsically conservative. It is this sort of confusion that led to Stephan Hermlin's misunderstanding of the Communist Manifesto along with thousands more socialists like him in the 20th century. The reality is far more complex than this, and probably always was. individualistic values can be associated not only with more progressive attitudes but also with more conservative ones and *vice versa*.

As an alternative to the simple terms 'individualistic' and 'collectivist' values, it seems more accurate to make internal differences within both categories, or, as in this case, to oppose 'personal' attitudes to more 'organic' ones. The first of these concepts can be related to what we can call 'new versions of progressive values' and the second to 'new versions of conservative values' (neo-liberal hegemony). To be more personally oriented and to have more diversified interests can mean being more idealistic,

The spark in the engine: creative workers in a global economy

having a preference for content over form, being less utilitarian and having less consumerist attitudes (Stiglitz, 2003:118). These can contribute to the development of a modern, progressive, anti neo-liberal or altermondialist[6] culture and value system.

© *Armando Fernández Steinko, 2006*

REFERENCES

Bouffartigue, P. (2004) 'Ouvertures', Bouffartigue, P. (ed.) *Le retour des classes socials. Inégalités, dominations, conflits*, Paris: La Dispute

Fernández Steinko, A. (2004) *Clase, trabajo y ciudadanía. Introducción a la existencia social*, Madrid: Biblioteca Nueva

Hermlin, S. (1979) *Abendlicht*, Leipzig: Reklam Verlag:23

Lippmann, W. (1955) *Essays in the public philosophy*, Boston: Little Brown

Marcuse, H. (1964) *One-Dimensional Man: Studies in the Ideology of Advanced Industrial Society*, Boston: Beacon

Stiglitz, J. (2003) *The Roaring Nineties. A New History of the World's Most Prosperous Decade*, Spanish Edition, Madrid: Taurus

ACKNOWLEDGEMENTS

This paper was published in French as Fernández Steinko, A. (2006) 'Valeurs des Employès Espagnols de la Nouvelle Economie: Repenser les Valeurs Conservatrices et Progressives' in Cojleine J. (ed) *Nouvelles Luttes des Classes*, Paris: Presses Universitaires de France.

---

6   The term 'altermondialiste' was developed in France as a preferable alternative to 'anti-globalisation' in order to distinguish demands for an alternative form of globalisation based on democratic values from more reactionary and xenophobic anti-globalisation demands.

Divided they stand:

Hollywood unions in the information age

Catherine McKercher
Vincent Mosco

Catherine McKercher is Associate Professor in the School of Journalism and Communication at Carleton University in Ottawa, Ontario, Canada.
Vincent Mosco is Canada Research Chair and Professor of Sociology at Queen's University in Kingston, Ontario, Canada.

ABSTRACT

In an effort to increase labour power, trade unions representing communications and creative workers in North America have pursued a form of convergence, merging with each other and restructuring themselves along similar lines to their employers. This paper examines the issues surrounding labour convergence by taking up the failed merger between the Screen Actors Guild and the American Federation of Television and Radio Artists. It finds that, although the leaders of both unions supported the merger, the particular characteristics of the unions, including their culture, sense of craft identity and the lived experience of members, derailed the effort.

Research has demonstrated the importance of information and communication labour in the modern economy (Dyer-Witheford, 1999; Huws, 2003; Terranova, 2004). In an era characterised by declining trade union penetration, increasing corporate concentration, and the rise of global conglomerates that feed into – and are fed by – the spread of new communication and information technologies, North American knowledge workers have begun to explore new ways to increase the power of labour. This is especially the case in the communication sector, which provides the equipment that makes globalisation possible and the production and distribution of the ideas that make it work.

One approach is to pursue trade union mergers, designed strategically to restructure labour unions along much the same lines as the corporations that employ their members. Convergent unions like the Communications Workers of America (CWA) or the Communications, Energy and Paperworkers Union of Canada (CEP) bring together workers in what were once independent industries – newspapers, telecommunications, sound recording, broadcasting – but are now part of cross-media conglomerates. These unions also recognise that it's not just the boundaries between employers that have become less distinct; the boundaries between what were once distinct forms of work have also been blurred through the spread of digital technology. Labour convergence, therefore, is seen as an appropriate response to technological and corporate convergence (Bahr, 1998; McKercher, 2002; Swift, 2003). A second approach is to create non-traditional worker organisations, which draw into the labour movement people who cannot or will not join a traditional trade union. Such groups provide a range of services and supports for workers, their families or their communities but do not engage in collective bargaining. In North America, they are particularly prominent in the high-technology area (Kline, Dyer-Witheford and de Peuter, 2003; Stone, 2004; Van Jaarsveld, 2004).

This paper focuses on the issue of trade union convergence and specifically takes up this question: why would two unions facing an increasingly concentrated set of employers in the film and media industries decide not to merge? To answer this question, we draw on interviews with key participants and access to primary documentation to provide a detailed case study of the failed merger between the Screen Actors Guild (SAG) and the American Federation of Television and Radio Artists (AFTRA). The case is instructive for a variety of reasons. First, there is considerable research on the value of merger or convergence among trade unions, including in the communication and information industries (Batstone, 1984; Katz, 1997; Stone, 2004). It is important to examine through a detailed case study why such convergence may not be attractive to workers. Second, whilst unions are often viewed as bureaucratic institutions which make merger decisions based largely on the basis of a cost-benefit analysis (Chaison, 1986), this case vividly demonstrates that unions are also political institutions with at least formal democratic procedures that may significantly influence decisions about mergers. Specifically, while a merger might help SAG and AFTRA deal with media conglomerates, it might also mean that members would have to give up some of their influence over union decisions simply because the union has grown larger. Trade unions are also cultural institutions and the distinctive cultures associated with a self-consciously guild-oriented group of film workers (SAG) and a union-oriented organisation of workers who come out of a broadcasting tradition (AFTRA) also matter. Finally, the story of these two unions provides important lessons for those who would see a natural path to unity among knowledge and cultural workers (Terranova, 2004). Unity is not a given simply because workers produce the same product, i.e., digital content. If a merger cannot succeed in a highly concentrated industry between two unions that share a substantial portion of their membership, then perhaps the road to unity among workers in the network society may not be as clear as some would contend. With that said, our conclusions, based on one case study, cannot be definitive. However, they do raise questions that need to be considered in knowledge worker theory, research on the cultural industry workforce and studies of union mergers generally.

Those who support trade union convergence argue that it stands to benefit the labour movement, though it is not without problems (Swift, 2003). It is difficult, for example, to see what a news reporter has in common with a telephone operator, yet both could theoretically be accommodated by a single, amalgamated communication workers' union. Workers in the converging communications industries are increasingly involved in knowledge labour that requires similar sets of skills and training. And while specific differences among jobs exist, these are eroding as knowledge workers go through similar processes of deskilling and reskilling, and often deskilling again, and face similar challenges such as the outsourcing of their work (Mosco, 2005). Convergence enables previously independent unions to pool resources to concentrate on different struggles as they arise. It was vital in the 2005 fight by the Canadian Media Guild against the Canadian national public broadcaster, the Canadian Broadcasting Corporation (CBC), which locked out its workers for nearly two months in a failed effort to gain the unlimited right to hire temporary workers. The Canadian Media Guild is a branch of the Washington-based Communications Workers of America (CWA), a cross-border form of convergent unionism, and, following a bargaining unit consolidation ordered by the Canadian labour board, its CBC unit contains both on-air and technical employees. During the lockout at CBC, journalists and technicians came together as never before. Their convergent union marshalled resources and talent to mobilise a degree of national support that surprised CBC management and many analysts. With the financial backing of the CWA, workers could afford to stay out longer. In addition to paying for half the strike pay and all the supplementary health benefits of locked-out workers, the CWA used its international networks to mobilise a pressure campaign that directed messages from media workers throughout the world to CBC management and the Canadian federal government. It also organised demonstrations at Canadian embassies in Washington, London and other power centres.

Convergence permits unions to speak with a voice that spans entire industries to get at the heart of central policy issues, as White concludes in a report for the Canadian Centre for Policy Alternatives on 'Losing Canadian Culture: The Danger of Foreign Ownership of Telecom' (White, 2005). Convergence also allows unions to work co-operatively as never before. In the United States the AFL-CIO recently threw its support behind a form of convergent unionism in the cultural sector by setting up an industry co-ordinating committee made up of ten unions covering the arts, entertainment, media and telecommunications industries. The committee's goal is to build labour power in industries that have been rocked by corporate concentration and technological change. It is worth noting that this action is also a response to the largest defection in the history of the federation, which occurred in 2005 when unions representing six million workers chose to leave and join the new Change to Win labour federation. Convergence, therefore, may also be a response to the failure of an organisation to maintain its membership.

While labour convergence has had its successes, there have been failures too. This paper tells the story of an unsuccessful attempt at creating a converged union of cultural workers in Hollywood, the heart of the US entertainment industry and still – despite challenges from Bollywood and other production centres – the film capital of the world. Unification has long been on the agenda of both the Screen Actors Guild (SAG) and the American Federation of Television and Radio Artists (AFTRA). In 1998, the two finally struck a deal and sent it to members for ratification. AFTRA's members endorsed it; SAG's did not. Five years later they tried again, with a new and different merger agreement. Again, AFTRA's members said yes, this time by a larger margin. So did a majority of SAG members. However, because the SAG vote fell short of the 60 per cent threshold required by both unions' constitutions for ratification, the merger was defeated. Says Mathis L. Dunn Jr., the Assistant National Executive Director of AFTRA,

'Had we been playing horse shoes or hand grenades, it would have been good enough. But that's not the case' (interview with the authors, February 2006).

Despite majority support in both unions for the idea of unity, achieving labour convergence is no easy task. Chaison (1986) argues that trade union mergers occur when the incentives to unite outweigh the drawbacks of uniting. In this case, the incentives were clear: a merger would have put the unions in a stronger position to deal with the challenges of new technology and of an increasingly concentrated media industry. It would have eliminated the need for film, television and commercial actors to pay dues to two unions. It would also have streamlined the bureaucracy and ended the potential for employers to play one union off against the other. But trade union mergers are not simply a matter of calculating benefits and drawbacks (McKercher, 2002). Unions are political institutions, with their own governing and dues structures, bureaucracies, histories and, especially, their own cultures. Unlike the corporate mergers that have transformed the communications sector in North America in recent decades, labour union mergers require the approval of the full range of players in each potential partner: the elected leadership, the staff who have day-to-day contact with the membership, and the rank and file members. The fact that potential merger partners often have a shared history of competition and conflict as well as co-operation complicates matters for trade unions. As a result, mergers between labour unions are often more like the unification of rival states than they are like corporate mergers.

This paper shows that in the case of SAG and AFTRA, the particular characteristics of the unions, including their history, culture, sense of craft identity and the lived experience of members, derailed the unity effort. We conclude that the failure to merge has had consequences for how Hollywood's cultural workers deal with a range of issues, from new technology to global production.

A tale of two unions

If ever a compelling argument could be made for a union merger, it is the case of the Screen Actors Guild and AFTRA. These unions represent workers in the same industry, doing the same work, often under identical contracts. Between them, they represent the elite of creative workers in the United States. While AFTRA covers a broader range of workers – sound recording artists, radio and television journalists, performers in soap operas, talk shows, reality shows and game shows – film, television and commercial actors are the core constituency of both unions. Roughly 44,000 actors belong to both unions, which means 40 per cent of SAG's 120,000 members belong to AFTRA, and 60 per cent of AFTRA's 70,000 members belong to SAG. Since the early 1980s, under an agreement optimistically called 'Phase One of Merger'[1], they have bargained jointly on their major national contracts with employers in the advertising and entertainment industries.

These unions did not start out as overlapping entities. Originally, they represented distinct groups of workers in distinctly different industries, working on opposite coasts of the United States. What pushed them together was a combination of new technologies and corporate concentration, a combination that continues to blur the lines that separate them today.

---

1 Phase Two was to be the creation of a new governing structure. Phase Three would have brought together the unions' health and pension funds (Prindle, p. 138).

The Screen Actors Guild was founded in Los Angeles in 1933[2]. Right from the beginning, SAG was different from a standard trade union. To get around the possibility of individual members being held financially liable for collective action – a quirk of US. law that would change with the New Deal – it was set up as a corporation (Prindle 1988:22). This meant that SAG was a centralised organisation, run by a board of directors that would be elected by the full membership and would serve without salary. Voting membership in the union was limited to working actors. One of the unusual features in SAG's constitution was a requirement that strike votes had to be approved by a margin of 75 per cent. This bylaw continues to be in effect today (Constitution, 2003).

The American Federation of Radio Artists (AFRA) was founded in 1937 in New York, home of the US radio industry. AFRA's constitution vested power in local bodies, which elected their own boards and chose representatives to the national board. In this respect, it was much more like a traditional North American trade union than SAG. Both unions belonged to the Associated Actors and Artistes of America (AAAA), the American Federation of Labor's umbrella organisation for performers' unions. Performance was the common denominator of the two unions, but their jurisdictions were clearly and sharply delineated. Performing on radio was AFRA work[3]; acting before the cameras for later projection on a screen was SAG work. Actors who wanted to perform on both radio and film had to join both unions, and many did[4].

When the radio networks expanded into new technology – television – the neat divisions began to break down. AFRA saw television as an extension of radio, and in terms of corporate ownership, the geographical location of the industry, and the way shows were produced and broadcast, that was certainly the case. It found allies in other New York-based performers' unions – representing theatre actors, singers, variety artists and musicians – who formed the Television Authority (TVA) and joined with AFRA in an effort to co-ordinate labour's response to the new technology. But television also meant projecting moving images on a screen, and therefore it held the potential for showing filmed programs. Film work was SAG work.

As television burst into North American homes after the end of the Second World War, the two unions wrangled over jurisdiction. In 1950, the AAAA awarded jurisdiction over television to AFRA (Prindle 1998, p76). SAG fought back, appealing to the federal labour regulator for certification elections to allow performers to decide for themselves which union should represent them. SAG won all but one of these elections and in 1952 AAAA gave up its attempt to create one big television union. SAG won the right to represent actors in filmed television programs. AFRA was given jurisdiction over live television. It merged with TVA and changed its name to AFTRA to reflect its expanded jurisdiction.

---

2   It was not the first union in Hollywood – the Screen Writers Guild appeared a few months earlier – nor was it the first to attempt to organise film actors. Actors Equity, the New York-based theatrical workers union, ran an unsuccessful recognition strike in 1929 ('The history of SAG', www.sag.org).
3   Radio was live work. In 1941 AFRA asserted jurisdiction over radio transcriptions, or recorded performances that could be broadcast later.
4   Indeed, Eddie Cantor, SAG's president from 1933 to 1935, became the first national president of AFRA two years later. Cantor began his career in vaudeville and starred on Broadway, in motion pictures and on radio.

Over the next three decades, this division began to break down. The television business migrated west, from AFTRA's New York base to SAG's home ground in Los Angeles. Evolving technologies like videotape – which allowed for productions that were neither live nor on film – created confusion over jurisdiction. Television's ability to reuse material by showing theatrical films or broadcasting reruns of programs launched the unions on long and costly fights for what are called 'residual payments' for members. Meanwhile, actors complained about having to pay dues to two unions for doing essentially the same work. Writes Prindle, 'Periodically, the notion of eliminating the tangle of jurisdiction by merging all screen actors into one union would gain favor. SAG and AFTRA would consult about it and hire a professional researcher to do a study, there would be a good deal of argument back and forth, and after a while the impulse would peter out' (Prindle 1998:77).

By the early 1980s, however, the talk had become much more purposeful. Merger discussions were promoted in large part by the introduction of cable television and the videocassette recorder, which threatened both the movie theatre business and conventional network television and put the residuals question back on the table. SAG still had jurisdiction over film and AFTRA over live performance and over tape. But these distinctions became less and less significant, and there were instances when a producer's decision to change studios – moving a television series from a facility that shot on film to one that shot on videotape, for example – meant changing unions (Prindle 1998:125). Because the unions had separate contracts, producers could use one against the other.

In 1981, the unions took a significant step toward uniting by signing the Phase One of Merger agreement that allowed them to jointly negotiate and ratify all major film and television contracts. Phase Two of Merger – bringing together governance of the two unions – never appeared. Instead, it became the victim of an internal struggle at SAG.

Not only does SAG have an unusual structure for a North American trade union, it also has an unusual political history. This is a union, after all, whose past presidents include the arch-conservative Charlton Heston and the radical Ed Asner – not to mention Ronald Reagan, the only trade union president ever to serve as president of the United States. From its earliest days, SAG has had both progressive and conservative elements. Indeed, the decision to call itself a 'guild' reflected the fact that many of the more conservative founding members felt uncomfortable about joining a union[5]. For its first four decades, conservatives dominated the SAG board, though the struggle between progressive and conservative actors provided a 'constant but muted' undercurrent in SAG politics (Prindle 1998:8).

The split between left and right is not the only fault-line in the union, however. There have also been tensions between the Hollywood, New York and regional divi-

---

5   The use of the word Guild was a popular choice among cultural workers in the US. It harked back to the artisans' associations of the mediaeval era, rather than to the factory-based trade union movements of the 19th and early 20th centuries. A guild could be seen as a professional association, and the name suggested exclusivity. In choosing the title of their organisation, the actors took their cue from the Screen Writers Guild. A few years later, the directors chose the name Screen Directors Guild, keeping the designation when they later changed their name to the Directors Guild of America. The union representing US newspaper journalists made the same choice, naming their organisation the American Newspaper Guild. Within a few years, however, it became a fully-fledged industrial union, seeking to represent a broad range of workers in the newspaper industry.

sions, and between people who want to make their living as actors and people who see acting as a side line (and SAG membership as a status symbol). In addition, the income structure of SAG members is wildly skewed. Elite members earn millions of dollars per film, while the majority struggle to make ends meet. At any one time more than 80 per cent of SAG members are unemployed.

Since the 1980s, SAG has developed a de facto party system, an extremely rare feature in North American trade unions[6]. It is not a formal or institutionalised party system, in that the names (and at times the composition) of the parties change depending on the issue grabbing their attention, or on the views of the caucus of members promoting or contesting a particular issue. Competing slates of candidates for national office have become a regular feature in SAG elections. And this has had an enormous impact on attempts to merge with AFTRA.

In 1980 a group known as the Caucus of Artists for Merger, upset with the leaders of both unions and angry over what they saw as a botched strike that year, set out to gain power and influence on both the SAG and AFTRA governing structures, hoping to use that platform to bring about a merger. They won control of AFTRA's Los Angeles local the next spring, persuaded the well-known television actor Ed Asner to run for president of SAG a few months later, and in that year's election took control of the SAG board. Their hopes for a speedy merger were derailed by the creation of a conservative coalition, Actors Working for an Actor's Guild, whose members objected to Asner's radicalism in particular, and to the direction in which SAG was heading in general. The two factions tore at each other for much of the decade, ultimately sidelining the AFTRA merger talks in 1988[7].

In the early 1990s, the unions decided to try again, going at things more slowly but also more steadily. Finally, in 1998, they made a deal. The agreement called for a full merger of the two unions into a new bod, to be called SAG/AFTRA, whose structure would reflect the traditions of both unions. It would have a strong national board of directors (a SAG feature) and 30 semi-autonomous locals (an AFTRA feature). The new union would have a new dues structure, but the two unions' health and pension plans would remain separate (Robb, 1999a). In promoting the merger to their members, the leaders of SAG and AFTRA argued that the merger would end jurisdictional disputes between the two unions, including a looming battle with the media conglomerates over revenues from high-definition television. It would also streamline operations and give the union more power at the bargaining table.

The merger agreement provoked a strong and vigorous reaction under the banner of a group called Save SAG. This largely conservative opposition group, a faction of a broader coalition known as the Performers Alliance, dismissed the prospect of a jurisdictional dispute as a scare tactic. The group also objected to the idea that dues would increase after the merger, and questioned the decision on health and pension plans. But

---

6   Another communications union, the International Typographical Union which represented printers, was the only other North American trade union with an institutionalised two-party system (See Lipset et al., 1956).

7   The SAG-AFTRA merger effort was knocked off the agenda by a vicious fight over a tangentially related merger between SAG and the Screen Extras Guild, which was to be a prelude to the larger merger with AFTRA. That deal was rejected by the SAG membership twice, the second time more decisively than the first (Prindle).

perhaps the biggest success of the Performers Alliance was in convincing SAG members to embrace a narrow, craft-based view of trade unionism – to choose the 'purity of an actors' union rather than merging into a union with broadcasters and musicians' (Cooper, 2001).

Ballots went out to members in November 1998, with polls closing in January 1999. Both unions' constitutions require a merger vote to pass by a margin of 60 per cent. When the votes were tallied, 67.6 per cent of AFTRA voters supported the merger but only 46.5 per cent of SAG members voted for it (Kiefer, 2003; Robb, 1999).

Soon after, SAG went through another period of political turmoil. Its pro-merger president, Richard Masur, was replaced by the conservative William Daniels, who promised to get tough with the employers and presided over a divisive and combative two-year term that included the longest strike in the union's history, the six-month SAG/AFTRA commercials strike in 2000. Assessments a year later suggested that SAG's hard-line approach prolonged the dispute unnecessarily (Cooper, 2001). Daniels decided not to seek re-election in 2001, throwing his support to Valerie Harper. She lost the election to Melissa Gilbert, but the result was nullified because of balloting irregularities. Gilbert won the rerun election. A moderate, Gilbert headed a coalition known as Restore Respect, whose platform included support for a merger with AFTRA. Negotiations were on again, and in 2003 they resulted in a new agreement.

This deal, based on a set of principles drawn up by a joint committee of the two unions, tried to avoid some of the stumbling blocks that tripped up the previous merger. To recognise that SAG members didn't want to lose their identity or their traditions, the deal proposed an affiliation rather than a full merger. The new organisation would be called the Alliance of International Media Artists. It would have three autonomous, self-governing affiliates: SAG, covering actors; AFTRA, covering broadcasters; and the American Federation of Recording Artists, covering singers and recording artists. Each affiliate would have its own board and officers. Again, the health and pension plans would remain separate, but the trustees of both would look into the possibility of consolidating them (Connell, 2003; Kiefer, 2003).

In announcing the details of its consolidation plan to members, AFTRA's Magazine pointed out that one of the 'common perceptions' in the 1999 merger result was that there was 'no imminent or compelling need to take action ' (Winter 2003:5). This time, it argued, things were different:

'The emergence of digital production has rapidly escalated the jurisdictional conflict. This serves to: 1. Drive down terms and conditions for performers. 2. Divert resources from critical union initiatives ' (Winter 2003:5).

If new technology was a compelling factor in favour of a merger, so was industry consolidation. The same issue of the magazine summarised the changes: the number of major employers of performers and broadcasters had declined from 26 in 1985 to six, five of them in the television and motion picture industry; eight studios controlled 88 per cent of all domestic theatrical production and distribution; five record companies controlled 84 per cent of the recording industry; cable revenues increased from $5 billion in 1990 to $35 billion in 2002, and the cable market was controlled by five companies; two cable system owners, AT&T and Time Warner, accounted for 40 per cent of all cable households; two companies owned more than 1,400 radio stations and one, Clear Channel, was comprised of what used to be 70 separate companies. The magazine put it this way:

'While AFTRA and SAG have been thinking about consolidating, our employers have actually done it. The industry already has consolidated' (Winter 2003:4).

As with the previous merger vote, the campaign was heated. A reinvigorated Save SAG argued that the plan would result in a loss of direct fiscal control over SAG's budget, and that the actors' union would be reduced to a 'glorified committee' of a larger union (Kiefer, 2003). In an interview with the *New York Times*, former SAG president Daniels brusquely dismissed the idea that a merger would make SAG stronger:

'AFTRA is a crummy little union, and they're undercutting our contracts, so we should join them? To us it's a very, very bad deal' (quoted by Connell, 2003).

The opponents also made much of the uncertainty about the future of the pension and health plans (Connell, 2003) – a tactic that frustrated members of the committee that negotiated the deal. Matt Kimbrough, AFTRA's National Recording Secretary, explains that because the plans were created and governed separately from the unions,

'you couldn't even begin the process of merging the plans until you actually merged the unions.' (interview with the authors, 2006).

But this meant that merger advocates could not offer clear answers to questions about what the merger would mean for actors' pensions, a situation that opponents to the merger used to fan actors' fears about the future.

The voting took place in the summer of 2003. AFTRA members overwhelmingly endorsed the merger, with 75.8 per cent of votes in favour. At SAG, the deal lost by a hair. The merger needed 60 per cent of votes to pass; it got 57.8 per cent (Kiefer, 2003).

Pamm Fair, the Deputy National Executive Director of SAG, says post-election polling of SAG members found that the vast majority wanted a merger; 'they just didn't like that plan'. They also objected to the idea that the new union would have a different name.

'Our people said, "What, are you crazy? We have worldwide branding with the name we have now. Why would you think about changing it?" The pension and health care issue also resonated with members, especially since SAG's plans are comparatively healthier – and less expensive for members – than AFTRA's.' (interview with the authors, February 2006).

Kimbrough, who is also a member of SAG, says that the opponents of the merger came up with a short and simple slogan to sink the deal: 'If you don't know, vote no'. It worked brilliantly.

'The members were sold on the notion that if you vote no now, there's going to be another vote later, when there was never any intention from the people trying to defeat it that there should be a merger agreement.' (interview with the authors, 2006)

He agreed that the name of the new organisation was an issue, as it had been in 1998. Hollywood is, after all, SAG's town, and the SAG name is known throughout the world. Kimbrough says that if two sides had simply agreed to call the new union SAG, the merger might have passed. But that would have been unacceptable to AFTRA, since it would imply an absorption by another union. Leslie Simon, Director of Legislative and Public Affairs for AFTRA's Los Angeles local, adds another reason for the failed merger:

'Fundamentally, there was a lack of recognition of how the industry has changed, of why it is that two unions are no longer acceptable and no longer can do the job for actors.' (interview with the authors, 2006)

Finally, as in 1999, the pro-merger side was unable to overcome the opponents' appeal to craft solidarity: the notion that actors are artists who shouldn't be co-mingled in a union with broadcast journalists or musicians. Ron Morgan, President of AFTRA's Los Angeles local and a SAG member as well, says this argument was strictly an emotional one. But when all was said and done it 'resonated stronger than anything else' (interview with the authors, 2006).

Divided they stand

After the merger was defeated, each union had to chart a new course based on maintaining the status quo of two unions rather than the synergy of one. SAG elected a new president, Alan Rosenberg, whose Membership First coalition currently holds a majority on the national board (Armbrust, 2005). Rosenberg opposed the AFTRA merger; instead, he would prefer to see all actors come to SAG. Rosenberg is a political liberal who was an anti-war activist during the Vietnam War, has worked in the civil rights movement and is an advocate for social justice. He pledges – as did the conservative Daniels – to get tough with the employers. He told the *Los Angeles Times:*

'Until now, the studios have looked at how fractured we are as a union and haven't taken us very seriously. So my philosophy is that we have to take an adversarial position and stand strong and never leave the negotiating table until we make progress and prevail.' (quoted in Goldstein, 2005)

Since taking office, Rosenberg has presided over the firing of the union's executive director, who had been a key player in negotiating the failed AFTRA merger. He has also begun to work more closely with two other Hollywood unions that have fought their own internal battles: the Writers Guild of America and the Directors Guild of America.

'If we could present a united front with the WGA and the DGA, we'd be a lot stronger…Since late 2005, for example, the writers' and actors' guilds have been campaigning together for tougher rules on product placement, which the unions see as "stealth advertising".' (ibid)

Following the failed merger, AFTRA undertook a major restructuring. It plans to move its national headquarters from New York to Los Angeles, home of its largest local. It has also embarked on a series of structural changes – reducing the size of its executive board, for example – that are aimed at cutting costs, reducing its deficit and increasing its revenue (AFTRA Magazine 2004-05; Horwitch, 2005).

Both unions continue to work together on contract negotiations. This included successful negotiations in 2005 on a contract covering voiceover actors featured in video games, an area that is not included in the 1981 agreement on joint bargaining. Both are also active in the formation of the AFL-CIO's new industry co-ordinating committee, which covers unions in the arts, entertainment, media and telecommunications industries (AFL-CIO 2005; Eggerton 2005). The federation says that the council's goal is to build more power for workers by undertaking collaborative initiatives in four areas: organising, collective bargaining, contract standards and public policy. Pamm Fair of SAG, who works on policy and strategic planning, says she hopes the committee will serve as an arbitrator for jurisdictional problems that may come along. Kimbrough says that AFTRA is hoping to play a pivotal role in the creation of the council and is keen to see it succeed. But he is not certain about SAG's commitment to the idea. 'Right now I think that in a lot of these questions, the Guild is a wild card', he says.

Clearly, the unions have shown that it is possible to continue to work closely together despite the disappointment of the 2003 merger vote. But it is also clear that the failure to unite has created problems for both unions. Perhaps the most significant is the fact that they now find themselves competing over new digital technologies. A host of new devices and media have arrived since the last merger vote – podcasts, satellite radio, ipods with video screens, interactive blogs, cell phones with video and so on. These devices have all but obliterated the lines between various types of performance, and pose the most serious challenge yet to jurisdictional divisions. In January 2006, AFTRA president John Connolly set out his union's stance on digital technology, recording a podcast to do so:

'This message [is] an acknowledgement of AFTRA's readiness and resolve to organise the digital markets of the 21st century – proof positive that AFTRA is the future in media.' (AFTRA, 4 January 2006)

Shortly after that, the union announced that two new prime-time series shot in digital format were under AFTRA contract (Miller 2006). Because SAG also claims that its contracts cover digital production, this means the two unions are now competing for digital work. Both are aware that competition tends to benefit the employers rather than the workers. As AFTRA's Kimbrough puts it,

'The only way a union competes with another union for a job is to offer the producers a better deal. That's a hard truth and it's not good for the members'. But each union feels it has no choice.' (interview with the authors, 2006)

Another area where the failure to merge is likely to have consequences is in the campaign against what Hollywood likes to call 'runaway production' – the production of films and television shows in lower-cost, incentive-rich, non-Hollywood locales like Canada. SAG's approach has been to build a series of coalitions to address the issue in a number of ways. With the Directors Guild, it commissioned a ground-breaking economic analysis of the problem. It then helped the Directors Guild create a 19-member coalition known as the Runaway Production Alliance to fight for federal and state legislation to subsidise domestic film production. The alliance includes not just trade unions, but also professional and trade organisations, as well as groups representing marketers, distributors, promoters, talent agents and musicians – anyone in Hollywood with a stake in the issue. SAG has also extended its jurisdiction beyond the US border through its Global Rule One campaign, which says that SAG members can only work for producers who sign SAG agreements, regardless of where they film. AFTRA has been very much onside in this campaign, participating in the Runaway Production Alliance and issuing public statements in support of Global Rule One. Though they may be effective, informal coalitions are, however, inherently unstable. They work only as long as they meet the self-interest of the individual members. Kimbrough says that AFTRA is considering whether to continue the lobbying effort against runaway production at the same level because it is not that sure that it is worth the time, money and effort. He explains,

'We've spent a considerable amount of energy and capital in support of these bills,
and that has gravitated to the benefit largely of the Screen Actors Guild.
There has not been a terrific amount of growth in AFTRA work as a result of
these bills.' (interview with the authors, 2006)

Meanwhile, SAG is thinking about ramping up its fight. Its board voted in late 2005
to support a coalition of other unions that have been exploring the idea of launching
a complaint with the US trade representative office against Canadian film subsidies.
This would seek to have Canada's subsidies declared a violation of trade agreements.
Fair says SAG has not committed any funding to the initiative, but is helping with legal
research. AFTRA, by contrast, has no interest in the trade case. Says Kimberley,

'Politically we have voted it down every time it comes up in our boardroom. We
regard it as counter-productive.' (interview with the authors, 2006)

Ron Morgan, the president of AFTRA's Los Angeles local, says that focusing too much attention on runaway production misses the larger issue: confronting Hollywood unions.

'The real runaway production issue, to me, is not that the work is going to Canada, but
that it's going non-union. That's runaway production as far as I'm concerned.'
(interview with the authors, 2006)

Conclusion: going it alone in the age of convergence

If Morgan is right, the solution to the problem of the increase in non-union work is to
capture – or in some cases, recapture – the work. And this is where labour convergence
may play a critical role. We began this paper by suggesting that the twin challenges of
new technology and corporate concentration are prompting worker organisations to
explore new ways of increasing labour power. Few places offer as vivid an example of
both phenomena as Hollywood. Between them, corporate consolidation and technological convergence have undermined existing union jurisdiction, opened up new areas of
non-unionised work and tipped the balance between labour and management sharply
in favour of the employers. A merger between SAG and AFTRA would have helped the
members of both unions. It would have ended the competition for work between SAG
and AFTRA, a competition that chiefly benefits the employers. Individual actors would
pay only one set of dues, not two. The organisation resulting from the merger would be
simultaneously more united and, with AFTRA's non-acting membership, more diverse.
In short, the new union would have been more like a convergent union than a craft
union. The kind of craft-centred toughness displayed by the current leadership of SAG
can be effective in protecting a position, especially in the short term.

As this paper has shown, however, by rejecting AFTRA – twice – the Guild has lost
an opportunity to solidify its relationship with its closest ally. As a result, two unions
that are each other's best colleague find themselves having to devote resources to
competing with each other, all the while knowing that those resources might better be
spent promoting their joint interests. For those opposed to the merger – a minority
at SAG, but a large enough one to determine the outcome of the vote in 2003 – this
is a small price to pay for retaining political and cultural independence. The current
leadership of SAG believes its members will be better off because it is taking a tougher

political stance against the industry and those in Washington who support the industry. Moreover, the status quo preserves the independent guild culture of SAG, a culture deeply rooted in the history of a labour organisation that has struggled with seeing itself as a trade union. All this questions the perceived commonalities among communication workers that purportedly make them easier to organise and mobilise.

At this point, neither side is talking about taking another run at a merger. Both are committed to working side-by-side on contract negotiations, and on the AFL-CIO's industry co-ordinating committee for the media and telecommunications sectors. In the longer term, shoring up their mutual relationship while building strong bridges to other cultural worker organisations, in Hollywood and beyond, may be critical to whether they thrive or merely survive.

© *Catherine McKercher and Vincent Mosco, 2006*

REFERENCES

AFL-CIO (2005), 'AFL-CIO Executive Council Announces Formation of First Industry Co-ordinating Committee Covering the Arts, Entertainment, Media and Telecommunications Industries', News Release, Washington, 6 Oct

AFTRA (2004) 'AFTRA Board Approves Sweeping Overhaul of Union's Structure', News release posted on www.aftra.org 10 July. Accessed 16 March 2006

AFTRA (2003) 'AFTRA consolidation plan', AFTRA Magazine, Winter:3-5

AFTRA (2006) 'AFTRA introduces national president's message podcast on website', News release posted on www.AFTRA.org 4 Jan. Accessed 16 March 2006

AFTRA (2006) 'A Small Slice of AFTRA History', www.aftra.org. Accessed 16 March 2006

Armbrust, Roger (2005) 'SAG's Christie Rebuts Rosenberg, Who's N.Y.-Bound', Backstage.com, 3 Nov. Accessed 16 March 2006

Bahr, Morton (1998) *From the Telegraph to the Internet*, Washington: National Press Books,

Batstone, Eric (1984) *Working Order: Workplace Industrial Relations over Two Decades*, Oxford: Basil Blackwell

Chaison, Gary N. (1986) *When Unions Merge*, Lexington, Mass: Lexington Books

Connell, Angel (2003) 'AFTRA/SAG's Failed Consolidation and its Impact on New England's Acting Community', *New England Entertainment Digest*, 29 July. Posted on www.jacneed.com. Accessed 16 March

Constitution and By-Laws (2003) Screen Actors Guild, July

Cooper, Marc, (2001) 'Residual Anger', *The Nation*, April 2. Posted on www.thenation.com. Accessed 16 March 2006

Dyer-Witheford, Nick (1999) *Cyber-Marx: Cycles and Circuits of Struggle in High Technology Capitalism*, Urbana and Chicago: University of Illinois Press

Eggerton, John, (2005) 'Unions consolidate to face merged media.' *Broadcasting & Cable*, 11 Oct.

Goldstein, Patrick, (2005) 'His Union Divided Cannot Stand' *Los Angeles Times*, 4 Oct. 2005:E1.

Horwitch, Lauren (2005) 'AFTRA Tackles Finances', Backstage.com, 22 July 2005. Accessed 16 March 2006

Huws, Ursula (2003) *The Making of a Cybertariat: Virtual Work in a Real World*, New York: Monthly Review Press,

Katz, Harry C. (ed.) (1997) *Telecommunications: Restructuring Work and Employment Relations Worldwide*, Ithaca, NY: ILR Press

Kiefer, Peter (2003) 'SAG-AFTRA merger proposal shot down', The Hollywood Reporter.com, 2 July. Accessed 16 March 2006.

Kline, Stephen, Nick Dyer-Witheford and Greig de Peuter (2003), *Digital Play: The Interaction of Technology, Culture and Marketing*, Montreal: McGill-Queen's Press

Lipset, Seymour M., Martin A. Trow and James S. Coleman (1956) *Union Democracy: The Internal Politics of the International Typographical Union,* Glencoe, Ill.: The Free Press

McKercher, Catherine (2002) *Newsworkers Unite: Labor, Convergence and North American Newspapers,* Lanham, Md.: Rowman and Littlefield

McNary, Dave (2005) 'SAG looks to law on runaway prod'n', Variety.com, 26 Oct. Accessed 16 March 2006

Miller, A.L. (2006) 'AFTRA, the Monkey on SAG Actors Backs.', Posted on SAG Watchdog blog, www.sagwatchdog.com, 18 Jan. Accessed 16 March 2006

Mosco, Vincent (2005) 'Here Today, Outsourced Tomorrow: Knowledge Workers in the Global Economy', *Javnost/The Public* 12 no. 2:39-56

'National Board Begins AFTRA Restructuring', *AFTRA magazine,* Fall/Winter 2004/2005:3-4

Prindle, David F (1988) *The Politics of Glamour: Ideology and Democracy in the Screen Actors Guild,* Madison: The University of Wisconsin Press

Robb, David (1999) 'SAG-AFTRA ballots due at 5 p.m.', *The Hollywood Reporter,* 25 Jan. Hollywoodreporter.com, accessed 16 March 2006

SAG (2006) 'The History of SAG' www.sag.org. Accessed 16 March 2006

'It's still two parts for actors', *The Hollywood Reporter,* 29 Jan. 1999. Posted on www.performersalliance.tv/archive/hr_Jan2899.html. Accessed 16 March 2006

Stone Katherine V.W (2004) *From Widgets to Digits: Employment Regulation for the Changing Workplace,* Cambridge: Cambridge University Press

Swift, J. (2003) *Walking the Union Walk,* Toronto: Between The Lines

Terranova, T. (2004) *Network Culture: Politics for the Information Age,* London: Pluto

van Jaarsveld, D. D. (2004) 'Collective Representation Among High-Tech Workers at Microsoft and Beyond: Lessons from WashTech/CWA', *Industrial Relations* 43, no. 2 (April):364-85.

White, J. (2005) 'Losing Canadian Culture: The Danger of Foreign Ownership of Telecom', Canadian Centre for Policy Alternatives: Trade and Investment Series, 31 October, Available at: <http://www.policyalternatives.ca/documents/ National_Office_Pubs/2005/brief6_3_Losing_Canadian_Culture.pdf>.

INTERVIEWS BY THE AUTHORS

Mathis L. Dunn, Jr., Assistant National Executive Director, AFTRA; interim executive director of Los Angeles Local. Los Angeles, 6 Feb. 2006

Pamm Fair, Deputy National Executive Director, Policy and Strategic Planning, SAG. Los Angeles 3 Feb. 2006

Matt Kimbrough, AFTRA National Recording Secretary, Member of AFTRA National Executive Board and President's Strategy Cabinet. Also member of SAG. Los Angeles 6 Feb. 2006

Lise Lareau, National President, Canadian Media Guild, 2 March 2006

Ron Morgan, President of AFTRA Los Angeles Local; member of AFTRA national board. Also member of SAG. Los Angeles, 6 Feb. 2006

Leslie Simon, Director, Legislative and Public Affairs and Spanish Language Media Project, AFTRA Los Angeles local. Los Angeles, 6 Feb. 2006

ACKNOWLEDGEMENTS

The authors would like to acknowledge a grant from the Social Sciences and Humanities Research Council of Canada to support ongoing research on Trade Unions and Convergence in the Communication Industry. We also thank the Screen Actors Guild, the American Federation of Television and Radio Artists, and the Canadian Media Guild for agreeing to the interviews that provided vital information for this paper.

Immaterial Fordism:
the paradox of game industry labour

Leif Schumacher

Leif Schumacher *is a Ph.D. Candidate in Communication researching the political economy of the interactive games industry at Carleton University, Ottawa, Canada, .*

ABSTRACT
In different ways, Marxist autonomist, regulation school, and neoliberal theories all claim that work in the new economy is increasingly characterised by high levels of creativity, cooperation, and innovation, albeit accompanied by uncertainty and a relentless pace of work, introducing a new form of labour that differs fundamentally from past forms. This paper does not disagree with the proposition that capital is currently in the process of intensifying its search for more efficient value extraction. However, through a case study of lawsuits launched against the video game company Electronic Arts regarding its labour practices, it argues that the change in the nature of knowledge work and immaterial labour has been overstated by the adherents of these three schools and that what we are witnessing is not so much a replacement of traditional Fordist practices by post-Fordist ones as a new fusion of the two forms.

The starting point for this paper is a single blog entry in early November 2004 which stirred up enormous controversy and attention. Identifying herself as a 'disgruntled spouse' (or EA_spouse, as her signature read) this blogger described the experience of her partner who worked as a programmer for Electronic Arts (EA), the world's largest independent video game producer. His work involved 90-hour 'crunch' workweeks for which he received no compensation either in terms of overtime pay or extra vacation. These were labour conditions that had more in common with sweatshops than what would be expected in Silicon Valley – the leading beacon of the so-called knowledge-based economy. Rresponses to the blog posting were immediate, and within a day the trade press had picked up the story. Earlier the same year, the International Game Developers Association (IGDA) had released a comprehensive study that highlighted many of the same issues that EA_spouse detailed, but it had received scant attention. Now, the study was quickly revisited by the trade press, and in addition it came to light that EA had earlier the same year been hit by a class action lawsuit that claimed the company was breaking California labour law with their practice of requiring unpaid overtime.

This paper focuses on these class action lawsuits and subsequent settlements and what they reveal about the status of so-called creative workers in the new economy. It focuses on the computer and video games industry because it, and the commodities it produces, seem to epitomise the cultural content, marketing practices, production processes, consumption patterns, and labour conditions that are symptomatic of what

David Harvey (1989) has described as a sea-change in political, economic, and cultural practices related to a shift in the organisation of capitalism. The industry is based on a knowledge-based symbolic output geared towards entertainment, produced almost exclusively using modern information and communication technology, within an environment relying on creativity and innovation. If we understand how the video game industry operates we should be able to illuminate many aspects of the functions and consequences of the reorganisation of capitalism.

One aspect of this industry, labour conditions and organisation, is examined in this paper, drawing on a secondary analysis of a series of lawsuits that claim improper classification of video game production personnel as creative workers. The argument made by these lawsuits – that these workers are not engaged in autonomous creative labour – problematises Marxist autonomist, regulation school, and neoliberal theories that claim that work in the new economy is increasingly characterised by high levels of creativity, cooperation, and innovation, albeit accompanied by uncertainty and a relentless pace of work. The evidence from these cases suggests that, even though the labour involved may be immaterial, it still appears to be carried out under conditions that are more characteristic of some of the 'old' production paradigms.

Converging theories

Discussing what is variously known as the 'creative', 'information' or 'knowledge' economy, analysts and commentators as diverse as Robert Reich (1991; 2002), Frances Cairncross (1997), Diane Coyle (1998), Manuel Castells (2000; 2001), and Richard Florida (2002; 2005) have painted a picture of a new economic landscape, enabled by new information and communication technologies, where creativity, knowledge and information have become the key factors that determine increased productivity and competitiveness, and general economic growth. Because these factors largely reside inside workers' heads, the argument goes that we are witnessing a transformation where labour is increasingly valued for workers' mental inputs rather than their physical skills.

Such views can be seen as representing a convergence between three different theoretical traditions: neo-liberal theories, those of the French regulation school and those of Marxist autonomists. To the French regulation school, with its concepts of 'mode of regulation' (Aglietta, 1979) or 'regime of accumulation' (Lipietz, 1987) we owe the idea that we are currently witnessing the transition from a Fordist to a post-Fordist regime, where the development and use of new information technologies play a central role in the shift towards a regime of flexible labour and production, intensified consumption, and constant innovation (Jessop, 2002). In this view, the consequence for labour is that flexibility translates into uncertainty, contracts become more precarious and workers face constant pressure to update their skills. Marxist autonomists have critiqued this approach for taking insufficient account of the formative potential of class struggle (Gambino, 1996; Dyer-Witheford, 2004). Agreeing that the mass worker has been largely replaced by the socialised worker as a result of major change in the organisation of capitalism (the emergence of 'Empire') this approach emphasises the introduction of new network technologies and new accumulation strategies as an effort to disperse the collective power of the mass worker (Hardt and Negri, 2000). In this model the homogeneous mass worker is replaced by the heterogeneous 'multitude' engaged in 'immaterial labour', which is viewed as inherently cooperative, and contains a strong potential for liberation through the use of the very tools and tendencies introduced by Empire (Hardt and Negri, 2004). This view has been criticised for putting too much emphasis on the dichotomy of 'Empire' versus 'multitude' (Thoburn, 2001) and for failing to recognise divisions within the 'multitude' based on, for instance, gender and ethnic differences (Dyer-Witheford, 2001). Despite these differences, it can be argued that the overall context is one of convergence between these different theoretical approaches. From Harvey to Florida, from Negri to Jessop there is a common perception that capitalism has entered or is in the process of entering a new phase of expansion characterised by intensified creative/information/knowledge work, flexible work arrangements, and a post-modern culture of consumption.

Video game production is often viewed as the pinnacle of creative work, involving artistry in everything from the fantasy of the storyline and the ingenuity of the game mechanics to the spectacular graphics and sound that make up crucial dimensions of the video game experience. This type of labour should supposedly illustrate the work arrangements envisioned, for example, by Florida (2002) and Reich (2002), who describe a creative knowledge-based economy with labour markets full of new opportunities for those with the requisite skills. Dyer-Witheford (2002) speaks of this as the 'work as play ethos', where the prospect of a 'hip' creative workplace is welcomed despite the prospects of long hours and job insecurity.

This paper argues that the reality is much more contradictory than this and that there is clear evidence of working conditions within the industry that are standardised and closely monitored, with as many Fordist as post-Fordist characterisitics. The lawsuits studied do not only reveal knowledge work performed according to such Fordist standards; but they also demonstrate that the 'multitude' (or at least those parts of it represented by the workforce in these games companies) has chosen avenues of resistance that do not form part of the tools and tendencies put in place by 'Empire'.

The context – structure of the video game industry

Video game production has established itself as a strong and growing global industry. With major investment from large multinational corporations such as Sony, Microsoft, and Vivendi, it produced global revenues of approximately US $28 billion in 2005[1], and is expected to nearly double that by 2010 (Cole, 2005). According to PriceWaterhouse-Coopers the growth of the video game industry is set to outpace all other entertainment sectors by the end of the decade (Fahey, 2005). The map of the industry involved in developing and publishing computer and video games is constantly changing through takeovers, mergers, bankruptcies, and the emergence of new actors. However, some basic contours can be discerned.

[1]   All dollar figures mentioned from here on are in US dollars, unless otherwise mentioned.

At the top of the hierarchy we find the publishers (e.g. Electronic Arts, Activision, UbiSoft and Take-Two Interactive). They stand as gatekeepers between developers and the market, providing the financial muscle needed for distribution and marketing. Many publishers employ their own large in-house development teams (often the result of acquisitions of successful independent developers), but they also rely on contracting work out to independent developers. This helps mitigate the risk of operating in a hit-driven business with an alleged 95 per cent failure rate (International Game Developers Association, 2004). Independent developers range in size from a handful of people operating from a basement to large multinational operations employing hundreds of people. Acquisition is a common strategy in this industry, and as soon as an independent developer produces a successful game the chances are that a larger company will buy it out to capitalise on the prospects of continued sales and development of successful sequels.

The escalating costs associated with game production, as hardware has become increasingly sophisticated, are a growing concern. With the release of the next generation of consoles (Microsoft's Xbox 360, Nintendo's Wii, and Sony's Playstation 3) development costs are expected to reach $15 million per game. On top of this must be added the costs associated with marketing and SG&A (selling, general, and administrative expenses), which could bring total costs as $25 million (Gamedaily Staff, 2006). At this price point there is enormous pressure to produce games that stay on budget and sell in large quantities, since over a million copies might have to be sold just to break even. Several strategies are implemented in order to achieve this, and one consequence is that many firms put pressure on their workforce to increase their working hours in order to maximise output, even when they are engaged in so-called creative endeavours (Handman, 2005).

The labour process and the people engaged in it

About 100,000 people are engaged in game related labour in North America (Bass, 2005). It is uncertain exactly how many of these are directly working with game development since job descriptions range from public relations personnel and game testers to software engineers and product managers. However, it is clear that game development labour forms the foundation of the industry, supplying content and digital code (Kline, Dyer-Witheford and de Peuter, 2003).

Producing a game can take anything from six months to two years, and work is mostly conducted in teams involving up to 100 people. Designers create the vision for the game (what characters are involved, the mechanics of the game, etc.), artists provide the visual and audio content, and programmers build the code that acts as the engine of the game (de Peuter and Dyer-Witheford, 2005). Overseeing the project we find the producer, who is responsible for the overall functioning of the team. He (in the vast majority of cases it is a 'he') must coordinate all development efforts, schedule deadlines, manage budgets, provide the proper tools for his team, and ensure that development stays within the bounds of the overall vision of the game (Irish, 2005). At the lowest rung of the ladder we find the game tester who is involved in the quality assurance process. Testers are generally only paid the minimum wage.

Through interviews (about 40) conducted by de Peuter and Dyer-Witheford (2005), a quality of life survey (994 respondents) and a workforce diversity survey (filtered sample size of 3,128 respondents) carried out by IGDA (2004; 2005) [2] we have a fairly good idea of the demographics of the industry. The people involved in game development are overwhelmingly young white males, with an average age of 31 years. Most are between their early twenties and mid thirties, with the majority having worked in the industry for less than five years.

The picture that emerges both from the surveys and the interviews is of a workforce that is generally content with the work, enjoying flexibility and autonomy, a variability of creative work tasks, intellectual freedom, high levels of cooperation, and a playful work environment. This despite reports of high turnover rates, a culture of long hours, and complaints from immediate family that they do not get to spend enough time with their significant others.

According to de Peuter and Dyer-Witheford (2005) 'game development is an exemplary site of "immaterial labour"'. Following Hart and Negri (2000) they use the term immaterial labour to refer to the emotional, creative, networked, socialised work in which the 'multitude' is engaged in our era of high technology. Referring to the work of Maurizio Lazzarato, they point out how he 'emphasises the centrality of "inventive work" to contemporary production, an aspect of the performance of immaterial labour that he contrasts to the "reproductive work" characteristic of the mass production of similar goods in the Fordist era'. Their study found many features supposedly typical of immaterial labour in game development, such as individual creativity, digital and social networking, and a culture of subjective self-fulfillment, but also precariousness and uncertainty.

Rossiter (2003) points out the remarkable similarity that can be found between such arguments coming from the autonomists and the 'neoliberalism' of writers like Richard Florida and Charles Leadbeater who have discussed similar phenomena. Here, for instance is Florida on creativity:

'Creativity has come to be the most highly prized commodity in our economy – and yet it is not a 'commodity.' Creativity comes from people. And while people can be hired and fired, their creative capacity cannot be bought and sold, or turned on and off at will. … Creativity must be motivated and nurtured in a multitude of ways, by employers, by people themselves and by the communities where they locate.' (Florida, 2002: 5)

This description can be compared with Negri's (2003) notion of the multitude emerging 'when labour starts being regarded as something that can no longer be directly exploited.' Instead it is the social relationships between workers – their cooperation – that is exploited. This notion is further developed in de Peuter and Dyer-Witheford's (2005) description of game labour, as involving the 'capture of human creativity' made possible through work processes focusing on the combination of cooperation and individual creative freedom.

---

2   The complete results of the Quality of Life survey (including the raw data) can be downloaded at: http://www.igda.org/qol/whitepaper.php The complete results of the diversity survey (including the raw data) can be downloaded at: http://www.igda.org/diversity/

Florida (2002:327-328) does not speak of the 'multitude', but he postulates the emergence of a new class of workers valued for their creativity, and who, according to his calculations, make up about a third of the total American workforce. Workers who are involved in the production side of video games are not only included in this class but, because they belong to the US Bureau of Labor Statistics 'computer and mathematical occupations' category, would even form part of what he calls the 'super-creative core'. Florida's argument in many ways reflects the features identified by Leadbeater (1997) as key to the economic success of Silicon Valley in the mid-90s. Leadbeater saw a culture dominated by creativity, individualism, diversity, meritocracy, risk, and high performance. In his view this culture was the driving force behind the re-emergence of the Californian economy from its troubles in the late 80s and early 90s resulting from the loss of manufacturing jobs. Here we also find similarities to the regulation school, which speaks of innovation and knowledge work as characteristic of the demands made of labour in the emerging regime of accumulation based on post-Fordist production processes.

Combining these converging views, albeit simplistically, leads to the presumption that workers in the gaming industry are likely to be more highly skilled and creative than their Fordist counterparts but that this may come at the price of uncertainty and a volatile work/life balance. It would thus be expected that any lawsuit launched by workers against firms in this field would focus on these issues.

The case study firm

The lawsuits examined here were all targeted at Electronic Arts (EA), a behemoth of the gaming industry, which stands out as the largest independent publisher/producer of video games. According to EA's 2005 annual report the company had a net revenue of $3.1 billion, and published 31 titles with worldwide sales of over a million copies[3]. EA has established development studios in North America, Europe and Asia. Two of these studios, employing a total of 6,800 people, are located in California, in Los Angeles and Redwood City in Silicon Valley. According to *Develop Magazine*'s annual ranking based on sales in the UK market (the world's third largest video game market) these are among the most successful production studios in the world (Graft, 2006a).

The lawsuits

On July 29, 2004, Schubert & Reed LLP and Shapiro, Haber & Urmy LLP filed a class action lawsuit before the San Mateo County court on behalf of Jamie Kirschenbaum, who at the time worked as a so-called 'image production employee' at EA's Redwood studio (InterNet Bankruptcy Library, 2005a).

The class action lawsuit alleged that EA unlawfully classified image production employees as workers exempt from overtime pay under California labour law. The term 'image production employees' covers several different job titles including modellers, texture artists, lighters, background effects artists, and environmental artists (Feldman, 2005). These are the people who produce the visual and audio content of the games

---

3   EA's 2005 annual report can be found at: http://ccbn.mobular.net/ccbn/7/1169/1228/

which form the industry's core products, performing work that most observers would expect to be described as 'creative' or even 'artistic'.

The California labour code sets out minimum standards for workers' regular and overtime compensation, working hours, health and safety, protection against discrimination, appeals processes, etc[4]. In 1999, the California Assembly, through Bill 60, reinstated California's original eight-hour overtime law that had been repealed in 1998 (Jordan and Steen, 2000; Bar-Cohen and Carrillo, 2002). This applied to numerous professionals, and mandated extra pay for any work exceeding eight hours a day or 40 hours a week (Smith, 2004). Bill 60 met with stiff resistance from Silicon Valley executives. Intense lobbying led a year later to the introduction of Senate Bill 88 which amended the overtime legislation, making certain types of workers (computer and health-care professionals) exempt from receiving overtime pay (Jordan and Steen, 2000; Marsh, 2000). This exemption applies to workers that are 'primarily engaged in work that is intellectual or creative and requires the exercise of discretion and independent judgment' (State of California, 2003). In addition, the workers must earn $41 per hour (equivalent to an annual salary of $85,280) in order for the exemption to apply.

EA's image production employees were not paid overtime, and the Kirschenbaum v. EA complaint filed before the court provided detailed information about the type of work performed and the hours required. The main argument was that image production employees were not engaged in creative work that required independent judgement and therefore should be eligible for overtime pay. The complaint alleged that the employees covered by the lawsuit frequently worked more than eight hours a day and 40 hours a week, including weekends and national holidays, without overtime compensation. Regardless of their salary, it was argued, they should not be exempt from overtime pay, because they worked under strict supervision and their task was simply to mount images that were the result of the creative labour of others. The complaint described a hierarchical work process where independent creative decision-making took place among producers, designers, concept artists, and art directors. The image production employees were to be found further down the ladder, being required to follow the orders handed to them strictly, to the point where art directors and producers would monitor their work over their shoulders. The work duties described, it was argued, would not allow these workers to be exempt under California overtime laws. The complaint went on to claim that EA had a

'common policy and practice of classifying all Image Production Employees as exempt from the California overtime laws – while at the same time [assigning them] duties inconsistent with exempt status.' (Schubert, Reed, Kolbe, Urmy, and Heyman, 2004)

The Kirschenbaum v. EA lawsuit was eventually successful. In October 2005, the company released a notice to the press announcing that the suit had been settled. EA was to pay $15.6 million to cover all claims by the class members (Muller, 2005) in a settlement covering 618 current and former employees (Heyman, n.d.a). Another

---

4   The complete up-to-date California Labor Code can be found at http://www.leginfo.ca.gov/cgi-bin/calawquery?codesection=lab&codebody=&hits=20. Details of exemptions can be found at http://www.dir.ca.gov/dlse/faq_overtimeexemptions.htm.

similar lawsuit (Leander Hasty v. Electronic Arts) involving software engineers (programmers) was settled on April 25, 2006. This settlement was worth $14.9 million, and covered 600 class members (Brightman, 2006; Heyman, n.d.b; Muller, 2006).

Improper exemption practices are not only limited to a single company, state, or industry. Sony Computer Entertainment America, Activision, Electronic Arts in Florida, IBM, and Siebel Systems (a world-leading producer of Contact Relations Management software) have all been hit with similar lawsuits (Associated Press, 2006; Graves, 2004; InterNet Bankruptcy Library, 2005b; Schubert, Reed, Kolbe, Urmy, and Heyman, 2005; Smith, Urmy, and Heyman, 2005; Urmy and Heyman, 2006). The case against EA in Florida was settled in October 2005 for a total of $785,000 covering 119 class members (Heyman, n.d.).

Conclusions

What do these results tell us about 'immaterial labour' in the new economy?

In a memo sent to North American employees in late 2004, EA's Vice President of Human Resources, Rusty Rueff, responded to the improper classification allegations by stating that the company considers many of its employees to be creative and skilled professionals that relish flexibility in an environment built on a spirit of entrepreneurialism and innovation (Frauenheim, 2004b). This kind of rhetoric is in line with Richard Florida's argument that they form part of a creative class. Florida (2002; 2005) postulates an inherent creative knowledge-based individuality that is shared by the entire creative class, and that is attractive to prospective employers. He argues that these employees enjoy a privileged class position in their capacity as creative workers:

'Those in the Working Class and the Service Class are primarily paid to execute
　　according to plan, while those in the Creative Class are primarily paid to
　　create and have considerably more autonomy and flexibility than the other
　　two classes to do so.' (Florida, 2002:8)

As we have seen, the regulation school and the autonomists share similar sentiments regarding the position of workers in the new post-Fordist era of capitalist organisation. Jessop (2002:99) speaks of a post-Fordist virtuous circle of growth that would among other things involve 'rising incomes for skilled manual and intellectual workers (often jointly reclassified as 'knowledge workers')'. Specifically addressing game production labour and drawing on Hardt and Negri (2000), Dyer-Witheford (2002) claims that 'such 'immaterial labour' is completely unamenable to Taylorist/Fordist management techniques.'

However, the reality examined in this paper demonstrates a class of workers that are engaged in immaterial labour, but basically employed as production workers who are not expected to exercise independent judgement or contribute creatively to the value-adding process. Although they are employed for the sake of their mental capacity and knowledge rather than their physical skill, the method for extracting the value of this knowledge mirrors the closely monitored standardised work processes of the assembly line. It could be argued that what we are witnessing here is a form of immaterial Fordist labour, a form which does not fit into any of these three characterisations of the new era. In response, both the autonomists and the regulation school would probably argue that what is theorised as a new phase, at the moment constitutes tendencies towards reorganisation, rather than a complete break with the past. As 'Empire' attempts to establish itself, and a new regime of accumulation is becoming visible, old assembly line mass production methods still exist hand in hand with flexible production and immaterial labour (de Peuter and Dyer-Witheford, 2005; Jessop, 2002). This study, however, suggests not so much a scenario in which assembly line Fordist production exists *alongside* knowledge work based on creativity and symbolic manipulation, but rather a *fusion* of Fordist and knowledge work practices. Furthermore, this new form does not seem to constitute an isolated exception but appears to be a dominant form of work amongst a large segment of workers in the game production industry.

De Peuter and Dyer-Witheford (2005) acknowledge the existence of what they call corporate-style management in large game development companies, which can dampen creative spirits, and lead to workers leaving to set up shop on their own. However, the newfound creative freedom can be short-lived:

'Ironically, over the period during which we conducted our interviews, two of the developers who had waxed most eloquent to us about self-management, flattened hierarchies, and creative control sold their studios to multinational publishers for millions.' (de Peuter and Dyer-Witheford, 2005)

They also acknowledge that the lawsuits are a form of resistance posed by what they call 'play slaves,' but they do not discuss the implication of the avenue chosen for this resistance. Instead, they focus on what they see as a counter-mobilisation of 'the multitude' through the subversive practices of game labour. These practices include the production of anti-capitalist games with subversive content, 'modding'[5], and piracy. This is done in an attempt to re-appropriate 'the general intellect of games, re-organising it autonomously, and re-directing it toward a critique of Empire' (de Peuter and Dyer-Witheford, 2005).

However, at the same time, a large number of people working in the game production industry and other so-called knowledge industries are struggling against capitalist exploitation, using a very different approach, the framework of labour law that was developed as a result of working class struggle in the era of Fordism. This is very different approach from the kind of resistance the autonomists expect from the 'multitude'.

Clearly, more qualitative research on the experience of the creative knowledge worker and more reliable use of statistics (with clearer definitions) are needed to establish a definitive picture, but the evidence of these lawsuits suggests that it is difficult to claim that we have or are just about to move into an era of reorganised capitalism, whether this move comes as a result of new technology, capital's search for a new stable regime of accumulation or labour's continued struggle against capitalist exploitation.

It is of course easy to caricature theories of the knowledge-based economy. Many would claim that what is underway is a process that is still being negotiated through a

---

5   'Modding', according to Wikipedia, 'is a slang expression for the act of modifying a piece of hardware or software to perform a function not intended by someone with legal rights concerning that modification', http://en.wikipedia.org/wiki/Modding (accessed October 28, 2006).

landscape of state regulation, new technology, right-wing ideology, and reorganisation and re-skilling of labour. It could, perhaps, be more fruitful both for our understanding of these processes and for promoting the interests of the workers in these industries to focus on this hybrid of Fordism/post-Fordism that we are currently experiencing rather than theorise about ideal typical potentialities that might be the end result. As Ned Rossiter (2003) puts it in his critique of Negri:

'There has not been a revolution [of work and production practices]. Rather, capital has transmogrified into an informational mode of connections and relations, a mode that does not so much come after industrial and post-industrial modes of production as incorporate such modes within an ongoing logic of flexible accumulation.' (Rossiter, 2003)

We need to acknowledge that capitalism today does not function quite as it did in the heyday of Fordist production practices; however there is little evidence to support the idea that it has moved into an entirely new mode of operation. Instead, new theories, or modifications of existing ones, are needed to better understand the fusion of creative work and Fordist production practices that we are currently experiencing.

© *Leif Schumacher, 2006*

REFERENCES

Aglietta, M. (1979) *A theory of capitalist regulation: The US experience.* London: New Left Books

Amar, A. D. (2002) *Managing knowledge workers: Unleashing innovation and Productivity,* Westport, CT:: Quorum Books

Bar-Cohen, L. & D.M. Carrillo (2002) 'Labor law enforcement in California 1970-2000', *The state of California labor 2002,* 135-170. Retrieved April 14, 2006 from http://iir.ucla.edu/scl/pdf02/scl2002ch6.pdf

Bass, D. (2005) 'Microsoft aims for video game heights', *Seattlepi.com,* March 5. Retrieved Aug. 4, 2006, from http://seattlepi.nwsource.com/business/214593_msftgames05.html

Brightman, J. (2006) 'EA settles overtime suit, Pays $14.9 Million', *GameDailyBiz,* April 26. Retrieved April 27, 2006 from http://biz.gamedaily.com/industry/feature/?id=12522

Campbell, C. (2006) 'America's top 20 publishing giants', *NextGeneration,* June 1. Retrieved September 6, 2006 from http://www.next-gen.biz/index.php?option=com_content&task=view&id=3133&Itemid=2

Cairncross, F. (1977) *The death of distance: How the communications revolution will change our lives,* Boston: Harvard Business School Press

Castells, M. (2000) *The rise of the network society. Volume 1: The information age: Economy society, and culture,* Oxford: Blackwell Publishing

Castells, M. (2001) *The Internet galaxy: Reflections on the Internet, business, and Society,* New York: Oxford University Press

Cole, D. (2005) 'Interactive entertainment industry to rival size of global music Business', *DFC Intelligence.* Retrieved May 1, 2006 from http://www.dfcint.com/news/prnov92005.html

Coyle, D. (1998) *The weightless world: Strategies for managing the digital economy,* Cambridge, MA: MIT Press

de Peuter, G. & N. Dyer-Witheford (2005) 'A playful multitude? Mobilising and counter-mobilising immaterial game labour', *Fibreculture,* 5. Retrieved August 3, 2006 from http://journal.fibreculture.org/issue5/depeuter_dyerwitheford.html

Dyer-Witheford, N. (2001) 'Empire, immaterial labor, the new combinations, and the global worker', *Rethinking Marxism,* 13(3-4): 70-80

Dyer-Witheford, N. (2002) 'Cognitive capital contested', *Multitudes,* October 10. Retrieved August 3, 2006 from http://multitudes.samizdat.net/Cognitive-Capital-Contested.html

Dyer-Witheford, N. (2004) 'Autonomist Marxism and the information society', *Multitudes,* June 3. Retrieved August 3, from http://multitudes.samizdat.net/Autonomist-Marxism-and-the.html

Fahey, R. (2005) 'Videogames to lead entertainment sector boom through 2009, says PWC', *GamesIndustry,* October 10. Retrieved May 1, 2006 from http://www.gamesindustry.biz/content_page.

php?aid=12135

Feldman, C. (2005) 'EA settles labor-dispute lawsuit', *Gamespot*, October 5. Retrieved April 16, 2006 from http://www.gamespot.com/news/6135106.html

Feldman, C. & T. Thorsen (2006) 'Electronic Arts cuts staff by five percent', *Gamespot*, February 1. Retrieved April 13, 2006 from http://www.gamespot.com/news/6143510.html

Florida, R. (2002) *The rise of the creative class: And how it's transforming work, leisure, community, & everyday life.*, New York: Basic Books

Florida, R. (2005) *The flight of the creative class: The new global competition for talent*, New York: HarperCollins Publishers Inc.

Fraser, J. A. (2001) *White-collar sweatshop: The deterioration of work and its rewards in corporate America*, New York: Norton

Frauenheim, E. (2004a) 'For developers, it's not all fun and games', *CNET News*, November 18. Retrieved April 18, 2006 from http://ecoustics-cnet.com.com/For+developers%2C+its+not+all+fun+and+games/2100-1022_3-5457274.html?tag=nl

Frauenheim, E. (2004b) 'Electronic Arts promises workplace change', *CNET News*, December 3. Retrieved April 18, 2006 from http://ecoustics-cnet.com.com/Electronic+Arts+promises+workplace+change/2100-1022_3-5476714.html?tag=nl

Frauenheim, E. (2005) 'Overtime coming to Electronic Arts', *CNET News*, March 11. Retrieved April 16, 2006 from http://ecoustics-cnet.com.com/Overtime+coming+to+Electronic+Arts/2100-1022_3-5611293.html?tag=nl

Gambino, F. (1996, October) 'A critique of the Fordism of the Regulation school', *Wildcat-Zirkular*, 28/29. Retrieved August 6, 2006 from http://www.wildcat-www.de/en/zirkular/28/z28e_gam.htm

GameDaily Staff (2006) 'Are Big Budget Console Games Sustainable?' ,*GameDailyBiz*, March 10. Retrieved March 11, 2006 from http://biz.gamedaily.com/industry/advertorial/?id=12089

Graft, K. (2006a) 'Develop names top 100 power studios', *NextGeneration*, April 16. Retrieved May 1, 2006 from http://www.next-gen.biz/index.php?option=com_content&task=view&id=2748&Itemid=2

Graft, K. (2006b) 'Game developers turn to outsourcing', *NextGeneration*, March 9. Retrieved March 10, 2006 from http://www.next-gen.biz/index.php?option=com_content&task=view&id=2447&Itemid=2

Handman, D. H. (2005) 'Electronic Arts settles a class action overtime lawsuit for $15.6 million: Red flags and practical lessons for the entertainment software industry', *Entertainment Law Reporter*, 27(6) Retrieved April 19, 2006 from http://www.entertainmentlawreporter.com/archive/v27n06/270601.htm

Hardt, M. & A. Negri (2000) *Empire*, Cambridge, MA: Harvard University Press

Hardt, M. & A. Negri. (2004) *Multitude: War and democracy in the age of Empire*, New York: Penguin Press

Harvey, D. (1989) *The condition of postmodernity: An enquiry into the origins of cultural change*, Cambridge, Mass: Blackwell Publishing

Heyman, T. S. (n.d.a) *Electronic Arts California artists overtime litigation*. Retrieved April 17, 2006 from http://www.shulaw.com/unlawful/EAovertime_new.asp

Heyman, T. S. (n.d.b) *Electronic Arts California software engineers overtime litigation*. Retrieved April 28, 2006 from http://www.shulaw.com/unlawful/EAovertime_California.asp

Heyman, T. S. (n.d.c) *Electronic Arts Florida artists overtime litigation*. Retrieved April 16, 2006 from http://www.shulaw.com/unlawful/EAovertime_Florida.asp

Holloway, J. (2002) 'Going in the wrong direction: Or, Mephistopheles – not Saint Francis of Assisi', *Historical Materialism*, Volume 10(1): 79-91

International Game Developers Association (2004) *Quality of life white paper*. Retrieved April 18, 2006 from http://www.igda.org/qol/whitepaper.php

InterNet Bankruptcy Library. (2005a) 'Electronic Arts: Plaintiffs amend employees' lawsuit in CA court', *Class Action Reporter*, 7(27). Retrieved April 16, 2006 from http://bankrupt.com/CAR_Public/050208.mbx

InterNet Bankruptcy Library. (2005b) 'Siebel Systems: Faces amended overtime wage lawsuit in N.D. CA.', *Class Action Reporter*, 7(231) Retrieved April 16, 2006 from http://bankrupt.com/CAR_Public/051122.mbx

Irish, D. (2005) *The game producer's handbook*,. Boston: Thomson Course Technology PTR

Jessop, B. (2002) *The future of the capitalist state*, Cambridge, UK: Polity Press

Jordan, H. & M. Steen (2000) 'New law exempts some from overtime applies to high-tech professionals making $41 or more an hour', *San Jose Mercury News*, September 20:C1

Kline, S., N. Dyer-Witheford, and G. de Peuter (2003) *Digital play: The interaction of technology, culture, and marketing*, Montreal & Kingston: McGill-Queen's University Press

Leadbeater, C. (1997) 'A slice of the Silicon pie', *New Statesman*, 126(4335)

Liepitz, A. (1987) *Mirages and miracles: The crisis in global Fordism*, London: Verso

Lombardi, R. (2006) 'Oppressed gaming workers liberated by IT best practices', *Globe and Mail*, April 12. Retrieved April 15, 2006 from http://www.theglobeandmail.com/servlet/story/RTGAM.20060412.gtgameapr12/BNStory/Technology/AtPlay

Loughrey, P. (2006) 'Probst performing well as EA CEO', *GamesIndustry*, April 24. Retrieved

May 1, 2006 from http://www.gamesindustry.biz/content_page.php?aid=16301

Marsh, M. C. (2000) *New California law creates overtime exemptions for some computer personnel*. Retrieved April 14, 2006 from http://www.yourlegalcorner.com/employment/oct2000.html

Mieszkowski, K. (2004) Santa's sweatshop, *Salon.com*, December 2

Muller, T. (2005) *EA settles class action on overtime*, October 5. Retrieved April 17, 2006, from http://www.info.ea.com/news/pr/pr691.pdf

Muller, T. (2006) *EA settles engineer class action on overtime*, April 26. http://www.info.ea.com/news/pr/pr767.pdf

Negri, A. (2003) 'Public sphere, labour and multitude', *MakeWorlds*, 3. Retrieved April 17 2006 from http://makeworlds.org/node/11

Pham, A. (2004) 'Working too hard in an industry of fun and games', *Los Angeles Times*, November 17:C1

Reich, R. B. (1991) *The work of nations: Preparing ourselves for 21ˢᵗ century capitalism*, New York, NY: Knopff Publishing

Reich, R. B. (2002) *The future of success: Working and living in the new economy*, Toronto: Random House

Richtel, M. (2005) 'Fringes vs. basics in Silicon Valley', *New York Times*, March 9:C1

Robinson, E. (2005) *Why crunch mode doesn't work: six lessons*. Retrieved April 25, 2006 from http://www.igda.org/articles/erobinson_crunch.php

Rossiter, N. (2003, December) 'Report: Creative labour and the role of intellectual Property', *Fibreculture*, 1. Retrieved August 3, 2006 from http://journal.fibreculture.org/issue1/issue1_rossiter.html

Schubert, R. C., J.J. Reed, M. P.Kolbe, T. V.Urmy, & T.S. Heyman (2004) *First amended class action and representative action complaint*. Retrieved April 13, 2006 from http://www.eaovertimecase.com/First%20Amended%20Complaint.pdf

Schubert, R. C., J.J. Reed, M. P.Kolbe, T. V.Urmy, & T.S. Heyman. (2005) *Class action and representative action complaint*. Retrieved April 13, 2006 from http://www.schubert-reed.com/Sony%20Complaint.pdf

Shepherd, C. and K.Graft (2006a) 'GMC: Hardware guys to blame', *NextGeneration*, March 8. Retrieved March 9, 2006 from http://www.next-gen.biz/index.php?option=com_content&task=view&id=2440&Itemid=2

Shepherd, C. and K. Graft (2006b) 'GMC: Innovation is Key Challenge', *NextGeneration*, March 8. Retrieved March 9, from http://www.next-gen.biz/index.php?option=com_content&task=view&id=2438&Itemid=2

Smith, D. (2004) 'EA Faces Class-Action Overtime Suit', *1UP.com*, November 12. Retrieved, April 15, 2006 from http://cgw.1up.com/do/newsStory?cId=3136538

Smith, R. W., T.V. Urmy, & T.S.Heyman (2005) *First amended class and collective action complaint*. Retrieved April 16, 2006 from http://www.shulaw.com/documents/complaints/EA%20Florida%20First%20Amended%20Class%20and%20Collective%20Action%20Complaint.pdf

State of California (2003) *Exemptions from the overtime laws – Glossary*. Retrieved, April 13, 2006 from http://www.dir.ca.gov/dlse/Glossary.asp?Button1=E#employee%20in%20the%20computer%20software%20field

Stross, R. (2004) 'When a video game stops being fun', *New York Times*, November 21. Retrieved April 14, 2006 from http://www.nytimes.com/2004/11/21/business/yourmoney/21digi.html?ex=1258693200&en=40a60cc6d7971ab2&ei=5090&partner=rssuserland

Takahashi, D. (2005) 'Nicole Wong's story on Electronic Arts overtime lawsuit settlement', *Mercury News*, October 7. Retrieved April 16, 2006 from http://blogs.mercurynews.com/aei/2005/10/guest_posts_nic.html

Thoburn, N. (2001) 'Autonomous production? On Negri's "new synthesis"', *Theory, Culture & Society*, 18(5):75-96

Urmy, T. V. and T.S.Heyman (2006) *Activision overtime litigation*. Retrieved April 29, 2006 from http://www.shulaw.com/unlawful/Activision.asp

Wells, J. (2006) 'A city worthy of Buzz', *The Toronto Star*, March 11:L1.

Review

The Class of the New by Richard Barbrook

Christoph Hermann

Christoph Hermann *is is a senior researcher at Forschungs- und Beratungsstelle Arbeitswelt (FORBA), the Working Life Research Centre in Vienna, Austria.*

Richard Florida's *Rise of the Creative Class*' has become an academic bestseller in the United States and beyond.[1] In his *Class of the New* Richard Barbrook contests the concept of the creative class on two major accounts:[2] First, the scientific invention of new classes has a long history and can be traced back as far as Adam Smith's comments on the *Nature and Cause of the Wealth of Nations*. From this perspective Florida's concept is only the latest in a long chain of concepts with expiry dates. Second, the concept is highly ideological, while empirically and theoretically flawed.

Barbrook has assembled 86 definitions of new classes from the past 230 years. It seems that at each turning point in capitalist development, researchers have found evidence that a new class is emerging which, depending on the political intention of the author, will either lead capitalist society into a new phase of economic prosperity or overthrow the existing system and bring about socialism. In both cases the future will certainly be better than the past. Florida's creative class in no exception. Despite promoting postmodern values such as individuality and diversity, it is deeply modernist insofar as it promises a better world full of happy and self-sufficient workers. Perhaps the modernist optimism is rooted in a bleak technological determinism which, remarkably, seems to be shared by all these authors regardless of their political backgrounds.

'Over the past two centuries, the restructuring of working methods and the development of better machinery have been the driving forces of this economic system. Each wave of organisational and technological change has required another reordering of the hierarchical relationship between capital and labour. In successive generations, the concept of the new class has been used to analyse the impact of these processes upon the structures of modernity.'(page 20).

The information and communication technologies and the world wide web which allegedly boosted workers' creativity, or, in a left version, their independence and cooperation, are only the latest examples of a long list of technological inventions.

Barbrook hopes to reveal continuities and discontinuities with his encompassing list of concepts.

'By analysing what has changed and what has remained the same, we come closer to comprehending the political and economic significance of this social prophecy in the present.' (page 19).

---

1   Richard Florida, The Rise of the Creative Class (New York: Basis Books, 2002).

2   Richard Barbrook, The Class of the New (London: Openmute, 2006). Downloadable at http://www.theclassofthenew.net/

Barbrook assembles a montage of quotations which is supposed 'to create its own meaning'(ibid).[3] It would have been more interesting if he had analysed the role played by different class definitions as part of an ideological struggle over how the future of work is seen, including its division of labour and hierarchical structures, since such visions always work as a legitimation or de-legitimation of the existing system. As Barbrook notes, 'the new class is prefiguring today how everyone else will work and live tomorrow'(page 17). Given that writers of the left have been particularly active in these exercises in class definition, it would have been interesting to read a discussion of how they have imagined a future socialist world of work and to which degree these imaginations have inspired revolutionary forces.

Barbrook's second point is a more practical one. He takes the example of London to demonstrate how Florida's concept has been translated into a local development strategy, thereby simultaneously legitimising the existing order and giving hope for a better future. After a period of painful deindustrialisation, London, like so many other Western cities, has discovered the creative industries as its new source of competitive advantage in an increasingly globalised world. In contrast with many second- or third-ranking urban centres, London actually acquired its competitive advantages as one of the few global cities in Europe on the basis of its banking and finance sectors rather than its creative industries. Yet, according to a study published by the Greater London Authority in 2002, the media, cultural and computing sectors have grown faster in the 1990s than any other section of the local economy. After business services, the creative industries have become the second largest source of new jobs.

Barbrook quotes statisticians' estimates that in 2000 ten per cent of London's population were already members of the creative class, including artists, designers, programmers, technicians, writers, musicians, architects, actors, directors, copywriters and tailors, a proportion that, according to these sources, will continute to rise (page 33). This ten per cent is modest by Florida's standards (he estimates that creative workers make up for as much as a third of the American workforce), but Barbrook disputes even this number as empirically unsustainable.

> '*Crucially, the British government's employment surveys lumped together people with very different jobs under the same category because they happened to work in the same industry. When they were on the payroll of a film company, security guards were transformed into members of the Creative Class ... When they were selling artworks and antiques, old-fashioned shopkeepers were counted as part of the new class.' (ibid).*

Confronted with the lack of statistical evidence, the defenders of the creative class have repeatedly argued that its significance lies in a qualitative change which cannot be measured quantitatively. Without empirical evidence the notion of the creative class becomes what it really is: 'feel-good rhetoric' or, more precisely, a deeply ideological concept. It gives super-exploited workers, many of whom do not even have unemployment insurance or pension coverage, a positive image to identify with while at the same time legitimising the neoliberal restructuring of London (pages 39-40). It

---

3   In producing a collage of definitions Barbrook follows the examples of Walter Benjamin and Humphrey Jennings.

also helps to conceal the increasing social divisions among the urban population, including those between the super-rich and the super-poor creative workers, and the reality that many creative people can no longer afford to live in the creative city (ibid. 41).

But the concept of a creative class is not only empirically weak, it is also theoretically inadequate. The strongest and most original point in Barbrook's critique is when he reveals the limits of Florida's thesis by exposing it to the London experience. 'Ironically, this theorist draws the boundaries of the Creative Class not only too widely, but also too narrowly. On the one hand, he includes people doing routine tasks, which require little or no imagination within this sector. On the other hand, this theorist ignores the extent to which contemporary culture is a participatory phenomenon. Creativity isn't a monopoly of the Creative Class. The majority of the population, who earn their living outside this sector, can also be cultural producers. When Florida praises cities with hip music scenes, he misses that some the coolest people in their clubs and bars aren't members of his new class. For them, creativity is what happens when they're playing outside work.' (page 46).

Perhaps the deeper contradiction which Barbrook is pointing to is the dependence of capitalism on one kind of creativity to create new commodities and innovate production and work organisations, while at the same time restricting other kinds of creativity through exploitative production relations and commodification.

© *Christoph Hermann, 2006*

The spark in the engine: creative workers in a global economy